Staging Ageing

Staging Ageing
Theatre, Performance and the Narrative of Decline

Michael Mangan

intellect Bristol, UK / Chicago, USA

First published in the UK in 2013 by
Intellect, The Mill, Parnall Road, Fishponds, Bristol, BS16 3JG, UK

First published in the USA in 2013 by
Intellect, The University of Chicago Press, 1427 E. 60th Street,
Chicago, IL 60637, USA

A catalogue record for this book is available from the
British Library.

Series: Theatre & Consciousness
Series editor: Daniel Meyer-Dinkgräfe
Series ISSN: 1753-3058

Cover designer: Stephanie Sarlos
Copy-editor: MPS Technologies
Cover image: Taken from Michael Mangan's play *The Inner Child's
    Compendium of Magic* (Exeter, Varadi Foundation, 2006).
    Copyright: Sarah Goldingay.
Production manager: Jessica Mitchell
Typesetting: Contentra Technologies

Print ISBN: 978-1-78320-013-9
ePDF ISBN: 978-1-78320-137-2
ePUB ISBN: 978-1-78320-138-9

Printed and bound by Hobbs, UK

Contents

Acknowledgements   vii

Introduction: Mind, Body and Ageing in Drama, Theatre and Performance   1

Part I: Frames and Contexts   **11**

Chapter 1:   On Gerontology   13

Chapter 2:   On Age, Stage and Consciousness   33

Part II: Tragedy and Comedy   **53**

Chapter 3:   On Liminality and Late Style: *Oedipus at Colonus*   55

Chapter 4:   On Negative Stereotypes in Classical and Medieval Drama   77

Chapter 5:   On Sex and the *Senex*: English Restoration Comedy   93

Chapter 6:   On Dirty Old Men and Trickster Figures   105

Part III: Memories   **119**

Chapter 7:   On Memory and Its Modes   121

Chapter 8:   On Reminiscence, Interaction and Intervention   151

Part IV: The Value(s) of Old Age   **171**

Chapter 9:   On Longevity   173

Chapter 10: On Institutions   197

Chapter 11: On Song and Dance   219

Epilogue: The Amazing One-Hundred-and-Sixty-One-Year-Old Woman   235

References   243

Index   259

Acknowledgements

I would like to thank the very many people who helped me in the writing of this book. A large number of friends and colleagues in the fields both of theatre and of gerontology who have offered me advice, helped me find time to write, lent me books, gave me opportunities to share my work in its early stages, responded when I did so, asked good questions, shared their wisdom, chatted over a drink, collaborated with me on practical workshops and seminars, pointed me in new directions and, in short, gave me all kinds of invaluable help. The list is too long to mention everybody, but I am particularly grateful to Roland Clare, Christopher McCullough, Fiona Macbeth, Graham Ley, Nick Kaye, Anne Beynon, Sarah Goldingay, John Somers, David Melzer and the Peninsular Ageing Research Centre, David Roesner, Nela Kapelan, Andrew Thorpe, Peter Thomson, David Ian Rabey, Bonnie L. Vorenberg and the ATHE Theatre and Ageing Working Group, Valerie Barnes Lipscomb, Steven Pennell, Rob Alexander and Pier Productions, Cassie Phoenix, Rob Hallett, Tim Malone, David Amigoni, Lyn Greenwood, the staff and residents at The Lodge care home in Exeter, and Janice Hayward and staff at the Kathleen Rutland Home in Leicester. I hope that any of the friends and colleagues whose names I have omitted will have the generosity to attribute this to the failing memory of an academic who is investigating ageing experientially as well as theoretically.

My thanks are due, too, to the Arts and Humanities Research Council, who funded the *Staging Ageing* project of which this is the primary output; to Departmental and School Research Committees at the University of Exeter, who gave me additional time to work on this book; to administrative and technical colleagues at both Exeter and Loughborough Universities; and to the staff and curators at the University Libraries of Exeter, Loughborough, De Montfort and Leicester. The editorial team and peer-reviewers at Intellect have been both encouraging and scrupulous in their reading, advice and feedback, and I owe special thanks to Daniel Meyer-Dinkgräfe, who commissioned the book in the first place, and to Jessica Mitchell, who oversaw the publishing process.

Zara Mangan and Rachael Mangan, as ever, gave me their unfailing support, and the book is dedicated to my mother, Margaret Mangan, who taught me much of what I know about growing old, both gracefully and disgracefully.

Introduction

Mind, Body and Ageing in Drama, Theatre and Performance

Gerontideology, or acting your age and being as old as you feel

> Cultures include in their work self-presentations to their members. On certain collective occasions, cultures offer interpretations. They tell stories, comment, portray, and mirror. Like all mirrors, cultures are not accurate reflectors; there are distortions, contradictions, reversals, exaggerations, and even lies. Nevertheless, self-knowledge, for the individual and collectivity, is the consequence.
>
> (Barbara Myerhoff 1992: 233)

'What do you read, my lord?' asks the wise old counsellor. 'Slanders, sir', replies the rude young prince; 'for the satirical rogue says here that old men have grey beards, that their faces are wrinkled, their eyes purging thick amber and plum-tree gum, and that they have a plentiful lack of wit, together with most weak hams; all of which, sir, though I most powerfully and potently believe, yet I hold it not honesty to have it thus set down' (Shakespeare 1974: 1155). And thus Prince Hamlet flashes in front of Polonius's eyes a mirror in which Polonius may or may not see himself reflected.

Mirrors and theatre go hand in hand, of course. 'The purpose of playing', as Hamlet pompously reminded the travelling players who passed through Elsinore, 'was and is, to hold, as 'twere, the mirror up to nature' (Shakespeare 1974: 1161). The status and the reliability of that mirror is variable, debatable and frequently dubious, but on the whole the basic metaphor holds good, and the notion that performance may offer us a way of somehow seeing ourselves is deeply ingrained in our culture.

The metaphor of the mirror, in fact, is an important one for western culture in general. In cultural analysis, the mirror is perhaps most often associated with Lacanian theory, for example, in which the 'mirror stage' is the foundation upon which so much else rests. Lacan derived his inspiration from earlier studies comparing the behaviour in front of mirrors of young animals and human children (see Jalley 1998) then applied his own Freudian reading to the ways in which children (typically between the ages of six and eighteen months) attempted to understand, appropriate or control their own reflection in a mirror. This became the basis for his account of the development of human subjectivity.

But mirrors, both metaphorical and literal, are significant for other life stages beyond that of infancy. Not least, as Simone de Beauvoir discovered at the age of forty, they are vivid reminders of the onset of ageing:

The fact that the passage of universal time should have brought about a private, personal metamorphosis is something that takes us completely aback. When I was only forty I still could not believe it when I stood there in front of the looking-glass and said to myself, 'I am forty.'

(de Beauvoir 1972: 283)

The moment de Beauvoir describes is one which many will recognize, and the unbelief which she articulates is certainly a valid response. After all, the reflection that one sees in even the least distorted of mirrors both is and is not oneself: it is a two-dimensional image whose horizontal but not vertical symmetry has formed the subject of many a quasi-philosophical conundrum. Moreover, the thing you see in the looking glass is also younger than the you that looks at it – albeit only by the fraction of a nanosecond that it takes the light to travel between glass and retina. Why, then, does it look so much older?

De Beauvoir goes on to tease out the implications of her moment of incredulity:

Old age is particularly difficult to assume because we have always regarded it as something alien, a foreign species: 'Can I have become a different being while I still remain myself?' 'False dilemma,' people have said to me. 'So long as you feel young, you are young.' This shows a complete misunderstanding of the complex truth of old age: for the outsider it is a dialectic relationship between my being as he defines it objectively and the awareness of myself that I acquire by means of him. Within me it is the Other – that is to say the person I am for the outsider – who is old: and that Other is myself.

(1972: 283–84)

While de Beauvoir, like Lacan, uses the term the 'Other', we should not be misled by this. She is using it in a very different sense from Lacan, and while her own unique style of existentialist thought is influenced by Freud, she is not concerned with developing a neo-Freudian theory of ageing. Her meaning is more akin to the way in which she described woman as the 'Other' in *The Second Sex*, with its connotations of abjection and hostility. But the force of de Beauvoir's insight lies in its understanding of the multiple consciousness that is involved in the 'complex truth of old age', and the difficulty that is involved in struggling to come to terms with its various components. As the brilliant pioneer of age studies, Kathleen Woodward, put it: 'if the mirror stage of infancy is distinguished by the perception of binary opposition, the mirror stage of old age is more problematic. It is inherently triangular, involving the gaze of others as well as two images of oneself' (1991: 69).

Culture teaches us at an early age to recognize and interpret the bodily identifiers of biological ageing that we may see in the mirror; and even if, like Hamlet, we hold it not honesty, or at least courtesy, to have them thus set down, we sense in them something that seems reassuringly – or perhaps disquietingly – objective and empirical. However, as recent research suggests, signs such as grey hair and wrinkles do not actually translate with any degree of accuracy into objective standards of chronological age. Ten years and twenty million dollars worth of research funded by the American National Institute on Ageing have not delivered the hoped-for result for determining the biomarkers of age – those objective biological features by which we might classify people into age groups and categorically define the 'old' and the 'young'. In any case, that 'satirical rogue,' whose 'words, words, words' Hamlet is reading, is telling only a part of the story. Biological ageing is one thing; social ageing is another – whether we understand this as patterns of intergenerational relationships, as a sequence of ages and age statuses, or as age-based normative expectations. In recent years, social gerontologists have been quick to insist that age cannot be taken for granted as a biologically grounded 'given'; rather it should be understood as one of the key bases for the production of social identity. And, like any kind of identity construction, it does not operate in a vacuum, but as part of the complex web of beliefs, assumptions and power relations that make up the ideological formations of a culture. Woodward's mirror stage of old age is deeply implicated in the social ideologies of ageing; and what I have termed 'gerontideology' is, like the mirror stage of old age, 'inherently triangular, involving the gaze of others as well as two images of oneself'.

So, too, is theatrical performance. Any kind of theatrical performance brings into play both the body and the mind, together with the signifier and signified, with the physical/ biological organism that is the performer and with the questions of self and identity which the performance generates. But age, like gender, brings a particular sharpness to some of these questions. Even more than gender, in fact, ageing draws attention to the gaps that can exist between *esse* and *percipi*: between how one feels oneself to be, and how one may be perceived. Time and again, researchers into the social psychology of aging have found that when interviewees in their sixties, seventies and eighties were asked directly about how they saw themselves in terms of age

> scarcely any of them thought of themselves as old. There was an apparent contradiction – a kind of disconnection, therefore, between how they looked, how they were, how they felt, and what they thought.
>
> (Thompson, Itzin and Abendstern 1990: 113)

This book will explore various aspects of these signs, contradictions and disconnections as they emerge in a variety of dramatic, theatrical and performative contexts. Looking at a range of texts and performances, from classical tragedy to modern dance theatre, from music hall acts to contemporary playwriting, and from television sitcom to reminiscence theatre, it will consider what light can be thrown upon our understanding of ageing by looking at it from the perspective of drama, theatre and performance studies. Secondarily, it will ask what a consideration of ageing might teach us about drama, theatre and performance studies.

Content and context

In what follows, texts and performances for analysis are drawn from a range of different kinds of drama, theatre and performance dealing with age-related issues: classic and modern plays, contemporary theatre performances from both 'high' and popular culture, and performances from areas of applied theatre and paratheatrical activity (such as reminiscence work, therapeutic drama workshops, senior theatre groups, etc.) which focus on the elderly. Where possible, the book tends to emphasize a relationship between text and performance, and to take an interest in what happens when the text is absorbed into and transformed by 'the multifarious verbal and non-verbal discourses of theatrical production' (Worthen 1998: 1100). This involves a consideration of the physical conditions of a text's theatrical realization, both in its original stagings and, where appropriate, in later revivals, informed by recent methodological models in performance analysis. An emphasis on the performed text is particularly appropriate in relation to the theme of ageing, because in theatrical performance the physical presence of the actor's body itself – and the way that that body is used in conjunction with the codes and conventions of movement, gesture, make-up and costume – inevitably becomes one of the theatrical signs from which the audience constructs meanings. For obvious reasons, this is more immediately accessible, and will play a greater part, in the analysis of contemporary performances, which can be seen at first hand in their initial manifestations.

In the case of historical performances, where the immediacy of the first-hand encounter with the original event is not available, we face the common problem of all theatre historians: recapturing the texture of the past performances. In this, we can only get so far, and will be more reliant on the text itself and various kinds of 'archaeological' evidence from secondary sources. For some early performance texts this archaeological evidence is thin on the ground; for some mid-twentieth century performances, such as Patrick Magee's performance as Beckett's Krapp, or Frank Randle's comic old men, it is rich and illuminating. At best it includes video archive material of performances – sometimes modified for the purposes of the camera, but invaluable nonetheless.

The book, then, involves the use of selected dramatic texts and theatrical performances as an optic through which to view changing images, representations and understandings of old age, and it includes plays and performances from both past and present. There are some chapters where particular chronological issues become relevant: for example, in those chapters in Part Two, where a stereotype is traced from one period to another. Elsewhere, too, a specific historical or political context may be invoked. However, the main organizing principle of the book is thematic rather than chronological. While chronology is followed when there is no good reason *not* to do so, there is no overall attempt to develop an overarching chronological argument.

Selecting texts and performances on which to focus has presented a predictable problem, since actually most plays include representations of older people of one kind or another, and the challenge has been to select not just those featuring prominent elderly characters but also those which afford a significant degree of illumination to questions of ageing, and a range of responses to what Margaret Morganroth Gullette calls the 'master narrative of decline' (Gullette 2004: 129–35) – an issue which is central to this inquiry, and which will be looked at in more detail later. Other criteria included a reasonable thematic and chronological spread, balanced against a degree of familiarity and accessibility.

'Familiarity' and 'accessibility' are themselves culture-specific terms. I am writing from a British perspective, and as a result much of what I say relates primarily to British culture, and to British theatre and performance: consequently, many of the plays selected for analysis come from within the British and European canon. 'Britishness' in cultural history has traditionally been constructed in relation (and sometimes in opposition) to continental European and North American influences and experiences, and this study follows that tradition. It should be added, though, that there is another more modern and more varied kind of Britishness, the Britishness of twentieth- and twenty-first century multiculturalism; the present volume has little to say about that, but it recognizes the pressing need for a greater understanding of the additional issues which this sector of the ageing population faces. A generation of scholars is emerging who will be better equipped than I am to investigate these complexities and all their cultural articulations.

As this study moves closer to the present day, there is a broadening of the generic focus. UK theatre practitioners (from the commercial to the avant-garde) employ a wide range of strategies to address the theme of ageing: traditionally 'authored' plays are supplemented by musicals, devised performance, verbatim and reminiscence theatre – and all of these will come under consideration. Live theatre is at the heart of the study, but a number of mediatized performances, including television and radio programmes, are also included, and a word needs to be said about this, since it goes somewhat against the grain of much contemporary writing in Theatre and Performance Studies, which tends to stress the differences between the various media rather than what is shared. However, as Philip Auslander pointed out a few years ago (Auslander 1999), the barriers and boundaries between the live and the mediatized or recorded are now less clear, less permanent and less important than they once were. On an aesthetic level, the multimedia experiments which seemed so radical in Beckett's *Krapp's Last Tape* are now the bread-and-butter techniques of theatrical *mise-en-scène*; on an archival level, records of the live performances which took place seventy or more years ago are documented on YouTube. Moreover, the inclusion of texts and performances from television and radio reflects a pragmatic reality about contemporary British performance culture. In the UK – much more so than in America – actors, directors and other practitioners still find the boundaries between theatre on the one hand, and film and broadcast media on the other to be fairly permeable. Television and radio, therefore, feature in the book – not only for this pragmatic reason but also because their presence within the culture is one of the key ways in which the narratives of old age circulate and (especially now, with the proliferation of digital channels in both media that specialize in repeat broadcasts) *keep* circulating. I have, however, not dealt with cinema or film culture in this volume. This is partly because the film industry is so deeply rooted in, and so influenced by, the specifics of North American culture that, in order to do it justice the focus on UK performance culture would have had to be even further reduced, to the detriment of the book as a whole. Beyond that, the subject of old age in cinema is so vast, and the discipline of film studies so well defined, that it demands a separate study altogether. And, indeed, such studies are emerging: there is an impressive and growing area of film studies (e.g. Beugnet 2006, Chivers 2011) which deals with precisely this subject.

Both quantitatively and qualitatively, radio turned out to be an important medium for the subject matter, and sound recordings of various kinds (in the shape of conventional plays, radio ballads, experimental performances and documentaries) feature rather more prominently in the book than I had expected. I should not have been surprised. The BBC's public service mandate means that issues of importance such as ageing come high on its agenda and are treated, for the most part, thoughtfully and intelligently, whether as drama, documentary or 'feature'. And while television remains the elderly person's entertainment of choice, talk-radio channels such as BBC Radio 4 speak to a predominantly older audience. Many of these listeners, who grew up with the radio, have treated it as a lifelong companion; it will be interesting to see how important the radio is to future generations of older people.

This, then, is the material which will be investigated in the course of this book. The theoretical context within which this investigation will take place is provided by one of the pioneers of age studies, Margaret Morganroth Gullette, whose own work has involved a continual engagement with, and resistance to, age ideology and the 'master narrative of decline'. Broadly speaking, the master narrative of decline is that invisible but dominant cultural 'message' which encourages men and women to experience and articulate growing older essentially in terms of loss, isolation, and diminished physical mental and material resources. As such, decline ideology is an

> invisible producer of economic differences, an omnipresent regulator of age-inflected discourses, a constant pressure on our sense of life time, [and] its master narrative needs to be revealed in all its workings … The master narrative starts … as a story of progress and becomes a peak-and-(early)-decline story … According to the prevailing script, even if we also make progress, we are supposed to internalize decline as our dominant private age identity.
>
> (Gullette 2004: 130)

The master narrative appears in many specific differentiated versions, depending on whether it is being 'told by or about men, women, various classes, races, sexualities, ethnicities' (Gullette 2004: 130). It informs the dominant fictions of our culture and in doing so it shapes our own subjectivity, identity and desires.

And, of course, these dominant fictions include theatrical fictions. Indeed, theatre is more inextricably bound up with age ideology than is the case with most art forms. The primary medium of theatrical performance, after all, is the human body. And the human body is always of a specific age – whether that be old or young. The specificity of that age becomes part of the meaning of the theatrical experience as a whole. Moreover, the master narrative of decline may find that the fictions of theatrical performance offer it a particularly convivial home for other reasons. Theatre is, among other things, a sign-system; but it is a sign-system which necessarily refers to other sign-systems. In particular, it draws on and quotes the signifiers, codes and modalities of everyday life. If the master narrative of decline is indeed, as Gullette suggests, 'omnipresent' in the discourses which dominate our lives, then it is to be expected that it will find frequent expression in plays and performances.

But if theatre is inherently complicit in the contradictions and complexities of the ideologies of a culture, that is not to say that it is doomed only to articulate those ideologies uncritically. It may also play with them, question them or contradict them. As it has repeatedly shown, theatre can critique and subvert hegemony as well as comply with it. And, like other forms of ideology, age ideologies can be resisted.

> There is a way out [of being overwhelmed by the bleakness of the narrative of decline] if one recognizes that decline is an ideology, learns more about its techniques, and invents resistances.
>
> (Gullette 2004: 135)

This book will be looking at plays and performances both in order to learn the techniques of age ideology, and also in order to explore resistances to it. And if it sometimes inclines towards the former, I still hope that in the very process of learning the techniques of an ideology, an implied resistance may be communicated.

PART I

Frames and Contexts

Chapter 1

On Gerontology

The first gerontologist?

As yet, social gerontology as a distinct academic field is itself hardly of pensionable age. Nonetheless, the social aspects of ageing have been the subject of inquiry for thousands of years. One of the founding texts of western philosophy, Plato's *Republic*, opens its inquiry into politics, metaphysics, philosophy and truth with a consideration of old age. It begins with Socrates and his friends visiting the house of Polemarchus in the Piraeus. There they meet with Polemarchus' aged father, Cephalus, a man who seems very much at peace with himself in his old age. He is an affectionately drawn caricature, whose initial greeting is immediately followed by an old man's stereotypical complaint that Socrates does not come to see him as often as he should. Socrates is eager to avoid any imputation of ageism. He says:

> There is nothing which for my part I like better, Cephalus, than conversing with aged men; for I regard them as travellers who have gone a journey which I too may have to go, and of whom I ought to enquire, whether the way is smooth and easy, or rugged and difficult. And this is a question which I should like to ask of you who have arrived at that time which the poets call the 'threshold of old age' – Is life harder towards the end, or what report do you give of it?
>
> (Plato [c. 380 BCE] 1970: 85)

Socrates is, of course, an inveterate questioner – his whole dialogic technique is based on asking clever questions which lead his interlocutors into more and more untenable logical positions, eventually demonstrating triumphantly that he – Socrates/Plato is right. His question to Cephalus, though, is not one of his rhetorical tricks: Socrates is asking a genuine question. He himself has not reached Cephalus' time of life, and he does not know what it feels like to be old. The supreme philosopher recognizes that the *experience* of old age is only available to the old themselves. So he asks Cephalus. And to that extent he is in a position not unlike most gerontologists today. Some of us are, it is true, no longer spring chickens, and many of us are pushing retirement age – or have already passed it. But most of us are studying something that is not quite ourselves. The subject of our study is not, for the most part, reflected in ourselves as we are now, so much as in ourselves as we imagine ourselves to be at some point in the future.

And in this respect, work on the cultural aspects of ageing is very different from work on gender and culture. Gender work – whether done by literary critics, sociologists, historians, geographers – nearly always has an element of autobiography about it. When I wrote a book a few years ago about staging masculinities (Mangan 2002) I felt the need to start it by placing myself in terms of the gender issues that it raised about my own negotiations between the stage and masculinity, and the writing of it continually returned me to my own sense of a gendered self – both in its similarities to the issues that the texts raised for me and in its differences. I had imagined that writing a book on theatre and ageing would be very similar to writing one about theatre and gender, since both raise such pressing questions about identity construction. It took me a little while to see just how great a gulf lies between them, and how most gerontologists of whatever hue are basically in the same position as Socrates – knowing that there is much that they do not know about what it is actually like to be old, and contemplating those 'travellers who have gone a journey which I too may have to go, and of whom I ought to enquire, whether the way is smooth and easy, or rugged and difficult'.

But if Socrates' question offers something pertinent to contemporary gerontologists, then so does Cephalus' reply:

> I will tell you, Socrates, he said, what my own feeling is. Men of my age flock together; we are birds of a feather, as the old proverb says; and at our meetings the tale of my acquaintance commonly is – I cannot eat, I cannot drink; the pleasures of youth and love are fled away: there was a good time once, but now that is gone, and life is no longer life. Some complain of the slights which are put upon them by relations, and they will tell you sadly of how many evils their old age is the cause. But to me, Socrates, these complainers seem to blame that which is not really in fault. For if old age were the cause, I too being old, and every other old man, would have felt as they do. But this is not my own experience, nor that of others whom I have known. How well I remember the aged poet Sophocles, when in answer to the question, How does love suit with age, Sophocles – are you still the man you were? Peace, he replied; most gladly have I escaped the thing of which you speak; I feel as if I had escaped from a mad and furious master. His words have often occurred to my mind since, and they seem as good to me now as at the time when he uttered them. For certainly old age has a great sense of calm and freedom; when the passions relax their hold, then, as Sophocles says, we are freed from the grasp not of one mad master only, but of many. The truth is, Socrates, that these regrets, and also the complaints about relations, are to be attributed to the same cause, which is not old age, but men's characters and tempers; for he who is of a calm and happy nature will hardly feel the pressure of age, but to him who is of an opposite disposition youth and age are equally a burden.
>
> (Plato [c. 380 BCE] 1970: 85)

He goes on a bit, it is true, but he is worth hearing out because he makes a crucial point. His reply has been interpreted in various ways by various critics. Stephen Marx sees Cephalus as a positive exemplar of 'the pastoral of old age' (Marx 1985: 39). Helen Small, on the other hand, in

The Long Life, finds the old man interesting only insofar as he anticipates something of Cicero's later argument in *De Senectute* about old age bringing with it a respite from the mad and furious mastery of passions such as love and sexual desire; beyond that she is rather dismissive of him, concluding that he 'is not presented as a philosopher of any great merit' (Small 2007: 28).

But, whether he is a philosopher of any merit or not, Cephalus is raising an important point for researchers into ageing: it is not just that the experience of ageing is diverse. More than this, he suggests to Socrates that he might be asking the wrong question. Old age simply is not the point: he tells Socrates that 'these complainers seem to blame that which is not really in fault. For if old age were the cause, I too being old, and every other old man, would have felt as they do. But this is not my own experience, nor that of others whom I have known.' Again, it is a very salutary point for gerontologists! It is all too tempting to generalize about old age and ageing: but Cephalus does not want simply to be pigeonholed as a data source in Socrates' gerontological research project. It is not because I am old that I feel this way, he says. It is because I am me.

In the same way, when we ask questions fuelled by our own current research obsession, it is important to be aware that the answers we receive might not, after all, be entirely determined by the terms of our own investigation. 'The truth is, Socrates, that these regrets, and also the complaints about relations, are to be attributed to the same cause, which is not old age, but men's characters and tempers.' One of the themes of this book will be the extent to which old age needs to be understood, not as a phenomenon in itself, but as part of a network of social realities and constructions.

Socrates, as we might expect, gets the last word. He, too, seems to think that questions about old age may not really be the point – and indeed this is not, after all what *The Republic* is really about; in the rest of the volume Socrates turns to exploring a series of questions about truth, justice and metaphysics on their own terms. But before doing so he also scores a point off the venerable old man – and he does so in a way that once more reverberates through gerontological research. He accepts the point that the experience of old age may not be universal, but he adds that the philosophical tenets that Cephalus bases upon his own particular experience may not be entirely generalizable either. He replies:

> Yes, Cephalus, but I rather suspect that people in general are not convinced by you when you speak thus; they think that old age sits lightly upon you, not because of your happy disposition, but because you are rich, and wealth is well known to be a great comforter.
>
> (Plato [c. 380 BCE] 1970: 86)

Socrates here suddenly becomes the cultural materialist. If the experience of old age is indeed culturally diverse, he suggests, one of the most important factors in that diversity – in Cephalus' case, the factor that has enabled him to live comfortably and contentedly in his old age – may simply be money. When we talk about old age – historically or in the present, fictionally or factually – there are some things from which we cannot divorce it: things such as gender, class and the material conditions of life.

From Plato's short dramatic scene, then, five points arise – all of which indicate some of the problems of research into ageing.

- Researching into old age usually involves, to some extent, investigation at second-hand.
- It is hard to generalize about ageing.
- Not everybody experiences ageing in the same way, and the disposition of the individual plays an enormous part.
- Social and material factors are also crucial. Socrates talks about Cephalus' wealth – we might also consider aspects such as his race and gender.
- Ageing is not the cause of all age-related phenomena, and as researchers we would do well to be aware of the extent to which our own interest in the issue of ageing might distort our perspective.

Being old, then, is not just about being old; it is about being old and rich, or old and poor, or old and a citizen, or old and a slave, or old and a woman, or… . It is about values and politics, and it is – above all – about meaning. That, in essence, is also the standpoint of 'modern age studies', or 'gerontology' (the two are sometimes defined separately but I am considering them here as a single entity and will use the terms more or less interchangeably). Contemporary gerontologists tend not to be satisfied, of course, with Cephalus' somewhat essentialist attribution of everything to 'men's characters and tempers'. Nonetheless, the general point that comes out of the dialogue between Cephalus and Socrates, about the interconnectedness of things, is one of the tenets of contemporary age studies. On a theoretical level, the interdisciplinary nature of much of age studies reinforces this. In practice, so do the methods and procedures of much age-related work with individuals – so that life-course perspectives, for example, stress the ways in which a person's present experience of ageing is linked to his or her own earlier life, to the lives of other individuals, and to their historical contexts. And the big questions to which contemporary gerontology continually returns are the questions of meaning: what does it *mean* to be old? To the old person? To others?

I shall be using theatre and performance to investigate these questions in various contexts, and theatre and performance are also continually concerned with making and exploring meanings. In Shakespeare's plays, for example, old age may at times be equated with hatred and destruction (*Romeo and Juliet*) or foolishness (Polonius in *Hamlet*); at other times it may seem to embody a kind of transcendent wisdom (*The Tempest*). The theatrical meanings of old age are sometimes social and shared, sometimes metaphorical, and sometimes painfully subjective.

Reading age studies against performance studies: Orientations

The broad tendency of this book will be to read age studies against performance studies – and vice versa. By this I mean that I will be investigating a series of selected plays and performances which deal significantly with old age and ageing, and analysing them (sometimes explicitly, sometimes implicitly) in relation to ideas, terms and theories drawn both from contemporary gerontology and from performance and literary studies. So, for example, in the course of examining both historical and contemporary plays and performances, we will also be looking at gerontological theories of life review, reminiscence and self-narrativization, biological theories of ageing, the recent social history of the care home, questions of gender, liminality, generational conflict and so on. In juxtaposing the procedures of performance analysis with the concerns and insights of age studies, the intention has been to discover what light each might throw on the other. In the process, I have tried to avoid being programmatic, and to resist the temptation to privilege one paradigm over the other. My proposition is a simple one: that there might be mutual benefit in this dual perspective.

In order to work in this way, however, it is necessary to provide a broad-brush picture of some of the concerns of contemporary age studies. As I suggest previously, Plato begins to map out some of the research questions and methodologies, and many of the points which arise from the beginning of *The Republic* continue to speak to us today. But modern gerontology has developed a further agenda and an intellectual framework of its own. At this point, then, I want to sketch out some of the aspects of this agenda and framework, and to locate some of the broad agreements that exist and within which this book operates. To do so is inevitably to oversimplify, and I offer my apologies to those many scholars and researchers whose nuanced work shows up these oversimplifications for what they are. Even so, this book is aimed at readers whose background lies in theatre and performance studies as well as those with an in-depth understanding of gerontology, and the former, I hope, may find such an introductory sketch helpful. In what follows, then, I shall offer a brief review of some of the key tenets and positions that are characteristic of contemporary age studies – with an occasional brief sideways glance at their theatrical implications.

a) Crisis?

The first point on which most gerontologists would agree is that there is currently a 'crisis' of ageing, both on global and local levels. A number of major national and international studies have established empirically what many people suspect instinctively – that what is going on now in terms of global population ageing is unprecedented, pervasive, profound and enduring. One of the most influential of these, the United Nations' report on *World Population Ageing*, first published in 2002 and updated in 2009, describes the current situation as

> a process without parallel in the history of humanity … At the world level, the number of older persons is expected to exceed the number of children for the first time in 2045 … [I]t is affecting nearly all the countries of the world … [and it] has a direct bearing on both the intergenerational and intragenerational equity and solidarity that

are the foundations of society ... In the economic area, population ageing will have an impact on economic growth, savings, investment, consumption, labour markets, pensions, taxation and intergenerational transfers. In the social sphere, population ageing influences family composition and living arrangements, housing demand, migration trends, epidemiology and the need for healthcare services ... As long as old-age mortality continues to decline and fertility remains low, the proportion of older persons will continue to increase.

(United Nations 2009: viii)

What is happening today, then, is unique and talk of a crisis in population ageing is by no means an exaggeration. But 'crisis' is a loaded word, with connotations of disaster and catastrophe; in a study such as this it is well to remember that crises are as frequently caused by people's attitudes as they are by natural forces. While the demographic statistics of global ageing are hardly subject to dispute, the different interpretations which can be put on those statistics are constantly debated. In 2002, the Executive Summary of the UN report on population ageing ended with the upbeat reminder that '[t]he profound, pervasive and enduring consequences of population ageing present enormous opportunities as well as enormous challenges for all societies' (Population Division 2002: xxxi). In the 2009 update, however, that cheerfulness is notably absent.

b) Cultural ageing

The second commonplace is that ageing is socially constructed as well as biologically or chronologically determined.

Although knowledge of old age can come to us from our infirmities (our own bodies can speak to us of old age) I want to insist again that old age is in great part constructed by any given society as a social category, as is, for example, adolescence.

(Woodward 1991: 66)

There are various 'hard' and 'soft' versions of this social constructionist position: Margaret Morganroth Gullette, for example, emphasizes the social over the biological. 'The next provocative proposition of age studies', she suggests, 'might be that we are aged *more* by culture than by chromosomes' (2004: 101; my emphasis). This is not a simple territorial battle between the 'two cultures' (Snow 1959) of the arts and the sciences: the social and cultural factors involved in the process of growing old have long been recognized by researchers in the humanities and the sciences alike. They have also, more importantly, long been recognized by the elderly themselves.

Cultural factors, after all, influence our experiences of ageing in very material ways: our economic and social situation, and the access that this affords us to benefits such as a good diet, a healthy lifestyle, effective medicines and work that is not physically debilitating – all these are cultural factors which determine the ways in which we experience the ageing process. At the level of ideology, however, our experience of ageing is also determined by the ways in which our culture constructs the very concept of old age: by the kinds of spoken and unspoken assumptions and messages that circulate about what old age 'is', and, most importantly, by the ways in which we internalize such messages. There are crucial links between the social construction of age, ageing, the life-course in general and the subject's sense of the self, and our culture contains a 'master narrative of decline' (Gullette 2004: 129ff.) which makes 'positive ageing' increasingly difficult.

Theatrical performance, too, is socially constructed. All art forms are, of course, but theatrical performance wears its social constructivism most proudly on its sleeve, as this famous passage from Shakespeare's *Henry V* (which rarely fails to finds its way into my teaching) demonstrates. Charming his audience into collaborating with the fictions of the stage, the Chorus urges the spectators to

Piece out our imperfections with your thoughts;
Into a thousand parts divide one man,
And make imaginary puissance;
Think when we talk of horses, that you see them
Printing their proud hoofs i' the receiving earth;
For 'tis your thoughts that now must deck our kings

(Shakespeare 1974: 936)

It is a perfect acknowledgement of the imaginative complicity between the audience and the actors on which theatrical performance depends – a complicity which translates descriptions of horses into a sense of their actuality, and the material presence of the few actors on the stage into a perception of the vast hosts that they come to represent in the consciousness of the audience. As William Demastes puts it, theatre 'rarely effectively discounts the world of consciousness in its efforts to deal with the materiality of existence. *Either* consciousness *or* materiality is not really a choice. Inevitably, theatre uses a both/and proposition of confronting consciousness integrally through materialism' (Demastes 2002: 41; original emphasis).

But this has ideological implications. Drama, theatre and performance are very public arts, depending for their success on the creation of a temporary sense of community with the audience whose job it is to 'piece out [the stage's] imperfections with [their] thoughts'. This (as was pointed out in the Introduction) gives theatrical performance a complex and difficult relationship with hegemonic structures, since to some extent it is already, by its nature, implicated in those structures. The theatre's dependence upon the complicity of the audience is absolute; and consequently the theatre is *also* complicit in societies' ideological and cultural structures, in all their complexities and contradiction. And among these is …

c) Ageism

The issue of cultural ageing leads almost inevitably to the question of 'ageism': perhaps one of the most pressing issues in social gerontology. If our subjectivity is in part constructed by ideology, then social messages or assumptions which encourage or tolerate prejudice against the old is, self-evidently, harmful. The term is usually attributed to Robert Butler, writing in 1969, in a short article in *The Gerontologist* which proposed it as a deliberate analogy to other forms of bigotry such as sexism and racism. Butler originally defined ageism as a systematic process of stereotyping and discrimination against people purely on grounds of their advanced age. More recent usage tends to include *any* age-related discrimination, but the original meaning, that of prejudice against old people, remains central, as does the issue of negative stereotyping. It is important to have a working definition of the term, and the one which was formulated by Bill Bytheway and Julia Johnson, and reiterated in Bytheway's book *Ageism*, is still useful:

Ageism is a set of beliefs originating in the biological variation between and relating to the ageing process ... In consequence of this it follows that:

(a) Ageism generates and reinforces a fear and denigration of the ageing process, and stereotyping presumptions regarding competence and the need for protection.
(b) In particular, ageism legitimates the use of chronological age to mark out classes of people who are systematically denied resources and opportunities that others enjoy, and who suffer the consequences of such denigration, ranging from well-meaning patronage to unambiguous vilification.

(Bytheway 1995: 14)

There is a moral imperative on us today to treat the elderly with respect, but, like racism and sexism, ageism has many forms, and it is articulated and perpetuated in a variety of ways, both explicit and implicit: through demeaning language, through negative images and stereotypes, through restrictive employment practices, through legislation – and simply through distorted information about and negative expectations of the elderly.

And some of the cultural forms that ageism takes can be quite subtle. It can lurk, for example, in the implicit assumption that all old people are somehow the same; and also in the assumption that old age, both in society and in the individual, is automatically 'a problem'. The aged themselves can be 'ageist' in this sense – as can those of us who work with or study them. By focusing on the very questions of age, by making generalizations (as we inevitably do) about a social category, we risk, however inadvertently, contributing to some of those very cultural constructs which define old age as a problem. It is the problem that is touched upon in *The Republic*, when Cephalus warns the well-meaning Socrates that he may be seeing not Cephalus the individual but Cephalus the type.

The study of 'old age' can turn its subjects into objects – as many social gerontologists are well aware. Sarah Arber and Jay Ginn, for example, enter a plea for sociologists of ageing to develop

> research methods [that can] capture the rich diversity of ageing and provide a sociological understanding building on the perspectives of older women and men. It is vital that quantitative research *on* older people is balanced by research *with* older people, in which older people are the subjects of research and their perspectives and concerns orient the research ... [and that] older people are studied as active subjects and given a voice.
>
> (Arber and Ginn 1995: 13)

It is hard for even an avowedly anti-ageist sociology of ageing to disentangle itself entirely from the discourses of ageism.

And in the study of theatre and performance it is particularly difficult. One of the ways in which ageism is articulated and perpetuated is through stereotypes; and theatre and performance has always made extensive use of stereotypes and stock characters. The latter term, indeed, derives from nineteenth-century theatrical 'stock companies'. The stock company comprised a tightly defined group of actors, each of whom specialized in a certain type of character: typical stock characters included the Leading Man (or Tragedian), the Juvenile Lead, the Heavy Lead (often a villain), the Leading Lady, the Low Comedian – and the Old Man and the Old Woman. But these nineteenth-century companies simply formalized theatrical custom and practice which had been going on for hundreds of years: the masks of the sixteenth-century *commedia dell' arte* companies were similarly stylized and stereotyped, with Pantalone in particular as the caricatured Old Man. Caricatures and stereotypes such as these continue – as we shall see – in contemporary performance culture, and have an important bearing on the master narrative of decline.

d) Chronological relativism

A further commonplace of social gerontology is that there is no single universally agreed point at which old age begins, so that definitions of old age are culturally and historically relative. To put it bluntly: what counts as old in one society – or, indeed, in one dramatic 'world' – may not count as old in another.

Even at the simplest level, talking about contemporary western society, things are not straightforward. As Ian Stuart-Hamilton observes in the opening section of his *Introduction to Gerontology*,

> providing a watertight objective definition is surprisingly difficult ... [W]hen do we decide that 'old age' begins? If we want a single 'threshold age' that marks the transition to becoming 'elderly', then this inevitably creates problems of inclusion and exclusion.

For example, suppose we choose 70 years of age as marking the onset of old age. A high proportion of people aged 70 and older have the stereotypical characteristics of old age, but not all do. And there are many people younger than 70 who have 'elderly' characteristics.

(Stuart-Hamilton 2011: 1)

And once the focus widens to include non-contemporary and non-western culture, it becomes even more complex. In Ancient Rome, for example, the onset of old age could be defined as anywhere from forty-two to seventy-seven (Parkin 1998: 19–42). In medieval Europe, old age could be defined as beginning at anything from thirty-five to seventy-two, depending on context (Shahar 1998: 43). Gerontologists thus tend to be wary of defining old age on a purely chronological basis – and indeed chronology itself is rarely 'pure'. Much of the best evidence we have concerning the definitions of old age in various historical periods derives from legal documents, laws and ordinances which stipulate exemptions from certain kinds of civic or military taxes or duties, or certain kinds of entitlements. Thus in England during the thirteenth century the Statute of Winchester expressly exempted men over sixty from the necessity of equipping themselves with arms for military service (Luders, Tomlins and Raithby [1810–38] 1963: 97). In ancient Rome, similar exemptions for men were often lower depending on the physical activity necessitated by the duty. The age of Roman women, on the other hand, was not considered in terms of legal rights or duties; rather 'women were considered old with the onset of the menopause, which was thought to happen between the ages of 40 and 50' (Cokayne 2003: 1). Contemporary European and American definitions of old age owe a great deal to health and social care legislation dating back to the nineteenth century. In this context, the Belgian statistician Adolphe Quetelet's *Treatise on Man* (1836) had a great influence on those policymakers of the period who sought to establish a state pension system for the elderly, based on the concept of a 'pensionable age' which begins at about sixty or sixty-five, and which became a norm in twentieth-century social provision. The fact that now, in the twenty-first century, many western countries are busy redrawing the boundaries of what constitutes pensionable age is both a testament to the success of health-care systems which have enabled citizens to remain healthier longer; and also one of the predictable responses of capitalist economies to the welfare aspects of the 'crisis' of ageing mentioned earlier in this section.

As should be clear, a simple chronological definition of what constitutes old age is never likely to be sufficient, and most gerontologists would agree with the argument that

an adequate sociological theory of age needs to distinguish between at least three different meanings – chronological age, social age and physiological age – and how they interrelate. Chronological (or calendar) age is essentially biological, but needs to be distinguished from physiological age, which is a medical construct, referring to the physical ageing of the body, manifest in levels of functional impairment. Social age refers to the social attitudes and behaviour seen as appropriate for a particular chronological age, which itself is cross-cut by gender.

(Arber and Ginn 1995: 5)

Chronology is a convenience rather than an absolute, and in fact, as cultural historians have shown, throughout history the category of old age has been constructed in a variety of ways which combine a simple year-count with a variety of biological, medical, moral, social, legal, civic and economic factors.

e) Over-compensation

Across time and cultures, then, definitions of old age change, and as soon as one moves away from purely biological definitions on the one hand (old age begins when such-and-such a physical deterioration sets in) or socio-legal on the other (at sixty-five one is entitled to draw a pension), then cultural definitions of old age are as much about meanings as about anything.

But while historical and cultural relativism in the definition of what constitutes old age is real, it is not boundless. A tendency towards historical over-compensation, which asserted broadly that people in such-and-such a period 'were considered old from their forties' (Shahar 1998: 43), has been shown to be just as distorting as a bland assumption that everybody dates old age from the same point as our modern western welfare legislation. In certain contexts (and we will be looking at some of these) old age certainly begins much earlier than sixty or sixty-five; but it is also noticeable how much repetition can be found, across cultures and across periods, concerning the chronological definitions of old age.

A common misconception about the number of old people who existed in historical societies is based on a misunderstanding of the nature of population statistics and phrases such as 'average life expectancy'. For example the average life expectancy of a sixteenth-century Englishman – or woman – was much lower than today: less than forty years across the country and much lower in London (Rappaport 2002: 67–71). But this statistical average is distorted by the extremely high infant mortality rate: those who survived up to adulthood had a good chance of living into their fifties or sixties, while seventy or eighty was not uncommon.

This question of over-compensation raises its head in other ways, too. What is true of historical inquiry may also be true of intercultural inquiry, and although this present study is very much based in European culture, it is worth reminding ourselves of the need for a similar caution in considering relative cultural values and ageing. While it is undoubtedly true that industrialized western societies have much to learn from non-western cultures, about ageing as about so much else, there remains a need for balance. On the one hand, we should not mistake our own local societal assumptions and practices as universal or normative. On the other hand, though, neither should we demonize nor idealize those of other societies and cultures.

A cooler anthropological perspective would suggest that 'the position of the aged in a given society can be expressed in terms of how much old people contribute to the resources of the group, balanced by the cost they exact, and compounded by the degree of control they have over valuable resources' (Amoss and Harrell 1981: 5). With this in mind, we would do well to treat with care, and indeed scepticism, some of the familiar and well-meaning but over-generalized statements about how much better the old are treated in 'other' societies. Thus, for example, the much-repeated commonplace that '[t]he elderly in India are generally obeyed, revered, considered to be fountains of knowledge and wisdom, and treated with respect and dignity by family and community members' (Anon. 2011a: n.p.) needs to be placed alongside the 2011 HelpAge *Report on Elder Abuse and Crime in India*, which described high levels of both physical and verbal abuse at the hands of family members. Of those surveyed, 98 per cent reported not filing any report about the abuse they experienced; 68 per cent reported taking no action at all (HelpAge 2011: viii). These statistics, together with accounts of widespread financial and medical dependency, and of a general fear among the Indian elderly that they are soft targets of crime, should warn us against any generalized assumptions about cultural differences.

f) Subdivisions of old age

Another broad insistence among social gerontologists is that old age does not form a single 'category'. We spend – if we are lucky enough to avoid an early death – much of our life being old, and while the physical and mental changes that we may undergo in, say, our last twenty years of life might not be quite as dramatic as those we undergo in our first twenty, they are nonetheless both real and significant. And now in particular, in the late twentieth and early twenty-first centuries, as the number of people reaching 'old age' has increased, and as these people have arrived at old age with an increased life expectancy, 'the elderly' has become an even more heterogeneous group, covering a large number of years, and a great range of physical and mental conditions: individual variation means that 'some individuals remain fit and active into their ninth or tenth decades, whilst others show evidence of infirmity during their early sixties' (Woodhouse et al. 1988: 505).

A recognition of the different stages of old age has led social gerontologists to propose various modes of sub-classification of the elderly. For some the key division is between 'fit' and 'frail', based on the following definitions:

The fit elderly are individuals, over 65 years of age, living independently at home or in sheltered accommodation. They are freely ambulant and without significant hepatic, renal, cardiac, respiratory or metabolic disorder on either clinical examination or laboratory investigation. They do not receive regular prescribed medication.

The frail elderly are individuals, over 65 years of age, dependent on others for activities of daily living, and often in institutional care. They are not independently mobile – whilst they do not have overt cardiac, respiratory, hepatic, renal or metabolic disease, minor abnormalities may be revealed on laboratory investigation. They may require regular prescribed drug therapy. Conditions contributing to frailty commonly include Alzheimer's disease, multi-infarct cerebrovascular disease, Parkinsonism, osteoporosis, osteoarthritis, and healed fracture events.

(Woodhouse et al. 1988: 505)

Others prefer to remain chronologically based, but divide the elderly into three sub-populations commonly referred to as the 'young-old', 'old' and 'old-old' groups.

There is nothing particularly new about this. In *As You Like It* Shakespeare's Jaques famously distinguishes between the various ages of man, including two subdivisions of old age: on the one hand, 'the lean and slippered pantaloon, With … his big manly voice, Turning again toward childish treble', and on the other the 'mere oblivion, Sans teeth, sans eyes, sans taste, sans everything' by which he characterizes extreme old age.

Shakespeare was drawing on a well-established trope: in 1607 John Cuffe published *The Difference of Ages of Man's Life,* in which he outlined his own typology of ageing, drawing on classical 'humours theory' – the dominant Renaissance medical model which sees bodily and mental health as dependent on a balance between various fluids within the body. Cuffe broadly followed Aristotle in his divisions of the life-course. He tells us:

Aristotle setteth downe only three distinct ages, childhood, flourishing man-age, and old-age; the first plentifully abounding with heat and moisture; the middle age having the same two qualities of life, as well tempered as their nature possibly can be; old age declining and swarving from that good and moderate temper, and by little and little decaying in both these qualities, till at length they be both of them consumed.

(Cuffe 1607: 116)

But Cuffe was not quite satisfied with Aristotle's schema, and when it came to old age he subdivided it into two smaller groups.

And this last part of our life is resembled unto Winter, for that although it be in itself hot and moist (as life consisteth wholly in these two qualities) yet in comparison of the former ages, and in regard of death, unto which it leadeth us, is accounted cold, and this hath also its degrees or parts: the first wherein our strength and heat are evidently impaired, yet not so much, but that there remaineth a will and readinesse to bee doing, and this lasteth usually from our fiftieth yeere unto our three-score and five. The second part of this last part of our life, which they call decrepit old age, is when our strength and heat is so farre decaied, that not onlie all abilities is taken away, but even all willingnesse, to the least strength and motion of our bodie: and this is the conclusion and end of our life, resembling death itselfe, whose harbinger and fore-runner it is.

(Cuffe 1607: 120)

Subdivisions of old age, then, are nothing new, and the impetus that inspired Cuffe and Shakespeare at the turn of the seventeenth century is still relevant today.

g) Interdisciplinarity/multidisciplinarity

The final aspect of contemporary social gerontology that I want to highlight at this point concerns the discipline's sense of itself. Nearly all accounts of gerontology stress its interdisciplinary and multidisciplinary nature: because ageing as a human phenomenon affects so many areas of life, it is only to be expected that all sorts of intellectual disciplines and social practices have something to say about ageing.

In its early phase, however, gerontology was dominated by scientific and medical models and methodologies. In the study of old age – as of so much else – the early and middle years of the twentieth century saw a clear divide between the 'two cultures' (Snow 1959) of science and arts, and it was from the former that most of the founding texts of gerontology were drawn. A biomedical model of ageing became the norm, with the social sciences following in the footsteps of the natural scientists: demographic perspectives on ageing, connections between social class and health in old age, and analyses of public policy on ageing have been particularly fruitful areas of scholarship. But the dominance of modernist scientific method meant that until comparatively recently gerontologists 'stayed away from questions of meaning and value, of ethics, metaphysics, and spirituality … [or else attempted] to answer them from within the paradigm of modernist science' (Cole and Sierpina 2007: 245).

Towards the end of the twentieth century, however, there was a change of mood within the social 'sciences'; as a result these disciplines did begin to concern themselves more urgently with such questions about meaning and value – questions which could be answered more appropriately through the development of a broader range of qualitative methodologies.

It was – predictably – during this phase that humanities disciplines such as history, theology, literary studies and (eventually) performance studies began to make a significant contribution towards our understanding of old age. The engagement of humanities scholars with questions of gerontology coincided with broader social developments and new kinds of analyses of – and attitudes towards – social and ideological structures of oppression. In gender studies and race studies, humanities scholarship developed a sense of purpose, working openly to expose prejudice, to combat negative stereotyping, and to make a stand against sexism, racism and other such discriminatory 'isms'. This concern with combating forms of oppression and identifying and exploring possibilities for emancipatory social change soon became applied to questions of ageing, and Butler's term 'ageism' became widely accepted both in everyday parlance and as an underpinning theme of age studies. The broader question that humanities approaches to ageing sought to answer, however, was the question of the meaning – or the meanings – of old age. Writers sought to take up the challenge posed by Simone de Beauvoir in the Preface to *Old Age*:

Old age is not a mere statistical fact; it is the prolongation and the last stage of a certain process. What does this process consist of? In other words, what does growing old mean?

(de Beauvoir 1972: 10)

There is no single answer to the question: as has already been said, different cultures, and different communities, have answered it in a variety of different ways, based on a variety of different ethical, political, economic, theological, historical, psychological, social and personal considerations. The question itself has innumerable inflections – of which perhaps the most important is the distinction between the old age that is observed and the old age that is experienced: 'What does it mean for someone to get old?' does not always produce the same sort of answers as 'What does it mean for *me* to get old?' And if the contribution of humanities scholarship to gerontology can be summed up in a single phrase, it might be this: an investigation into the meanings of old age.

Philosophy, both ancient and modern, has always shown an interest in ageing. It is a topic, perhaps, which leads easily – as it did for Plato/Socrates in *The Republic* – into a consideration of the wider questions of human life: questions about purpose, questions about personal ethics, about bioethics, about the nature of wisdom, about the continuity of the self, the contemplation of death, the limitations of life. From Plato to Schopenhauer, thinking about the nature of old age has led philosophers into explorations of the nature of human existence, and vice versa. Contemporary philosophy has continued to contribute to our knowledge and understanding of old age. D. L. Norton's *Personal Destinies: A Philosophy of Ethical Individualism* (1976), for example, was an ambitious attempt to buck contemporary trends in philosophy towards narrower and more technical inquiries, and address the ultimate question 'What is the meaning of human life?' Norton's account of the individual's self-actualization includes a chapter on 'The Stages of Life'. In this (like Erik Erikson (1959), who approached the same idea from a psychosocial perspective) Norton explores the distinctiveness of the various phases of childhood, adolescence, maturity and old age, with all their various values, advantages, problems and obligations. However, the text from this period which most directly addressed the topic of ageing was indeed de Beauvoir's *Old Age* (1972). This did for age studies what her *Second Sex* (1949) had done for gender studies – presenting an existentialist critique of attitudes towards age and ageing which draws on Marx, Freud and Husserl, and which combines her own insights with a wide range of reference to medical, anthropological and historical literature.

As a discipline, it might seem that philosophy has been rather less active in its exploration of old age than might have been expected. This, though, has as much to do with disciplinary boundary-drawing within the modern academy as with any lack of interest in the philosophical aspects of the subject. Many of the themes which were historically the domain of the catch-all concept of 'philosophy' have been explored in recent years through the more fragmented disciplines, and the increasingly sharply defined methodologies, of the various humanities and social sciences disciplines; the rise of gerontology itself as an inter- or post-discipline has added to the complexities.

Of the humanities as a whole, perhaps the most significant contributions have been made by historians – although even in 1992 Paul Thompson could write, in tones of exasperation, that 'the social history of ordinary ageing has scarcely been started' (Thompson 1992: 24). But it did start, and it continued. It remains true, however, that the lives of *extra*ordinary old people – the very rich, the powerful, in particular – have always been more richly documented than the lives of those whom Thompson referred to as 'ordinary'. Much of the work of the historians of age has been focused upon dispelling traditional assumptions about what it was like to be old in the past. 'One of the lingering stereotypes about the past held by non-practitioners of history', say historians Lynn Botelho and Susannah R. Ottaway, 'is that there were few old people in it, that most died well before reaching old age, and that those that lived long were venerated as ancient sources of wisdom' (Botelho and Ottaway 2008: I, xi). They are writing in the general introduction to their magisterial collection of historical texts about old age, *The History of Old Age in England, 1600–1800* – a collection which puts that stereotype, along with several others, to rest once and for all. They go on to say, 'Our texts clearly demonstrate that more than just a few individuals lived and worked into old age and that there was no rarity value in being old. Instead, there were enough old people to allow for mockery and satire, as well as respect and care' (Botelho and Ottaway 2008: I, xi).

It is difficult, of course, to gather watertight statistical evidence about longevity in ages before centralized governmental census records began to offer demographers a more panoramic view of the lives of populations. In dealing with these periods, then, attempts to reconstruct the historical demographics of ageing have had to rely on the much more fragmentary evidence which can be gathered from local ecclesiastical records of baptisms, marriages and burials, and from anecdotes, legal documents and other public and private records. Even so, historians such as Pat Thane, Paul Johnson, Lynn Botelho and Susannah Ottaway have built up between them a sufficiently complex picture of old age in history for us to be able to move beyond those simple 'lingering stereotypes', both about the experience of age and about attitudes towards old age in the past. Indeed, collections such as that of Botelho and Ottaway, drawn as they are from the social, literary and cultural records of the time, are more valuable for what they have to say about social attitudes than for what they have to say about numbers and statistics. They reject not only the stereotypical assumption that elderly people in the past were venerated as sources of wisdom, but also its shadow side – the complementary assumption that old people have always been marginalized, rejected, ignored or treated with contempt.

There are, to be sure, some historians who see the history of old age in just such terms. Georges Minois' *History of Old Age* (1989), for example, concentrates on these negative meanings of ageing. Drawing on sources from classical Greece to the sixteenth century, he offers an effective history, not so much of old age, as of ageism. His work forms an interesting companion to de Beauvoir's *Old Age*: whereas de Beauvoir is particularly concerned with the way in which modern, industrial societies devalue old people, Minois sees nothing new in this: ageism, in his view, is age-old. We will explore Minois' argument, and some of its implications, in more detail in Chapter Three.

Neither of these two pictures tells the whole truth, though both contain some truths in them. In the past, as in the present, the elderly are seen in a variety of ways, and are the subject of a wide range of attitudes, beliefs and opinions. Moreover, these opinions and attitudes are themselves rarely stable: on the contrary they are subject to variation, alteration and slippage. More recent histories of old age have recognized this and have concentrated less on demographics and on treating old people as a unified category, or as the passive subjects of large-scale social and historical forces, and more on those things which differentiate them from each other, on their individual experiences, life stories, feelings and beliefs.

The experience of the individual, imaginative or otherwise, is one of the primary concerns of literary studies, where there has been a growing response to the subject of ageing. In a valuable review of humanities perspectives on gerontology, Thomas R. Cole and Michelle Sierpina point out that initially, and despite the pioneering work in the 1970s and 1980s of one or two scholars, most notably Kathleen Woodward, questions of ageing attracted little interest in English departments or in bodies such as the Modern Language Association. They cite Anne Wyatt Brown's taxonomy of the way that literary scholarship on ageing began to develop during the 1990s. Brown

> divided the scholarship into five categories: (1) analyses of literary attitudes towards ageing; (2) humanistic approaches to literature and ageing; (3) psychoanalytic explorations of literary works and their authors; (4) applications of the gerontological theories about autobiography, life review, and midlife transitions; and (5) psychoanalytically informed studies of the creative process.
>
> (Cole and Sierpina 2007: 249)

Novels and autobiographies were of particular interest in this context, while plays received comparatively little attention: Kathleen Woodward, for example, explicitly excluded the drama from consideration in her groundbreaking literary study *Ageing and Its Discontents* (Woodward 1991: 8). The late twentieth century saw a flowering of new novels in which older people featured as heroes and heroines (a consequence of the ageing of the baby boomer generation) and there was a renewed interest in the representation of old age in the works of eighteenth- and nineteenth-century novelists and autobiographers. With its capacity for representing the 'inner life' of a character – his or her thoughts, feelings and emotional development – in depth and over a period of time, studies of ageing in the novel formed a valuable corollary to the historians' interest in the life stories of elderly individuals.

It took a while for the scholarship of dramatic literature to catch up, but it is happening. For example, Antony Ellis' *Old Age, Masculinity and Early Modern Drama* (2009) analyses, from a literary perspective, representations of 'comic elders' in Italian and Shakespearean dramatic texts. Maurice Charney's *Wrinkled Deep in Time* (2009) focuses entirely on Shakespeare's treatment of old age. (The appearance of these two volumes as I began my own writing convinced me to go against what would be my normal instinct, and to pay comparatively little attention to Shakespeare in this current project.) Wider-ranging is Valerie Barnes Lipscomb and Leni Marshall's edited collection of essays, *Staging Age: The Performance of Age in Theatre, Dance, and Film* (2010), which looks, inter alia, at plays by Beckett, Molière and (again) Shakespeare, at movies which feature 'ageing cops', at Hollywood's cult of youth and at intergenerational dance.

Two scholars who have done most to integrate performance theory into gerontological debates are Margaret Morganroth Gullette and Anne Davis Basting. Gullette, in fact, draws brilliantly on performance studies in her writings, but is more concerned to develop 'age studies' as a companion to race and gender studies. Her *Aged by Culture* (2004) is essential reading for anybody with a serious interest in the analysis of the cultural aspects of ageing and ageism, while her more recent work, *Agewise: Fighting the New Ageism in America* (2011), is a call to battle against ageism as strongly as we do racism, sexism and other forms of bigotry.

Playwright and scholar Anne Davis Basting, too, uses performance studies as her starting point. *The Stages of Age: Performing Age in Contemporary American Culture* (1998) explores relationships between performance and ageing in the US theatrical mainstream and avant-garde; in applied and therapeutic contexts; and in what, in America, has become a recognized genre of community theatre: 'senior theatre'. From here, her work has taken her into developing practical interventions, as Director of the Centre on Age and Community at the University of Wisconsin, Milwaukee. Most notable is the improvisational storytelling of the *Timeslips* programme, which she devised as a method for working with people with dementia in ways which bring out their creativity through imagination rather than memory. The title of Basting's most recent work *Forget Memory: Creating Better Lives for People with Dementia* (2011) clearly indicates the recent trajectory of her work.

It is not only at the level of scholarship that literature and performance has turned its attention to the elderly in recent years. Publishers, theatre and media producers are turning out more novels, poems, plays and programmes about old age than ever before. In contemporary performance culture, it is true, youth still dominates the agenda at the institutional level, at the organizational level and at the level of policymaking. Arts Council England documents bristle with calls for theatres to 'work with young people aged eleven to twenty-five years, with a view to increasing opportunities and broadening the range of theatre-related activity in which young people can participate. This initiative is a priority within Arts Council England's national policy for theatre' (Arts Council England 2007: 1). But against such demands for a youth-oriented policy is a growing awareness of the size, the needs and indeed the audience potential of an ageing population, and the response has been a great increase in the number of recent programmes and performances which address the issues, the problems and the construction of old age. Some of these will, of course, form some of the subject matter of the rest of this book.

Chapter 2

On Age, Stage and Consciousness

'What is it like to be … old?'

There is something it is like to be a subject of experience. This is uncontroversial. There is something distinctive that it is like to be each and every one of us. This is more controversial. But it is true … What it is like to be you or any other subject of experience is closed off to me. This is controversial … The aim of this chapter is to show that the controversial claims are false.

(Flanagan 1992: 85)

Owen Flanagan's *Consciousness Reconsidered* is a contribution to the series of seminal debates that took place within consciousness studies during the nineties. Arguments between thinkers such as Daniel Dennett, Steven Pinker, Steven Jay Gould, Jerry Fodor and many others covered questions such as: the computer-like nature of the mind, the place of natural selection in the shaping of human nature, the nature of creativity and the function of art and religion. Flanagan's broader concern is to defend and develop a particular version of 'naturalism' (which, in the sense that consciousness studies uses the term, refers to 'the view that the mind-brain relationship is a natural one'; Flanagan 1992: xi), and the clarity with which he states key points of contestation in that debate makes his work a valuable starting point for a consideration of consciousness in relation to theatre and ageing.

One of the repeated conundrums of consciousness studies relates to the question 'What is it like to be … ?' And in a rather different tone, this is also one of the repeated conundrums of theatre. What is it like to be a bereaved Scandinavian prince? A failed East Coast salesman? A teenager whose lover belongs to the family of your family's greatest enemy? A homeless person stuck in the middle of nowhere, waiting for who knows what? A despised Jew in a city of Christians? A ruler who discovers that the curse which has fallen on the city is your own fault? It is the actor's job, through 'magic ifs', through emotion memory, through leaps of the imagination and empathic identification, and through whatever other tools are at his or her disposal, to 'get inside' these implied subjectivities – to try and answer for themselves the question 'What is it like to be … ?' And here we might seem to be in the presence of another kind of 'naturalism' – that kind of theatrical naturalism which became, in the late nineteenth and early twentieth centuries, the dominant vocabulary of western theatre. But the question of 'What is it like to be … ?' actually haunts a range of different theatrical forms, from the 'strong' naturalism envisioned by Strindberg in his Preface to *Miss*

Julie and by Zola in his essay on theatrical naturalism, through to the traces of representation that are present in many of even the most anti-naturalist of contemporary or popular performance pieces. It may be mediated by all kinds of theatrical conventions, but it is there. And it is there not only for the actor but also for the audience to whom he or she plays.

There are, it is true, theoretical ramifications to the way that the question is asked within consciousness studies, ramifications with which actors – or even theorists of acting – rarely have to engage. The fascination that consciousness studies has shown with the question is most famously articulated in Thomas Nagel's influential essay 'What is it like to be a bat?' (1974) in which Nagel argues with some plausibility that it is actually impossible for us ever to answer that question, for us ever to know exactly what that *is* like. The question – and more importantly, the implications of the ways in which the question might be answered – have acted as a touchstone for a series of debates about the relationship between the mind and brain, the question of whether or not subjectivity is impenetrable, and the extent to which consciousness (if such a thing even exists!) is mysterious, miraculous, measurable or describable. On this subject, various positions have been taken, developed and defended. The non-naturalist position holds that consciousness is simply not describable in conventional scientific terms. Positions such as that of 'principled agnosticism', 'anticonstructive naturalism' – or 'new mysterianism' – 'eliminative naturalism' all argue, with various degrees of vehemence, that while the properties of the brain can be described, their relationship to the experience of consciousness evades (and, some would add, will always evade) explanation. Flanagan's own belief that subjectivity is *not* impenetrable, is founded on yet another theoretical framework, that of 'constructive naturalism', which holds that 'there is reason for optimism about our ability to understand the relationship between consciousness and the brain' (Flanagan 1992: 2). And while the details of many of these debates about mind and brain have not yet been incorporated into theatre studies, three things are worth noting:

1. Firstly, on a practical level, body/mind relationships are very much a concern of performance studies, especially in the realm of performer training.
2. Secondly, there has been sufficient unease within theatre and performance studies itself about questions of the penetrability of subjectivity to generate a retaliatory raid on the discourse of cognitive science in order to shore up some traditional assumptions with some scientific evidence.
3. The third point is that in Flanagan's particular case, the arguments take him into various places which will be important to this study: most notably the importance of narrative in the construction of subjectivity.

We are, he later concludes, inveterate story tellers:

> Many thinkers have converged on the insight that a narrative conception of the self is 'the essential genre' of self-representation ... A self is just a structured life, structured in

part by its temporal components – its beginning, middle and end – and by the relations between the various characters who play on the stage of our lives. Continuity, coherence and comprehensiveness are the ideals of narrative explanation.

(Flanagan 1992: 198)

It is to this strand of consciousness studies, then, that this study owes the greatest allegiance: this strand which considers conceptions of the self and questions of subjectivity. These are issues which are particularly pertinent to any consideration of ageing. The phrase 'I don't feel old' throws into sharp relief the disjunction between subjective experience and objective perception. Just as one kind of 'double consciousness' is a feature of the actor's relationship to his or her role, so another kind of double consciousness is a feature of ageing. In this case it is that double – or perhaps more accurately multiple – consciousness of self to which Paul Johnson refers:

Unless they are physically ill or emotionally depressed, [old people] do not feel, in their real selves, that they are old. And given the common stereotypes of old age, they are absolutely right. Because later life normally brings losses of unprecedented seriousness – retirement from paid work, and the death of lovers, friends and kin – it is a time of active challenge. So far from implying passivity, it demands an exceptional ability to respond imaginatively to change. To succeed, older men and women have to be able to draw on their full resources, built up over a lifetime. They have to fight against the stereotypes of dependence to maintain their own sense of independent purpose and meaning in life. Denial of old age is defiance of a spoiled identity.

(Johnson 1992: 27)

Subjectivity and performance

If one of the big questions of human experience is 'What is it like to be … ?' another (probably anterior to it) is that simplest and most difficult of all questions, 'Who am I?' Answers to this question have been sought – and offered – in a number of ways and places: in religious dogmas and artistic activities; in political movements and contemplative practices; and in a wide variety of academic and intellectual disciplines, each with its own particular ways of asking and answering the question: philosophers, psychologists, theologians, sociologists, geneticists, psychoanalysts, lawyers, historians, anthropologists, neuroscientists, literary critics and researchers in consciousness studies and performance studies have all engaged, in various ways, with the question of subjectivity. And because subjectivity has been so very obsessively explored from so very many perspectives, it is a notion which has taken on a multiplicity of meanings. In terms of this study of old age, I will be looking at subjectivity as something multi-layered.

We can start with the subject's sense of her own subjectivity, her sense of self. To herself she is an 'I' – and she may suspect that nobody else knows quite what it is like to be that 'I' – not in the same way that she does, at least. This 'ontological subjectivity' (Searle 1997) is, perhaps, the most common sense of the word. Simultaneously, however, the subject exists in relation to those others – and they help to create her own sense of subjectivity. The way in which a child is treated by parents, for example, does much to affect the way in which that child develops in her understanding of herself. And in her increasingly complex dealings with other subjects, to whom she, in turn, *is* an 'Other', she is also objectified. Most particularly, she becomes implicated in the social environment, and the discourse of social institutions that – again – both help to constitute a sense of self and at the same time circumscribe its terms of being (see Gagnier 1991: 8).

I have just used the common example of a child and her development, but this multilayered concept of subjectivity is equally appropriate to someone in the later stages of life. And so when, for example, Alan Bennett gives voice to Violet, an old woman in a care home, he quickly gives his audience a sense of all these layers:

> *The speaker is an old lady in a wheelchair. She has a rug over her knees. The background is plain and uncluttered. Sometimes she is parked by a radiator, sometimes by a window or the end of a bed. The shots need not be continuous as written but can be broken up by a cutaway of Violet's hands, twisting her handkerchief, turning her wedding-ring or just folded in her lap. Sometimes when she is trying to remember things or express them she fills up with tears but these are only brief and she generally battles on.*
>
> I saw this feller's what-do-you-call-it today. Except that I'm not supposed to say 'what-do-you-call-it'. Verity says, 'Violet. What-do-you-call-it is banned. When we cannot find the word we want to describe, we do not say what-do-you-call-it'. Well, you won't find me describing that. Besides, 'what-do-you-call-it' is what I call it. Somebody's what-do-you-call-it. Anyway, I saw it.
>
> (Bennett 2007: 256)

The various levels of Violet's subjectivity are articulated both through the images of her and what she has to say. On the one level there is her sense of self – a sense which today includes the private memory of having seen a man's penis earlier in the day. On another level there is the interpersonal relationship with Verity (one of the nursing staff), in which Verity attempts to influence the way in which Violet articulates that experience – and thus, to some small degree, to define her and her world in Verity's own terms. This leads to Violet's own reaction – a rejection of Verity's language and a reaffirmation of her own ('Besides, "what-do-you-call-it" is what I call it. Somebody's what-do-you-call-it. Anyway, I saw it').

I didn't think anything about it only someone must have gone and alerted the office because next thing you know Bouncing Betty poles in. She says, 'Violet, I have to ask you this. Was the penis erect?' I said, 'Nurse Bapty. That's not a word I would use.' She said,

38

'Erect?' I said, 'No. The other.' She said, 'Well Violet. You've had what we call a stroke. You're sometimes funny with words.' I said 'I'm not funny with that word.' She said, 'Things have changed now, Violet. Penis is its name. All the other names are trying to make it more acceptable. Language is a weapon, Violet. We're at war.' I said, 'Who with?' She said, 'Men.'

(Bennett 2007: 256)

Nurse Bapty's language implicates Violet in two rather different kinds of discourse. First there is the institutional discourse of the care home ('You've had what we call a stroke. You're sometimes funny with words'), in which Violet is constituted as less capable, and in some ways less human than the staff who look after her. Secondly Bapty's whole attitude towards language involves a world-view – specifically, the world-view of a certain kind of gender politics, one which is very different from Violet's own.

The 'I'-self, the self-and-other and the socially constituted self are all present in Violet's monologue, and they point us towards the fact that as soon as we begin to consider subjectivity per se, it begins to disappear. Or at the very least we need to invoke notions of objectivity as well. One of Descartes' great (though problematic) contributions to modern thought was his distinction between objective knowledge and subjective apprehension. Kant, on the other hand, argued that subjectivity and objectivity are in fact – or at least in theory – coextensive. The nuances and complexities of this philosophical debate go way beyond the remit of this book, so I rather want to stress the inter-relationship between what we broadly understand as objective and subjective knowledge. We know ourselves and each other in a variety of ways, and these knowledges interact with, affect and transform each other.

One of the characteristics of theatre as an artistic practice is the way in which it plays between the objective and the subjective. Most art forms do this, in fact, but theatre does so in particular ways. An actor portrays a character, and as a result we, the audience, watch another person moving, talking, smiling, falling in love, suffering and so on; and, frequently, in this process, we are positioned somewhere between objective and subjective knowledges. Some forms of theatre invite us to inhabit one end of this spectrum rather than the other. For example, at the turn of the nineteenth and twentieth centuries, Stanislavski broke new ground as he started to ask his actors systematically to re-experience memories of their own emotional states: these were to inform performances so that an audience might then experience a sense of the subjective realities of the characters portrayed. As a result of Stanislavski's initial successes, an entire tradition of actor training became based on principles of subjective exploration and consequent notions of 'truth'. At the same time, however, another branch of the avant-garde saw Alfred Jarry create *Ubu Roi* – a play peopled by grotesque, puppet-like figures, in whose 'subjectivity' the audience was not expected to be interested. A few years later, the perceived dominance of a theatre which stressed subjective fellow-feeling spurred Brecht to theorize (though not always to create) an 'Epic' theatre.

Within a single play, too, an audience may be invited to take up very different positions in relation to different characters. Much of Stanislavski's work was tried out through working on Shakespeare's plays, for example – but not all Shakespearean plays, scenes or characters offer the same kind of subjective exploration, or ask for the same kind of emotional investment from an audience. We may identify closely with Lear, but not very much with Oswald. Equally, in a pantomime, we may shed tears of sympathy for Aladdin but not for Widow Twankey. Theatre, for the most part, operates in terms of a continually moving, kaleidoscopic spectrum of shared subjectivities and objectivities.

The question arises, of course, as to the possibility of sharing subjectivity at all; and there are many who would say it is not possible. But even if (as noted previously) real life suggests that it may be impossible for other people to understand the subjective 'I' from its own point of view, art can sometimes present us with literary or theatrical constructs which, on occasion, can offer us the valuable illusion that we *are* experiencing the world from a perspective other than our usual one. And in any case, while shared subjectivity may not be possible in the sense that would satisfy the strictest criteria of philosophers of mind, what does exist – both in everyday life and in the experience of theatrical performance – is empathy: the ability to suspend our focus on our own point of view and our own thoughts, perceptions and interests, and to focus on other people's interests, to intuit what someone else is thinking or feeling, and to respond appropriately to their thoughts or emotions (Baron-Cohen 2011: 10).

Empathy – 'the ability to share in another's feelings' (Fiske and Taylor 1991: 334) – is not a particularly sharply defined term in the human sciences. Different disciplines have different ways of approaching the concept, but even within any single one of them it can be difficult to find agreement as to how it should be understood. As a term, it dates back to the nineteenth century (a translation of the German 'Einfühlung' – 'in-feeling') and its earliest theorist was Theodor Lipps, who saw it as a central concept both of aesthetics and of the philosophy of the social and human sciences. Partly through Lipps' influence, in the early years of the twentieth century it became regarded as 'the primary means for gaining knowledge of other minds and as the method uniquely suited for the human sciences, only to be almost entirely neglected philosophically for the rest of the century' (Stueber 2008: n.p.).

Recent findings in neuroscience, however, have lent some empirical weight to Lipps' theoretical belief in the importance of empathy, and appear to have established a neurobiological basis for an understanding of what empathy is. Studies of neural circuit activity, not only in humans but also in other living creatures, suggest that 'there is significant overlap between neural areas of excitation that underlie our observation of another person's action and areas that are stimulated when we execute the very same action' (Stueber 2008: n.p.). These so-called mirror neurons are specialized cells in particular regions of the brain which fire not only when an animal performs an action itself but also when it observes the same action performed by another, and their discovery suggests a potential neurological link between our own, first-hand experience of sensations such as pain, and our perception of those sensations in other people. The human brain contains multiple and complex mirror neuron systems, and some neuroscientists have concluded that these enable us to understand the actions and intentions of other people, and are the neural basis of the capacity for many interpersonal aspects of human consciousness – including empathy (see Keysers and Fadiga 2008).

Because the concept of empathy is so very important to the art of theatre (without it actors probably could not imagine what it would be like to be another character, and audiences probably would not care) some theatre scholars and practitioners have become very interested in mirror neurons. For example, Bruce McConachie's *Engaging Audiences – A Cognitive Approach to Spectating in the Theatre* (2008) opens his argument with an account of how 'our mirror neuron systems are an important key to social intelligence, including our ability as spectators to empathize with actors in performance' (McConachie 2008: 20–21). What interests McConachie is the theory that it is the mirror neuron system in the brain that produces the possibility of empathy in the mind, both in relation to everyday life and to art. What a spectator feels when they 'project themselves into the emotional life of an actor/character on stage' involves the embodiment of another person's emotional state, and 'embodying other's emotions produces emotions in us. Even if the situation is an imagined or fictitious one' (McConachie 2008: 67). And, in this context, it is important to remember that the situation is not only 'an imagined or fictitious one' but is *known* to be an imagined or fictitious one. Actors do not, contrary to popular belief, lose themselves completely in their parts: the exhausted, sweaty, sobbing, broken figure onstage at the end of *King Lear* is also a craftsman who knows that he must position his body at *this* angle to catch the light and create the most effective stage picture, and must modulate his voice in *this* way so that his 'Howl, Howl, Howl' may be heard at the back of dress circle as well as at the front of the stalls. And the audience member whose eyes well up with tears knows perfectly well with another part of her mind that the curtain call is not far off and wonders whether there might be time for a drink after the show. Consciousness, both for the actor and for the audience member, is dual. But that need not prevent the fact that, in the moment, empathy may enable us to embody another's emotions, and 'embodying other's emotions produces emotions in us'.

The mirror neuron explanation of empathy may be especially attractive to non-scientists because it seems to offer an authoritative riposte to a more mechanical kind of late-twentieth-century scientism. But while the existence of mirror neurons has been proved beyond reasonable doubt, research into their exact workings and significance is at an early stage. Little is known about them and it is too early to say whether the excitement they initially generated will turn out to be well-founded; there is still much uncertainty – and some scepticism – within the scientific community as a whole about the workings, effects and implications of mirror neurons. Even so, it does seem that a neural basis for emotions such as empathy might well be found, whether in mirror neurons themselves or in what is described as the 'empathy circuit' in the brain. Studies using functional magnetic resonance imaging (fMRI) have led to a growing consensus among neuroscientists that when we empathize, there are at least ten interconnected brain regions that play a central role in the process: the medial prefrontal cortex, the orbitofrontal cortex, the frontal operculum and so on (Frith and Frith 2003: 459–73).

This basic question of the relationship that mind and brain have with each other needs to be acknowledged, even if only in passing. However, for our present purpose, the exact details of how physical/chemical processes map onto emotional/cognitive ones is not the main concern – although it is good to feel that it is not all simply a matter of wishful thinking. Meanwhile, the mirror neuron experiments have contributed to a new wave of interest in the concept of empathy. There are, once again, signs that it is being seen as central, rather than peripheral, to an understanding of human consciousness. Evan Thompson, for example, echoes Lipps in his argument that empathy is 'the precondition (the condition of possibility) for the science of consciousness' (Thompson 2001: 2). He distinguishes at least four different kinds of empathy:

1. The passive association of my lived body with the lived body of the Other.
2. The imaginative transposal of myself to the place of the Other.
3. The interpretation or understanding of myself as an Other for you.
4. Ethical responsibility in the face of the Other.

(Thompson 2001:17)

And he goes on to argue that 'we need to pursue a "science of interbeing" … that integrates the methods and findings of cognitive science, phenomenology, and the contemplative and meditative psychologies of the world's wisdom traditions' (Thompson 2001: 29). For others, however, empathy remains at best a fuzzy concept, at worst a distracting irrelevance. Philosopher Jesse Prinz, for example, argues that 'empathy is not all it is cracked up to be. The assumption that empathy is important for morality can be challenged. Indeed, empathy may even be a liability' (Prinz 2011: 214–15).

My own understanding of the concept lies somewhere in the middle, resonating with David Hume's famous statement:

When I see the effects of passion in the voice and gesture of any person, my mind immediately passes from these effects to their causes, and forms such a lively idea of the passion, as is presently converted into the passion itself. In like manner, when I perceive the causes of any emotion, my mind is conveyed to the effects, and is actuated with a like emotion.

(Hume [1739] 1978: 3.3.1)

As well as being the basis for a theory of mind, Hume's formulation appears to offer a lot for an understanding of effective theatrical performance. Oddly, though, Theatre and Performance Studies have followed the general trend of humanities' disciplines in downplaying, devaluing or ignoring the term in recent years. This may be because it has been identified primarily or exclusively with Stanislavskian or Method acting – themselves frequently seen as outdated. But it is a mistake to imagine that these are the only modes of performance that demand an empathic relationship between the actor and the person/thing he represents: Stanislavski and Strasberg simply codified certain modes of this empathy, and taught particular techniques for transforming it into performance. But, as elsewhere, the term is making a reappearance – not least through the work of scholars such as McConachie. Empathy, seen in this light, is both a social and aesthetic phenomenon. In everyday life most of us are capable of empathy – and capable, too, of suspending empathy. A theatrical performance can invite empathy between audience and character(s). Or it can invite the suspension of such empathy – or indeed, a tension between different modes and degrees of empathy and its absence.

And this is particularly relevant to the theme of old age in theatre, because ageing itself involves – on a number of levels – both ourselves and the other. If, as I suggested earlier in this section, the first meaning of subjectivity involves the subject's sense of her own subjectivity, her experience of self as 'I' – then ageing immediately problematizes this. Ontological subjectivity can embrace the 'I' that I am now. But the 'I' that I am now is older than the 'I' that I once was. Can my experience of that younger self be the same as my experience of my present self? Perhaps it depends on the detail: how much younger? A minute ago? Yes, surely. Yesterday? Maybe. Last week? Last year? Ten years ago? Thirty? Fifty? At what point does that 'I' start to feel like the other? And how much like the other does it feel? I suspect that the answer 'no' begins to creep in at different points for different people and in different contexts. Even more radically, to contemplate the older person is also to imagine myself as older, to imagine a subjectivity that I have not yet experienced, but which I will or might experience.

The multiple layers of subjectivity – self/other/society – are picked up by the kaleidoscopic interplay which theatre enables between self and other, subjective and objective, empathy and distance. And these are particularly appropriate ways of approaching the issue of ageing.

Impersonations

Not that theatre always engages terribly well with the idea of ageing. I own a rather ancient book of actor training called *Stage Movement* by Marguerite Battye. It was published in 1954, and chapters thirteen to nineteen are devoted to the different ways in which parts of the body – feet, hands, arms, eyes, mouth, and head – appear in youth, middle age and old age. The instructions to the would-be actor are frequently predictable.

> In youth the walk is buoyant and springy. The head is carried high, the arms swing into opposition, the stride is long and from the hips, and the feet are placed on one line, with central balance. In middle age the tendency is to walk more from the hips, and two lines begin to be used for the feet, widening as age advances ... The walk in old age becomes restricted. Movement is mainly from the knee joint. The joints are no longer braced back,

but are bent and stiff. The balance of the whole body is thrown forward. The feet are flat, and are placed flatly, with the toes turned well out.

(Battye 1954: 75–76)

Illustrated by a series of stick figures, *Stage Movement* was one of a series of theatre training books whose purpose was 'to reveal to students of the theatre the essential details of professional practice' (Battye 1954: 93). It further advises the student actor that

The arms begin gradually to set or to become less flexible from the age of forty years. At first this loss in flexibility will be revealed by less movement from the scapula and will not be noticed by the ageing person, but by the onlooker. As age advances, the loss increases, becomes apparent, and, ultimately, only restricted movement from the elbow is possible.

(Battye 1954: 68)

It makes for slightly embarrassing reading, not only in terms of the cultural politics of gerontology but also in terms of the history of actor training. *Stage Movement* was never a classic of acting theory, but it was high-profile enough to get glowing reviews from both *Plays and Players* and the *Times Literary Supplement*, and it was promoted by a foreword from Sir Donald Wolfit and a preface from Margaret Leighton. But nothing of what we think of as modern acting theory has penetrated here. There is no Lee Strasberg – though this may be because at the time that Battye's book was published he had only been heading up the Actors' Studio in New York for three years. Nor, more surprisingly, is there a trace of Stanislavski, whose work had been influential elsewhere for rather longer. Instead, the book offers an approach to 'acting old' which is so generalized as to amount to unacknowledged stereotyping. It might come as no surprise to find that elsewhere in the book a similarly essentialist and generalist approach is taken towards gender differences: 'In the standing position, the woman's feet touch and the man's do not. The principle is breadth and apartness away from the body (man's movements) and together and to the body (woman's movements)' (Battye 1954: 32).

It is not that Battye's physical descriptions of the characteristics of age are inaccurate. Compare, for example, the following extract from a medical handbook.

Degenerative arthritis of the junction between the *clavicle* (collar bone) and the *acromion* (top of the shoulder blade) is ... quite common in the elderly. This is mildly painful in most instances, producing discomfort or creaking when the arm is lifted fully away from the side, as in the follow-through of a golf swing. It may be marked by a painless bony prominence on the topmost part of the shoulder ... The most common shoulder problems in older people involve the soft tissues that surround this joint, specifically the tendons. The biceps tendon runs through a bony groove across the front of the shoulder joint. Chronic wear and tear produce inflammation, called *bicipital tendinitis*, with tenderness over the front of the shoulder and pain during flexing of the elbow or turning of a key. The inflammation diminishes with rest and heat, although steroid injection may be necessary ... The tendon subjected to perhaps the greatest stress is the broad 'rotator cuff,' which has the job of lifting the arm away from the side and rotating it outward. Autopsy studies have shown that 50 percent of men over 50 years old have a frayed and worn rotator-cuff tendon. A great deal of friction occurs where this tendon runs between the bones of the outer shoulder joint. Here, as in other high-friction areas, there is a bursa serving as a fluid-filled cushion. When inflammation of the tendon extends to the bursa, a bursitis develops, which is both painful and persistent.

(Duncan 1982: 29–30; original emphasis)

I have quoted this at some length in order to do justice to the deeper level of detail offered by the medical writer. However, what is being said here, while more nuanced, and written with the intention of offering advice on pain alleviation rather than dramatic characterization, is not that different from Margaret Battye's advice to the actor – though nothing quite so crassly definitive as the assertion that in old age 'only restricted movement from the elbow is possible'.

But what is so striking about Battye's advice to the actor is the complete absence of any sense that the task of the actor might involve engaging empathically with the character being portrayed. When Elia Kazan talks somewhat blandly about the Method actor 'going through what the character he's playing is going through' (Kazan 1988: 143) he starts a whole drove (or husk) of philosophical hares, and there are many actor trainers now who believe that the revolution that Stanislavski started has gone too far. Nonetheless, one of the foundations of twentieth-century realistic acting was its belief in the need for – and the possibility of – an art based on emotional understanding and human empathy, and on the rejection of generalization (both of which are important gerontological values). And generalization lies at the heart of Battye's approach. She speaks as if everybody – and every body – aged in exactly the same way, moving all together from the knees, and turning out their toes in uniform compliance with the theatrical signs of ageing. It is enough to make a good social gerontologist – as well as a good acting teacher – despair.

Even so, before we consign Battye to damnation in the nether regions of some thespian hell, let us just pause on that one phrase: 'the theatrical *signs* of ageing'. Let us not forget that the actor is engaged in playing with conventions as much as with reality. And the conventional signs of old age – the stiff knees, the flat-footed walk – have their own kind of truthfulness and value, in terms of the ways in which old age is perceived.

'That is proper old'

'How to act old' is less common as a feature of actor training today than it once was. There is still a need, to be sure, for actors to be able occasionally to play outside their own actual chronological age range, but much less so now than in the past, when there was a good living to be made by a 'character actor' (such as a Clive Dunn) who could specialize in elderly comic types, often much older than their actual age. Moreover, much contemporary actor training that looks to the commercial sector is dominated by a realist aesthetic derived from the dominant aesthetic of both screen acting and theatrical naturalism which means that the young actor's training starts with the present self. Acting old, however, might still be found in programmes with a psychophysical bent, such as the MA in Training Actors (Movement) programme at the Guildhall School of Music & Drama, one of whose students was recently quoted in the press, teaching a journalist how to be old.

> First, she says, I must think about what has happened to my body. My trunk is shorter, because the discs in my spine have lost fluid; my sternum has caved in, forcing my shoulders to drop forward. When I turn to speak to someone, I can't just swivel my head: I must move my whole body because my neck has fused. Worst of all, my ass has dropped way down, my weight is lower and my muscles in my haunches are weaker. Which means that I walk with a wide-legged, unsteady gait.
>
> (Turner 2012: 310)

The lesson was being given to *Times* journalist Janice Turner, who was about to undertake some immersive research into the condition of the elderly by going out and about in the London streets 'disguised' as an eighty-year-old woman. Unlike Battye's imagined actors, Turner's journalism *was* undertaken as an act of empathy – an attempt to walk a mile or two, literally, in the shoes of an elderly person. It was a performance – a piece of Boalian 'invisible theatre' – through which she was seeking to understand from the inside what it is like to be old in today's society. It was motivated in part by her awareness of the situation of her own eighty-nine-year-old father, awaiting a nursing-home place in a geriatric ward, and the sense of loss that she witnesses in him. So she put on a wig, had wrinkles applied to her face by a make-up artist, dressed herself in beige and walked the streets of London, experiencing for herself the marginalization and exclusion that can come from goodwill and helpfulness as well as from rudeness and ageism: 'It is not that the world is odious to the old', Turner concludes, 'It just forgets their needs, blusters on into the future, leaving them behind' (Turner 2012: 31).

Her pilgrimage through the streets of London was a search for an authenticity in her understanding of age – an authenticity which she sought through the medium of performance but which, paradoxically, she also defines *in contrast to* the fictions which modern dramas sell to us.

> But this is the future. Your future and mine. Not that we ever think about it, being shortsighted, in-denial fools. More of us will survive to extreme old age than any generation who ever lived – yet no generation has planned for it so inadequately. It's too grim to contemplate, so we don't … The average life expectancy for a man is 78, a woman 82.

A fifth of us will reach 100. That isn't twinkly, silver-fox Bill Nighy fellas holding hands with Helen Mirren types on sunset cruises. That is proper old. That is suffering the geriatric unholy trinity of confused, immobile and incontinent.

(Turner 2012: 28)

It left her feeling 'depressed ... patronized, pitied, excluded from everything whizzy and new' (Turner 2012: 28).

Janice Turner's invisible theatre illuminates some of the strengths and limitations of performance as a way of knowing. Clearly, from her own report, it gave her a more vivid understanding of the complex, subtle and often clandestine forms of ageism that elderly people have to face in society. It also gave her a way of articulating her feelings about her father's condition. And to some extent it enabled her to understand what it might be like to be old. But *only* 'to some extent'. Turner's report from the country of the elderly is written, still, by someone who is comparatively young, for whom the look in the mirror which shows her the grandmotherly face that both is and is not her own is a novelty rather than an accepted – or acceptable – reality. Her performed experience of old age remains that of old age understood as *difference*.

Most notably, she describes old age as if there were only two possible ways of understanding it: the grimly real ('proper old age') or the sentimentally fictional ('twinkly, silver-fox Bill Nighy fellas holding hands with Helen Mirren types on sunset cruises'). Faced with only these two possibilities she plumps for the one that is 'too grim to contemplate' – and which turns out to be the familiar narrative of decline. But other realities, other ways of experiencing reality, are available. It is one of the repeated themes of this book that old age – as Cephalus insisted to Socrates – is not singular but multiple.

Ageing games and empathy suits

Few would disagree that a greater empathy towards the elderly would be a good thing. There are courses in some medical schools aimed at enhancing this, especially among those working with the elderly. For example, a teaching programme called 'The Ageing Game', various versions of which are presented in different American medical schools, creates an experiential learning environment in which 'medical students experience simulated physical, sensory, and cognitive deficits that are associated with disability from chronic diseases' (Pacala, Boult and Hepburn 2006: 144). The aim is 'to enhance medical students' attitudes toward caring for elderly patients, enhance empathy for elderly patients, and improve general attitudes toward the elderly' (Varkey, Chutka and Lesnick 2006: 224), and evaluative studies have shown the game to be 'an effective tool for stimulating long-lasting awareness and understanding of key issues related to aging and geriatrics' (Pacala, Boult and Hepburn 2006: 144).

Similar initiatives exist in the UK, and are now being adopted by the private care sector. The following story appeared in *The Guardian* in November 2010.

> Your vision is blurry because your glasses have been smeared with Vaseline; your sense of sound is muffled by earplugs, and your right arm is bound to your body, inhibiting your movement. You lean heavily on the stranger who leads you into the day room, but she's talking over you, moaning to a colleague about her cigarette break. Out of nowhere, a spoon is pushed into your mouth full of slippery, tepid oats. You don't like porridge, but if you refuse, you'll be punished for kicking off.
>
> This is the new experiential training programme being undertaken by staff at a leading independent healthcare provider of care homes. It is designed to give staff a sense of empathy with their residents who have dementia, and to stop staff handing out unnecessary medication.
>
> (Davis 2010: n.p.)

This and the Ageing Game are also forms of 'acting old'; the motives in both cases are clearly admirable. But not all forms of imaginative identification are equally positive. Margaret Morganroth Gullette begins her seminal work, *Aged by Culture* with an iconic – and angry – account of an exhibit at the Boston Museum of Science in 2000 called 'Face Aging'. Aimed exclusively at children under sixteen, it presented the boy or girl with a digitized image of their own face, followed by computer simulations purporting to show how he or she will look in later life.

> In seconds the computer added grotesque pouches, reddish skin and blotches to their familiar features; the faces became elongated and then wider and then saggy; lines became more heavily rutted. Boys lost hair. Hair turned gray. The heads of both boys and girls grew and then shrank.
>
> The children were almost uniformly shaken. One eight-year-old girl in the hearing of a *Boston Globe* reporter moaned, 'I don't want to get old!' While viewing the show, gerontologist Richard Griffin heard a boy 'looking as if he had tasted something bad', say about another child's facial changes, 'He's disgusting at forty-two'.
>
> (Gullette 2004: 3–4)

This is the platform from which Gullette launches her inspirational cultural attack on contemporary ageism. What hits home is not only her critique of the so-called science of 'Face Aging', her convincing dismissal of its predictive power, the arbitrariness of its assumptions about physical change and the sheer *bad science* of the exhibit; it is also the way in which she reveals the ideological work which it is doing: the way in which it reinforces existing social prejudices about old age, the negative associations which it holds for western late capitalism, the insistent message that old age is a problem and that ageing is terrible. What angers her most is the way in which the apparent authority and objectivity of science is harnessed to prove the truth of the narrative of old age as nothing but decline. 'If you paid a quarter for this in an arcade', she suggests, 'the whole thing might be less troubling' (Gullette 2004: 8).

In the second decade of the twenty-first century, the technology has moved on a little, and the arcade experience that Gullette refers to is widely available in digital form. For example, iPhone users can download free applications such as 'Age My Face – Free Aging Tool', developed and marketed by PurplePenguin.com for Swartz Enterprises 2010. 'Age My Face' allows any of us to upload a photograph of our own face, and, by applying a series of Photoshop-style overlay masks which portray wrinkles, sagging skin, increasing greyness or baldness helps to gain an impression of what we will be like in an unspecified number of years time.

There are several other similar iPhone ageing apps to enable such performances; these include 'Age Face', 'Age Photo Kiosk', 'Face Older', 'Age Machine', 'Time Machine', 'Dr. Man's Age Simulator', 'Time Booth', 'Hour Face', 'Age Me', 'Oldify', 'In20Years' and 'AgingBooth'. With the exception of 'Dr. Man's Age Simulator' these apps tend not to claim any scientific accuracy. Most, indeed, are offered in the spirit that PiVi and Co.'s AgingBooth makes explicit in its warning that 'AgingBooth is a funny application made for entertainment purposes only and does not guarantee resemblance to the real aging process.' Like 'Age My Face', 'AgingBooth' is one of the more popular of these face-ageing apps, and it seems to have divided consumers pretty sharply. Customer reviews on PiVi and Co.'s iTunes app page tend to polarize between the enthusiastic – 'This app is brilliant, very realistic as well' – and the contemptuous: 'Can't believe I paid for this. What a total waste of my money'.

Apps like 'Age My Face' and 'AgingBooth' aim to mobilize the same sort of reaction that Gullette talks about in the science museum exhibit – that of horrified fascination. They aim to do so, however, in a mode that is different from the Boston booth in two respects. Firstly, the horror is (like a good postmodern horror movie) to be controlled by laughter and so not taken too seriously – 'a funny application … [which] does not guarantee resemblance to the real aging process'. Secondly, and closely linked to this, these apps do not position the subject as a participant in a scientific experiment, but as a player in a theatrical game 'made for entertainment purposes only'. They invite the iPhone owner (imagined as a young adult – the main target customer group for such apps) to put on the grotesque make-up of stereotypical old age, and to do so through digital technology rather than by slapping on Leichner #5 and #9, liner, highlights and shadows. They invite us, in fact, to perform a part – the part of ourselves in *x* years' time – and to become our own spectators in this digital performance. And then, by posting the result on the big stage of one of the Internet's social network sites – Facebook or an equivalent – to share that performance with a wider audience.

Gullette's twenty-five-cent arcade booth can now be carried round in your pocket 'for entertainment purposes only', and its result is a performance whose potential audience is worldwide – much larger, certainly than the audience for the Boston Museum of Science's exhibit. Moreover, these apps can be applied in a variety of ways, and users report that seeing an old-age version of one's own face is only part of the fun. Most common alternative uses are seeing the ageing process of one's friends, and of 'real' performers: film stars, pop singers, models and other celebrities. This latter, not surprisingly, is a game that seems to appeal to the popular press as well: during news droughts, UK newspapers, both tablet and broadsheet, have published online photo features with titles such as 'OAP celebrities: Photoshop masters imagine what the stars will look like in old age' (*Daily Telegraph* 2008), and 'Gosh, Posh, is this you in 2020? How our favourite celebrities might look in ten years' time' (*Daily Mail* 2009). It should be added, too, that ageing is only one form of digital distortion to which customers may subject their faces, and the faces of their real and imaginary friends: PiVi and Co., for example, have also produced BaldBooth and FatBooth, and there are many commercial digital photographic applications which offer a whole suite of special effects. The available roles are actually quite varied, and, like a cut-price Cindy Sherman, you can write yourself into a visual narrative in which you/not-you perform a different 'self': one which is fat, or bald, or pimply, or skinny, or sunburned, or ginger-haired – or even alien! It seems that many of us desire to see ourselves, and those with whom we are most familiar, in terms of an unfamiliar 'other' – or at least an 'other' which is only partially familiar, since the distortions available tend to turn the individual into a stereotype of a fat/bald/skinny/pimply/sunburned person.

But while there are many self-distortions available, for the moment, and for the purposes of this book, it is the face-ageing app that specifically interests me. Gullette suggests that if the face-ageing technology which she experienced as a scientific exhibit were to be presented as a game, or as holiday entertainment (or a performance?) then 'perhaps the whole thing would be less troubling' (Gullette 2004: 8). I am not so sure. It is true that apps like 'Age My Face' and 'AgingBooth' do not seem to have the disturbing effect of the exhibit at the Boston Museum of Science. Perhaps this is because they are packaged as 'Entertainment', rather than bearing the authoritative imprimatur of a scientific exhibition; or because there is little novelty value now that photo-distortion techniques are now rather old hat; or perhaps just because so often the artwork is simply not very good. But the sheer number and variety of these apps, and the way they have crowded the marketplace does seem to suggest that very many of us are indeed fascinated, on however superficial a level, with the idea of our own ageing appearance. They are still troubling – just troubling in a different way. While Gullette criticizes the 2000 Boston 'Face Ageing' booth because it is bad science, I have a rather different problem with its present-day smartphone equivalent. The trouble with these apps is not that they are bad science, but that they are bad performance.

Like most kinds of acting, they offer the opportunity to imagine what it is like to *be* something else – in this case, what it is like to be an old person. They appear to ask for a movement of empathy. And not all forms of theatrical empathy, after all, use Stanislavskian 'emotion memories' as the starting point for empathic understanding. There are many others which work from the 'outside in': the actor begins by trying out the walk, by putting on the costume or the make-up.

Face-ageing apps, then, offer a kind of performance experience. But even as they suggest that possibility of empathy, they snatch it away, replacing it with a self-consciousness – not self-awareness – whose required outlet is laughter ('a *funny* application') which mocks the subject with the very possibility of its own ageing. We laugh, very often, at that of which we are afraid, and – as generations of acting teachers and performer trainers from multitude of traditions will confirm – the greatest obstacle to performing is fear. In that moment of aborted empathy which the face-ageing app engenders, we can read our culture's fear of old age.

Empathy is important, but it is also hard to predict and control. While some methods of teaching empathy, such as the Ageing Game, have an established track record, other techniques have fared less well. In 2009 a Canadian professor of design called Glen Hougan attracted some media attention when he created an 'Empathy Suit' to simulate the effects of ageing. People who work with the elderly, or who design products for them, would strap on the suit to get an inside feel for the problems of growing old.

It restricts movement around the knees, hips, shoulders, elbows, neck, wrist and hands. A strap-on pot belly simulates weight gain and various mechanisms stoop posture. Two layers of gloves reduce tactility and simulate poor circulation. The legs are tied together to imitate reduced stride and bad slippers create poor balance … [G]oggles simulate a range of visual problems, from macro degeneration to eye hemorrhages and 'floaters' – spots on your eyes. A straw gives the user a sense of what reduced lung capacity feels like and ear muffs reduce hearing.

(Tattrie 2009: n.p.)

With the aid of the Empathy Suit, designers of products for the elderly would be able to understand the needs of their clients/customers and so revolutionize their designs. In one interview the enthusiastic Hougan said, 'The Empathy Suit is great because you put it on and it's like: OK, I get it' (Hougan, quoted in Tattrie 2009: n.p.).

Like a face-ageing app the Empathy Suit offers a way of enabling a younger person to try old age on for size. It is altogether a more serious and socially responsible project, however: its aims are more academically respectable, more carefully thought through and more benevolent. Hougan clearly wishes to help seniors live fuller and more comfortable lives, and to make a serious contribution to well-being in later life. He also wanted to raise the general standard of empathy that younger and middle-aged people have with the physical constraints of the elderly. It seemed like a good idea. Unfortunately, as Hougan himself reports, things did not work out quite as he had hoped.

In 2009 a producer on the PBS show Life Part 2 filmed a segment on an empathy/aging suit that I had developed. This suit simulates the various physical changes associated with aging and was used as a way for my design students to gain a better understanding of the physical issues associated with aging. The producer put on the suit, and after I adjusted the suit to the worst possible restriction, I asked him how he felt? He replied, 'I feel horrible!'

51

It was then that I realized that I had developed a tool that did not elicit empathy and a better understanding of aging but confirmed all the fears and stereotypes we have about getting old – ending up hunched over, shuffling and in pain. I had unwittingly developed an 'ageist suit'!

(Hougan 2011: n.p.)

The master narrative of decline is a powerful one, and can engulf our individual experiences: like the playwright, the dramaturg of everyday life cannot always determine the reactions of his audience – or even his actors – to his dramaturgy, and even those scenes that are scripted with the intention of engaging empathy can be sucked into a master narrative which turns them into 'all the fears and stereotypes we have about getting old'.

PART II

Tragedy and Comedy

Chapter 3

On Liminality and Late Style: *Oedipus at Colonus*

'Sorrowful old age'

The ancient Greeks, we are told, were pretty brutal towards their old folk.

If this was indeed the case, it is of some importance to us, since ancient Greek culture has always been a vital touchstone for later European thought. There is something foundational about it: we have long been in the habit of seeing in classical and pre-classical Greece not only the origins of our philosophical, moral and scientific thought, our literature and our drama, but also the very terms by which these should be defined. So the attitude of the ancient Greeks towards the elderly may well have a bearing on the concerns of today.

In his seminal *History of Old Age*, Georges Minois paints a bleak picture of attitudes towards old age in classical Greek civilization. Greek culture, he argues, fetishized youth, which represented 'human perfection, beauty and the achievement of full human potential' (Minois 1989: 43); conversely, the Greeks saw 'sorrowful old age' as a defect, an affront and a curse from the gods. Minois charts the decline of the authority of the family patriarch in ancient Greece, which diminished steadily from the seventh century BCE onwards, and he details the way in which philosophers repeatedly point to old age as a time of misery, cynicism and negativity. In the *Rhetoric*, for example, Aristotle describes old age as follows:

> The old have lived long, have been often deceived, and have made many mistakes of their own; they see that more often than not the affairs of old men turn out badly. And so they are positive about nothing … They think evil; that is, they are disposed to put the worse construction upon everything. Further they are suspicious because they are distrustful, and distrustful from sad experience … They are mean-souled because they have been humbled by life. Thus they aspire to nothing great or exalted, but crave the mere necessities and comforts of existence. And they are not generous.
>
> (Aristotle, quoted in Minois 1989: 60–61)

Minois, too, points to the wealth of Greek mythology which depicts a repeated pattern of the overthrow of the tyrannous old by the vibrant and vital young: Uranus castrated by Kronos, Kronos in turn overthrown by Zeus. And he argues that one of the key originary myths of Greek culture, the triumph of the Olympian gods (who are portrayed as enjoying eternal youth) over their predecessors the Titans, is a myth with all 'the marks of a conflict of generations, which ended with the inevitable triumph of youth' (Minois 1989: 43). If Minois is right, it should perhaps come as no surprise that a society for whom intergenerational conflict was so deeply woven into its cultural DNA should have generated the Oedipus myth – another myth of intergenerational conflict whose influence on twentieth-century thought, once it resurfaced in a new shape in Freud's writings, has been immense.

Minois makes a convincing argument that such a negative vision of old age *was* one aspect of classical Greek culture, and his general account of the Greeks' fascination with the values of youth, strength and heroism has much to commend it. He overstates his case, however: he ignores or dismisses any evidence of contrary aspects, asserting that any such evidence is overdetermined by context (while neglecting, at the same time, to apply similar criteria to evidence which supports his own view). Thus, for example, he dismisses Plato's positive portrait of Cephalus, the contented elderly man (see previous chapter) on the grounds that Plato was stating a hoped-for ideal rather than a reality, and so 'turned many aspects of the real situation upside down' (Minois 1989: 62). On the other hand, says Minois, Aristotle's unpleasant picture of old age in the *Rhetoric* was a result of him 'simply describ[ing] what he saw' (Minois 1989: 62). Athens actually had a large number of laws and charitable institutions which were designed to support the old and needy; Minois adduces these as evidence of the marginalized and underprivileged position of the old in Athens, and the frequent renewal of those laws as evidence 'that they were not obeyed at all' (Minois 1989: 62). And again, archaeologists have discovered and analysed a wealth of Athenian funerary inscriptions expressing affection or respect for the departed elderly; these are dismissed on the grounds that 'it is known … that funerary texts are the subject *par excellence* of pious lies' (Minois 1989: 63). At another point, Minois dismisses some of the classical philosophers' more positive statements about old age on the grounds that they themselves were old men when they made them (Minois 1989: 53) – as if first-hand knowledge disqualified them from clear thinking!

Minois' general point, that historical evidence can be read in various ways, is sound enough: texts make sense only in terms of their contexts, and the meaning of a text in context may well turn out to be rather different from its apparent decontextualized meaning. A hoped-for Utopian ideal may indeed sometimes emerge as a reaction to an unpleasant actual reality; and it is true that laws are frequently passed because of an urgent need to suppress activities that tend towards their opposite. But Minois does give the impression of protesting rather *too* much, and of being a little *too* keen to insist on the gerontophobia of our classical forebears. Besides – even if funerary texts *do* sometimes contain pious lies and idealized pictures, these are more likely to emerge in societies where those positive values have some force than in those where they do not; and while laws are *sometimes* honoured more in the breach than in the observance, sometimes, too, a law may articulate a society's true beliefs and aspirations, and welfare provision may be established in order to act upon those beliefs and aspirations. Even the myths of regeneration, which Minois reads as inherently gerontophobic, are actually much less black and white than Minois suggests. In Greek culture they are not single texts so much as recurring ideas, which are told and retold in multiple and often contradictory forms, and have multiple and shifting meanings.

At the same time, textual sources which give accurate accounts of old age in antiquity (both in the real world and in the mythical or fictional realm) are scarce and patchy. Frequently they amount to little more than lists of characters who have lived a prodigious length of time, or accounts of historical characters who *happened* to live to a ripe old age, but whose achievements throughout their lifetime are of greater interest than their age per se (Parkin 1998: 20). Their value as evidence of wider societal attitudes is uneven.

Minois seems to have fallen prey to what Jeremy Rifkin has described as the historian's tendency to see the past primarily in terms of a 'pathology of power' (Rifkin 2009: 10) to focus, that is, on the terrible moments, on the holocausts and genocides, on the confrontations and colonizations, on the exploitations and redress of grievances, on all those painful events, processes and actions that are 'newsworthy' precisely because they trigger our flight/fight mechanisms, because they stand outside the experience of the everyday. Rifkin cites Hegel: 'Periods of happiness are blank pages in [the history of the world], for they are periods of harmony, – periods when the antithesis is in abeyance' (Rifkin 2009: 10). With this in mind, let us open ourselves to the possibility that the gerontophobia which we undoubtedly encounter in *some* classical Greek sources was not the *only* cultural response available to that society, and that the place of the aged in classical Greece was as complex, contradictory and paradoxical as it seems to have been in most other societies. And in order to explore some of those complexities, contradictions and paradoxes, let us turn to some of the imaginative narratives which that society generated – not because the pathologies of power are absent from these imaginative narratives of the past (after all, the writers of tragedies, comedies and epics are no more concerned with 'blank pages' than are historians), but because the imaginative narrative gives us a different kind of access to their detailed workings and to the historically situated consciousness(es) that produced them and which are described by them.

In particular, that genre of imaginative narrative which we call tragedy may have a special affinity for the themes of old age. In life-course theories, old age tends to be the time for reflecting on life, for attempting to discover a sense of meaning which will reaffirm the identity of the ego. Similarly, tragedy is traditionally associated with asking – and possibly even answering – questions about existence:

> Of all artistic forms, tragedy is the one that confronts the meaning-of-life question most searchingly and unswervingly, intrepidly prepared as it is to entertain the most horrific of responses to it. Tragedy at its finest is a courageous reflection on the fundamental nature of human existence, and has its origin in an ancient Greek culture in which life is fragile, perilous, and sickeningly vulnerable.
>
> (Eagleton 2007: ii)

So, perhaps of all theatrical forms, tragedy offers us a particularly direct way into a consideration of old age. And while there are other classical Greek tragedies which have ageing protagonists (*Hecuba* is a striking example), there are few in which old age is so central as in Sophocles' *Oedipus at Colonus*.

A chorus of elders

The story begins – as so many Greek tragedies, with their customary efficiency, begin – at a point of crisis: in this case, Oedipus' arrival at the sacred grove at Colonus. Since the catastrophe at Thebes in which (at the height of his fame and fortune) he discovered his own unwitting incest and parricide, he has been an exile, wandering outcast and abject. He now appears to have reached that point of 'maximum dependence, minimum social utility' (Myerhoff 1992: 110), which is sometimes labelled 'senescence'. His plight, when we encounter him at Colonus, is described not just in terms of a moral punishment for his guilt, but as an extreme statement of the relationship between himself and society. At the height of his power, he had effectively *been* the state of Thebes; the discovery of his pollution was followed by banishment, exile and abjection. His years of wandering establish his status as an outcast, and now his old age accentuates this, as his first speech to his daughter establishes.

> Child of an old blind sire, Antigone,
> What region, say, whose city have we reached?
> Who will provide today with scanted dole
> This wanderer? 'Tis little that he craves,
> And less obtains – that less enough for me;
> For I am taught by suffering to endure,
> And the long years that have grown old with me

> (Sophocles [406 BCE] 1928: 62)

The tragedy of *Oedipus at Colonus* also belongs to that small, distinctively Greek sub-genre of 'suppliant' plays, in which an outcast or a refugee – or a group of them – asks for sanctuary from disaster or danger: other examples include *The Suppliant Women* and *The Heracleidae*. Oedipus' abject state, then, is a feature of more than just his old age. And yet the theme of old age is central to the play, not only in the figure of its central protagonist but also in the Chorus of Athenian Elders whose presence pervades the drama. And while Oedipus makes constant fleeting references to the woes of old age which afflict him, the Chorus has a full-blooded lament.

CHORUS:	Who craves excess of days,
(*str.*)	Scorning the common span
	Of life, I judge that man
	A giddy wight who walks in folly's ways.
	For the long years heap up a grievous load,
	Scant pleasures, heavier pains,
	Till not one joy remains
	For him who lingers on life's weary road

And come it slow or fast,
One doom of fate
Doth all await,
For dance and marriage bell,
The dirge and funeral knell.
Death the deliverer freeth all at last.

(*antistrophe.*) Not to be born at all
Is best, far best that can befall,
Next best, when born, with least delay
To trace the backward way.
For when youth passes with its giddy train,
Troubles on troubles follow, toils on toils,
Pain, pain for ever pain;
And none escapes life's coils.
Envy, sedition, strife,
Carnage and war, make up the tale of life.
Last comes the worst and most abhorred stage
Of unregarded age,
Joyless, companionless and slow,
Of woes the crowning woe.

(*epode.*) Such ills not I alone,
He too our guest hath known,
E'en as some headland on an iron-bound shore,
Lashed by the wintry blasts and surge's roar,
So is he buffeted on every side
By drear misfortune's whelming tide,
By every wind of heaven o'erborne
Some from the sunset, some from orient morn,
Some from the noonday glow.
Some from Rhipean gloom of everlasting snow.

(Sophocles [406 BCE] 1928: 110)

The Chorus' speech seems to substantiate Georges Minois' argument that the Greek attitude towards old age was a particularly negative one. Certainly this chorus of old men – speaking, as it were from the heart, of that 'most abhorred stage/Of unregarded age/Joyless, companionless and slow/Of woes the crowning woe' have little positive to say about growing old.

In fact, however, the Chorus in *Oedipus at Colonus* is itself a rather more complex dramatization of old age than may at first appear. Choruses of Elders are not uncommon in classical Greek drama, and it is sometimes assumed that these choruses are all intended to be seen as ineffectual bystanders, without authority or impact on the main action of the drama, by virtue of the very fact of their old age (see, for example, Faulkner 1995: 177). And indeed, Choruses of Elders in plays such as Aeschylus' *Persians* and *Agamemnon*, in Euripides' *Heracles* and *The Children of Heracles*, and in Sophocles' own *Antigone* frequently seem ineffectual. But this Chorus of Elders is of another order. Despite their lament about the commonplace miseries of old age, its members have a high degree of authority within the play, and are far from marginal to its action. It is repeatedly stressed in the text that these men have a strong ritual importance as guardians of the sacred grove of Colonus. They are also politically powerful: high-status figures in civic terms, advisers and counsellors, whom both Oedipus and Creon address in terms of nobility ('lords of this land' or 'noble dwellers of this land'). They are identified, too, as specifically Athenian, as opposed to the Theban 'foreigner' – Oedipus and his family – and this gives them another kind of status in the eyes of the Athenian audience to whom the play would first have been performed. And, significantly, for the current argument, it is their age that confers upon them much of this political and ritual authority – and which also gives them a powerful bond with the central figure, Oedipus himself. Although they are swayed by Theseus concerning whether or not to allow Oedipus access to the grove, they are not indecisive or weak – as are the members of the Chorus of Theban Elders in *Antigone*, for example, whose main aim is not to get involved in the difficult political decisions of that play. These Athenian Elders, on the contrary, are vigorous participants in the decision-making process. Age may set limits to their involvement in the physical confrontations which punctuate the play's action: when acts of violence take place both on and off the stage, the elders do not participate directly. But, once they have aligned themselves with Antigone and Oedipus, they speak staunchly in their defence against the threats of Creon and his soldiers, standing together with Theseus to protect the suppliants from harm. In an interesting article which interprets *Oedipus at Colonus* as 'a play "about" old age and the tension between action and inaction that old age can create', Umit Dhuga points out that 'the audience will have seen the Elders ... repeatedly defending the City and the Grove' (Dhuga 2005: 341–42).

One of the key questions for (and about) the old in classical antiquity was that concerning their relation to the state. In both Athens and Rome the individual's ability to take part in public life was an essential aspect of a man's sense of selfhood, and surveying the literature both of ancient Greece and ancient Rome, Tim G. Parkin concludes that

Two extremes in attitude towards the elderly have been seen to recur, explicitly or implicitly, in the ancient evidence: that old people have a definite role to play and contribution to make; and that old people are an unwelcome burden and at best must be tolerated. These are gross generalisations, but ... such attitudes, at both extremes, may co-exist, rather than be mutually exclusive. Different people at different times under different circumstances may hold one view or the other – if they hold any view at all – about different aged individuals.

(Parkin 1998: 34)

The authoritative status of the Chorus in *Oedipus at Colonus* frames this question by presenting a group of elderly citizens who clearly *do* have a role to play in public life. Meanwhile, the action of the play shows this impacting on Oedipus himself. He begins the play as a figure who seems to exemplify abjection: not only because of his age, but also because of his polluted status, he *has* no social identity. But as the various deputations from Thebes arrive, Oedipus discovers that he does have a use-value after all, and that his political status has been transformed from that of despised outcast to highly valued bringer of good fortune in the battle that is to come. The role that Oedipus has to play in the future of Thebes is, as it turns out, a symbolic rather than a practical one: his 'contribution' to the state is a simple result of the prophecy that has announced that he will bring blessings to the land where he lives out his last days, and a curse to the land which has rejected him.

First to arrive is Creon – the archetypal politician throughout the three Theban plays, and here acting as ambassador for Oedipus' estranged son, Eteocles. Significantly, his attempt to persuade Oedipus to return with him to Thebes involves playing not only on their shared kinship but also on their shared age:

> I come with no ill purpose; I am old,
> And know the city whither I am come,
> Without a peer amongst the powers of Greece.
> It was by reason of my years that I
> Was chosen to persuade your guest and bring
> Him back to Thebes; not the delegate
> Of one man, but commissioned by the State,
> Since of all Thebans I have most bewailed,
> Being his kinsman, his most grievous woes.
> O listen to me, luckless Oedipus,
> Come home! The whole Cadmeian people claim
> With right to have thee back, I most of all,
> For most of all (else were I vile indeed)
> I mourn for thy misfortunes, seeing thee
> An aged outcast, wandering on and on,
> A beggar with one handmaid for thy stay.
> Ah! who had e'er imagined she could fall
> To such a depth of misery as this …
> O, by our fathers' gods, consent I pray;
> Come back to Thebes, come to thy father's home,
> Bid Athens, as is meet, a fond farewell;
> Thebes thy old foster-mother claims thee first.

> (Sophocles [406 BCE] 1928: 92–93)

Creon, then, is acting out of pure self-interest. For all his protestations of concern, he needs Oedipus for his own purposes. This becomes abundantly clear when, after his attempts at persuasion fail, he resorts to violence: he kidnaps Antigone and her sister Ismene in retaliation for Oedipus' stubbornness.

Theseus rescues the sisters and sends Creon packing, but then the pattern repeats itself as Oedipus' other son, Polyneices tries in his turn to win Oedipus' favour – again, masking his self-interest with apparent concern for Oedipus in his old age:

> Ah me, my sisters, shall I first lament
> My own afflictions, or my aged sire's,
> Whom here I find a castaway, with you,
> In a strange land, an ancient beggar clad
> In antic tatters, marring all his frame,
> While o'er the sightless orbs his unkept locks
> Float in the breeze; and, as it were to match,
> He bears a wallet against hunger's pinch.
> All this too late I learn, wretch that I am,
> Alas! I own it, and am proved most vile
> In my neglect of thee: I scorn myself.

(Sophocles [406 BCE] 1928: 111)

Again, this apparent repentance for earlier neglect is pure humbug. Polyneices is terrified: he rightly interprets Oedipus' rejection of him as an effective death sentence.

Throughout the play, Sophocles' portrayal of Oedipus himself alternates between that of a figure in some kind of holy mystery and that of an angry and bad-tempered old man, railing against the world, against fate and against those who have persecuted him. Such apparent inconsistencies of both genre and character have led some critics to suggest that this example of Sophocles' 'late style' is evidence of failing artistic powers and loss of structural control – or even of lack of time to complete it satisfactorily (Reinhardt 1979: 195). The narrative structure, too, of *Oedipus at Colonus*, alternates jerkily between the sacred and the profane. It starts with the 'sacred' story of the old man seeking a peaceful end at a holy place; then it is interrupted by the *realpolitik* narrative of the Thebans' attempts to coerce victory from Oedipus' blessing by whatever means possible. Hardly has Polyneices left the stage than the action returns – though ambiguously – to a sense of the possibility of the sacred, as Oedipus disappears offstage to end his life.

Late style in *Oedipus at Colonus*

The Oedipus story is one of the key texts of western culture, although since the end of the nineteenth century it has been the early part of the Oedipus narrative to which most scholars have paid most attention, following Freud's prioritization of the incest motif and its articulation in the Oedipus–Laius–Jocasta triangle. Some later psychoanalytic theorists, admittedly, have followed Jacques Lacan in reading Freud's own development in terms of *Oedipus at Colonus*, and seeing in the relation between *Oedipus at Colonus* and *Oedipus the King* something which mirrors the relationship between Freud's early writings and his later insistence that we look *Beyond the Pleasure Principle*. Even so, for most general readers, 'Oedipus' means *Oedipus the King*.

But of course the Oedipus we encounter in *Oedipus at Colonus* is a very different figure from the hero in his prime who was the protagonist of *Oedipus the King*. This is a blind and broken old man, who has been wandering for many years, supported by his daughter Antigone, and who now arrives at a sacred grove at Colonus, a small settlement near Athens. The central action of the play is comparatively simple: much of it involves Oedipus, sensing his own impending death, seeking sanctuary from the inhabitants and the keepers of the grove. A prophecy of Phoebus has told him that a place like this should be where he ends his life:

'There,' said he, 'shalt thou round thy weary life,
A blessing to the land wherein thou dwell'st,
But to the land that cast thee forth, a curse.'

(Sophocles [406 BCE] 1928: 66)

Once they discover Oedipus' identity, the guardians of the grove, initially sympathetic to this aged suppliant, are very reluctant to allow him to stay in this sacred place, both because he is an outsider and because of his polluted status. Eventually, however, they agree, persuaded by the intercession of King Theseus of Athens – who represents Athenian wisdom and generosity, and Oedipus finds both sanctuary and death in the grove. All this, however, is played out against a backdrop of events in the outside world, and Oedipus' search for peace is interrupted on several occasions by characters who break into the environs of the grove bringing with them the violence and chaos that Oedipus thought he had left behind in Thebes. For Oedipus' sons, Polyneices and Eteocles, are preparing to go to war with each other, each claiming the right of succession to the throne. Moreover, the prophecy regarding Oedipus' final resting place has leaked out in Thebes, where it has been understood to mean that Oedipus' presence and his blessing will bring victory to one of the warring brothers. So, having previously rejected and ignored the outcast old man, both brothers suddenly discover that they desperately need him on their side. Representatives from both armies arrive, one after the other, to try to bring Oedipus away, but Oedipus, defended by Theseus, resists, remains at Colonus and eventually – having seen off the Theban interruptions – goes off into the grove to die alone, a mysterious and holy death, witnessed only by Theseus.

Tradition holds that Sophocles himself had also experienced rejection and neglect from callous sons who were interested in him only for their own benefit. Towards the end of his life, according to the story, Sophocles' sons (like Polyneices and Eteocles – and Goneril and Regan in *King Lear*) decided that he was incapable of handling his own affairs, and that he 'should be ruled and led/By some discretion, that discerns [his] state/Better than [he him]self.' As a consequence, these sons brought a legal action against their father in order to challenge his right to self-determination – demanding, in effect, power of attorney. According to Plutarch in his *Moralia*, however,

> it is said that Sophocles, when defending himself against the charge of dementia brought by his sons, read aloud the entrance song of the chorus in the *Oedipus at Colonus*, which begins:

> > Of this region famed for horses
> > Thou hast, stranger, reached the fairest
> > Dwellings in the land,
> > Bright Colonus, where the sweet-voiced
> > Nightingale most loves to warble
> > In the verdant groves;

> And the song aroused such admiration that he was escorted from the court as if from the theatre, with the applause and shouts of those present.
> > > > (Plutarch [c. 100 CE] 1936: X, 88–89)

It may well be apocryphal, but this story of Sophocles' personal fight against his own marginalization and disempowerment is a fine parable: it is the riposte of hearty old age to self-seeking youth. And quite apart from its legal implications, it reminds us that the artist in his or her final years may be as powerful, as authoritative as they had been in their younger days – perhaps even more so. And certainly in *Oedipus at Colonus*, the elderly playwright is writing – with passion and fire – a play which is about old age.

A renewed interest in biographically inflected readings of texts is one of the contributions which ageing studies has made to literary and performance criticism: the impact of ageing on the life and work of creative writers has attracted philosophers and critics of art, literature and music. Theodor Adorno first used the phrase 'late style' in an essay fragment about Beethoven first published in 1937 (Adorno 1964: 13–17) addressing questions about what it is that leads some artists (though by no means all) to produce in their old age works which are notably different from the achievements of their earlier years, and the relation between these changes and apparent deterioration of the physical self. Beethoven's deafness is an obvious example, but we might also think of the near-blindness of a Titian or a Monet, or the physical weakness that led Rodin to turn from sculpture to drawing.

Not all artists, of course, discover their 'late style' in old age: Rembrandt's famous 'late' self-portraits were painted in his fifties. And in any case, the deterioration of the body is only one element in 'late style'. Might, then, old age itself bring about some change? And if so, what causes that change? Can it be down to the technical mastery that is the result of a lifetime of creative work? Or to financial independence, or the assurance that comes with success? Or does old age bring with it, for some, a new kind of creative energy – a liberation, perhaps, that amounts to a new kind of freedom? Adorno started a line of enquiry which has continued into the twenty-first century, the question of whether 'the work of some great artists and writers acquires a new idiom towards the end of their lives' (Said 2004: 3). And what, if any, are the shared features of 'late style'? Is it possible to point to generally identifiable 'marks of lateness in the work of major artists in their last years' (Kermode 2006: 7)? If they amount to something more than simply the signs of failing powers, and loss of precision and control, then what is that 'something'? It is, perhaps, tempting to look to an artist's works for evidence of a sense of wisdom, authority and serenity. These are the kinds of qualities that critics have seen, for example, in the work of the late (fifty-ish) Shakespeare, whose Last Plays seem to insist on motifs of reconciliation, forgiveness and intergenerational harmony.

Adorno suggested that an artist's 'late style' involved a growing sense of distance from the present, something which amounted to a sense perhaps of exile or disengagement. More recently, in his own final and unfinished work, Edward Said picked up and responded to some of Adorno's analyses.

> The accepted notion is that age confers a spirit of reconciliation and serenity on late works, often expressed in terms of a miraculous transfiguration of reality. In late plays such as *The Tempest* or *The Winter's Tale*, Shakespeare returns to the forms of romance and parable; similarly, in Sophocles' *Oedipus at Colonus* the aged hero is portrayed as having finally attained a remarkable holiness and sense of resolution.
>
> (Said 2004: 3)

It is not entirely clear whether Said himself subscribes to the reading of *Oedipus at Colonus* as full of a spirit of reconciliation and serenity. Certainly, he is alive to the possibility that 'late style' might have nothing to do with this: he goes on to ask, 'But what of artistic lateness not as harmony and resolution, but as intransigence, difficulty and contradiction? What if age and ill health don't produce serenity at all?' (Said 2004: 3). And this, certainly, is how Jacques Lacan reads *Oedipus at Colonus*: he sees it as a play in which the hero 'is shown to be unyielding right to the end, demanding everything, giving up nothing, absolutely unreconciled' (Lacan 1992: 310).

Late style as serenity and reconciliation? Or late style as intransigence and difficulty? Which to choose regarding *Oedipus at Colonus*? Which to choose as a dominant characteristic of 'late style' in general? Or are there, perhaps, two *kinds* of late style? It may be that 'late style' lies as much in reception as it does in production. As readers and spectators we may have become culturally habituated to the notion that there may be some kind of consolation in art – and especially in tragedy. Perhaps, as a result, it has become 'natural' for us to see, or to seek, in the 'final words' of an artist, those notes of reconciliation, resolution, integration and serenity which are the keynotes of Said's 'accepted' reading of *Oedipus at Colonus*. As should be clear from my analysis of the play, I do not agree that *Oedipus* demonstrates much of a 'spirit of reconciliation'. But nor do I see that there is any clear choice to be made between one reading and another, either of late style in general or of *Oedipus* in particular.

A valuable model for understanding what is going on in the play – and perhaps a valuable model for understanding the concept of late style altogether – may be found in the work of Erik Erikson, the neo-Freudian psychoanalyst who, in the mid-twentieth century, turned his attention towards the ways in which, throughout their life cycle, people create themselves, constructing who they are and what they might become. Downplaying Freud's own insistence on issues of sexuality and repression, Erikson turned instead to the development of the ego through the life cycle, from early childhood to old age. He outlined a scheme of eight psychosocial stages that humans encounter throughout their lives. These were structured as a sequence of binary oppositions, comprising positive or negative tendencies, each appropriate to a different stage in the life cycle. Thus Stage 1, typically encountered in the first year of life, is characterized by an opposition of Trust versus Mistrust, as the infant begins to learn who and what to trust in his or her environment – and in him or herself. Stage 2 (ages two–three) is dominated by a conflict of Autonomy versus Shame and Doubt, as the infant discovers a limited sense of self-control and independence.

As with Shakespeare's seven ages of man, the two stages that most concern us here are the last two. The characteristic opposition of Stage 7 is Generativity versus Stagnation: late middle age is a time when the individual's own knowledge can be passed on; but if he or she feels that they have done nothing to help the next generation then the experience may be one of stagnation. Stage 8, the final stage, is characterized by the opposition of Integrity versus Despair. As the individual reflects back on her life, she may negotiate this phase either successfully or unsuccessfully. If unsuccessful she may feel that her life has been wasted; old age for this person becomes a time of regret, bitterness or despair. The individual who completes this phase successfully, however, will feel a sense of integrity, being able to look back on her life with few regrets, and a general feeling of satisfaction and wisdom.

The word I would like to concentrate on here is 'versus'. In Erikson's scheme, these crises represent crucial moments in which 'a decisive turn one way or another is unavoidable' (Erikson 1959: 222). However, it is important to stress that these life stages are not (as they may first seem) simple chronological steps. The individual typically oscillates between two stages, moving into new phases as the demands of a subsequent crisis make themselves felt. Moreover, while each polarized pair has a time when it is particularly dominant, it is not *only* at that one stage in the life cycle that it influences the individual: tensions between trust and mistrust, for example, will reoccur throughout life in different forms. Erikson insists, moreover, that the scheme is essentially dialectical: it is not necessarily a case of choosing the positive pole of the pair – Trust over Mistrust, for example. Some kind of balance between the two may be essential, and a healthy degree of mistrust may be necessary for the individual to cope successfully with an unstable world. Positives and negatives, in Erikson's scheme, are dynamic counterparts at the end of life as well as at the beginning, and both can play a part in the development of a healthy ego. And what Erikson sees as true for the ordinary person is even truer for the artist, one of whose tasks is to travel to places that in real life we may want to avoid, and to push to the limit the tension between the opposite poles which each stage of the life cycle brings. One of the predominant characteristics of late style, I would suggest, is not so much 'reconciliation and serenity' – nor even 'intransigence and difficulty', but an intense tension between these positives and negatives.

This at least, I would suggest, is what constitutes the 'late style' of *Oedipus at Colonus*. The play was the last that Sophocles wrote, and it was not performed until after his death – in a production which was sponsored, we are told, by his grandson, who seems to have shown Sophocles more filial devotion than his actual sons ever did! In terms of narrative chronology, however, it is the second of his three Theban plays: preceded by the tragedy of *Oedipus the King* and followed by that of *Antigone*, Oedipus' daughter. In the first, *Oedipus the King* of course, Oedipus has been catastrophically thrown down from his position of ruler of Thebes, and his life destroyed by the revelation that – unwittingly – he himself was the man who had brought a curse upon the city by murdering his father and marrying Jocasta, his mother. The Oedipus legend is, from the very beginning, concerned with youth and age. Oedipus' original sexual sin is not only incestuous but also trans-generational, and the famous riddle of the sphinx – the solving of which set the younger Oedipus on the throne of Thebes – establishes the theme: 'Which creature goes on four legs in the morning, on two at mid-day, and upon three in the evening?' The answer – as Oedipus guessed – was 'Man': crawling on all fours as a baby, walking upright as an adult, and hobbling with the aid of a walking stick in old age. The sphinx's riddle describes the three ages of man, and the penalty for those who failed to recognize this pattern was a premature and violent death.

Endings: Redemption song?

Oedipus at Colonus is a difficult play. In a famous essay of 1978 George Steiner asked the question 'What do we mean when we say "this poem or this passage in this poem is *difficult*?"' (1978: 19). He attempted to answer the question by offering a 'typology of some of the principal modes of difficulty as one meets them in poetry' (1978: 19). One of these was what he called *modal difficulties* – mainly caused by a cultural or historical distance from the society that produced the poem which is so great that the poet's 'idiom and orders of apprehension are no longer natural to us' (1978: 33). For a modern audience *Oedipus at Colonus* is riddled with such modal difficulties. We have to contend with multiple 'orders of apprehension' which take as self-evident those 'truths' about the realities of pollution and ritual cleansing, about sacred groves and the sanctity of place, about the practical effects which blessings, curses and oracular pronouncements have upon the world of *realpolitik*. And any attempt to read it (as I am doing) as part of an enquiry into old age on the classical stage, must peer through a tangled thicket of modal difficulties which are anything but 'natural to us'. How, in particular, are we to read the ending of this extraordinary play about an old man approaching death? Surely, however we read it, the one thing that stands out is how different its world is from 'ours' – and how far removed Sophocles' story is *both* from a secular view of old age and end-of-life care *and* from any Christian sense of tragic resolution or redemption?

Which makes it ironic that Sophocles' play – not one of his most frequently-performed in recent years – is probably best known to modern audiences in the Gospel-musical adaptation by the innovative American director Lee Breuer titled *Gospel at Colonus*, in which Breuer 'take[s] Greek myth and fuse[s] it with the charismatic religion of the Black Pentecostal Church to form a unique mythological form' (Runnell 1989: 42). Originally produced in 1980, *Gospel at Colonus* has been revived and expanded on several occasions – most recently at the 2010 Edinburgh Festival, where it played to packed houses and rave reviews. Charles Spencer's *Telegraph* column provides a typical example:

Hallelujah! The Edinburgh International Festival has just delivered one of the most original and joyful shows I have seen in years. You leave this fantastic production in a state of blissed-out wonder.

(Spencer 2010: n.p.)

Spencer's approbatory phrase 'blissed-out wonder' is a marker of the extent to which Breuer has succeeded in taming the alien pagan experience and translating it into a Christian Pentecostal one.

Adaptations, rewritings and re-incorporations are part and parcel of theatrical production, of course. Moreover, even among some classical scholars, *Oedipus at Colonus* does seem to lend itself to religious interpretations, and sometimes these have been couched in specifically Christian language (see Burian 1974, Linforth 1951). Even Edward Said's account of Oedipus as having 'finally attained a remarkable holiness and sense of resolution' has something of this residual Christian spiritualization lingering about it. *Gospel at Colonus*, then, is a perfectly valid theatrical experiment in its own right, and one which fulfils Breuer's own programme of 'cross-cultural American classicism' (Runnell 1989: 7) in a melting-pot of theatrical culture which draws not only on Greek theatre and Gospel music, but also on Japanese traditional drama, and in which the powerful vocals of The Blind Boys of Alabama and the extraordinary performance of the eighty-year-old Jimmy Carter as Oedipus, play themselves out on a stage whose design is inspired by *kabuki* theatre.

Few classical scholars, however, have read Sophocles' play in the wholeheartedly Christian revivalist terms that Breuer's adaptation presents. The religious sensibility which the play articulates marks its distance from, rather than its proximity to, our own culture. Moreover, cross-cultural experiments and intercultural theatre do not exist outside broader patterns of cultural hegemony, and the effect of Breuer's fusion – as with so many 'intercultural' experiments – is to translate the strange and alien into the local and familiar, to modernize and westernize Sophocles' drama, and in the process to subordinate or even obliterate those 'orders of apprehension' which do not immediately fit with our own.

Liminality: Margins and thresholds

The ending of *Oedipus at Colonus*, then, is a more complex and problematic one than Spencer's 'blissed-out wonder' suggests. In fact, it is quite hard to tell just how Oedipus' story *does* end. In the final moments of the play, the conventional Messenger returns to tell Antigone, Ismene, the Chorus and the audience how Oedipus met his end. His message, though, is unusually unclear.

> After brief space we looked again, and lo
> The man was gone, evanished from our eyes;
> Only the king we saw with upraised hand
> Shading his eyes as from some awful sight,
> That no man might endure to look upon.
> A moment later, and we saw him bend
> In prayer to Earth and prayer to Heaven at once.
> But by what doom the stranger met his end
> No man save Theseus knoweth.

(Sophocles [406 BCE] 1928: 121)

And Theseus, bound by an oath of secrecy to Oedipus, is not telling. The end of *Oedipus at Colonus* is a zone of perpetual uncertainty – a zone into which all sorts of interpretations rush. And if some of these point towards an almost Christian 'assumption' into heaven, others are infinitely more down to earth – such as the suggestion that he simply jumped off a cliff (Jebb, quoted in Sophocles 1955: 256–57, Ahrensdorf 2008: 171). There is no consolation at the end of the play for Antigone or Ismene – and we are left uncertain as to what resolution or integration, if any, Oedipus himself has actually found. It is an extraordinarily open-ended text.

Even the satisfaction of a good theatrical death is denied to the spectator. Did he ascend into heaven or jump off a cliff? Or both? The play withholds the information from us, as Theseus withholds the information from Antigone and Ismene. And yet, however ambiguous the ending, we are left with a sense that Oedipus himself *has* crossed some kind of threshold – whether we imagine that threshold to lead to some kind of spiritual integration which amounts to a redemption, purification, or whether it is a threshold to oblivion. For the rest of us, however, the threshold remains uncrossed. For Antigone and Ismene there is little consolation or resolution in the play – indeed we watch with sadness as they turn their steps towards Thebes, and towards the bleak burial which Antigone will undergo due to the lack of any resolution between Oedipus and his sons. The play offers no closure for the sisters or for us. It might be Sophocles' final play, but structurally it is the second play in a three-part sequence: not technically a trilogy, this second part nonetheless leaves its meanings open in the way that second plays in trilogies traditionally do, pointing towards further catastrophes, further miseries.

Oedipus spends much of his time in the play – as he has spent much of his later life – in a position of liminality: marginalized, excluded, abjected. Liminality is a concept that is familiar – some would say over-familiar – to workers in the field of performance studies. The term (which means, roughly, 'in between') derives from the work of anthropologist Arnold van Gennep and his consideration of the

> division [of a society] into generation or age groups. The life of an individual in any society is a series of passages from one age to another and from one occupation to another. Wherever there are fine distinctions among age or occupational groups, progression from one group is accompanied by special acts ... Among semicivilized peoples such acts are enveloped in ceremonies.
>
> (van Gennep [1908] 2004: 2–3)

In his classic study, van Gennep classified and described rites of passage relating to various phases of a person's life: pregnancy and childbirth, childhood, initiation rites, betrothal and marriage, and funerals. In the rites themselves he perceived a common pattern – a progression in which the initiates moved through three transitional stages. The first phase (Separation) was that of being identified and segregated; the second (Liminality) involved a period of isolation from the rest of society; the third (Reaggregation) of being reincorporated into full membership of that society.

Liminality, then, is from the very first an age-related concept. But van Gennep's work has had a powerful influence, and one which he could not have foreseen, on the development of performance studies, through the writings of Victor Turner and his work on the relationship between social dramas, rituals and performance. Turner summarizes van Gennep's rites of transition as 'rites which accompany every change of place, state, social position and age ... [They] are marked by three phases: separation, margin (or limen) and reaggregation' (1977: 36), but when he adapted van Gennep's work for a new generation, he focused in particular on the second, liminal, stage – that ambiguous and transitional phase of separation and isolation, when the individual is neither fully part of a society nor entirely divorced from it.

The Greek term *limen*, from which van Gennep and Turner derived the word liminal, is usually translated as 'threshold'. *Limen* can also, however, mean 'margin' – the word with which we started at the beginning of this chapter, and which we are far more used to seeing in association with old age. In his analysis of rites of passage, in fact, Victor Turner, actually preferred the term 'marginal' but felt unable to use it because it had been 'pre-empted by various sociologists ... for their own purposes – so we are left with "liminal"' (Turner 1977: 36).

Largely through the work of Victor Turner – and then Richard Schechner – the notion of liminality has become a key concept in performance studies; indeed – it has become commonplace within the discipline to see both performance cultures and performance studies themselves in terms of the liminal. As Schechner wrote in a 1998 essay titled 'What is performance studies anyway?'

> Performance studies is 'inter' – in between. It is intergeneric, interdisciplinary, intercultural – and therefore inherently unstable. Performance studies resists or rejects definition. As a discipline, PS cannot be mapped effectively because it transgresses boundaries, it goes where it is not expected to be. It is inherently 'in between' and therefore cannot be pinned down or located exactly.
>
> (McKenzie 2004: 27)

By now, in fact, there is some danger that the term has become a little overworn. Paradoxically, as Jon McKenzie points out, 'the persistent use of this concept within the field has made liminality into something of a norm' (McKenzie 2004: 27).

In the process, the term has moved on somewhat from van Gennep's original empirical formulation, and has taken on a metaphoric quality – one which also links the study of performance with a certain kind of transgressive and resistant approach to culture. Liminality in this sense is divorced from the purely temporal: it *may* be a short period of dislocated existence which is quickly followed by reintegration into the community, or it may become a permanent state of being, one which is identified with principles of uncertainty, exploration, innovation and rebellion. This extension of the meaning of the concept is easy enough to pinpoint. Less easy, perhaps, but still noticeable, is the way in which this transgressive, resistant liminality of performance has also come to be associated with a kind of youthful energy. In terms of cultural generalizations, resistance and transgressiveness are most easily and frequently associated with adolescence and young adulthood – a life stage which is also frequently marked by an ambiguous relationship with society (Reuter 1937, Furstenberg 2000). By the same token, the radical and transgressive in performance is linked in the popular imagination (and often in reality) with younger, emerging companies, practitioners and writers: the Romantics' association of youth and rebellion remains a powerful cultural image. At the same time, in terms of van Gennep's original analysis, the most frequently cited example of a liminal stage in a rite of passage refers to that of the young male's passage from childhood to maturity. So it is, perhaps, unsurprising that although Turner and van Gennep both insisted that the rites of passage which they explored were ones which 'accompany every change of place, state, social position and age' (Turner 1977: 36), there has also been an unspoken tendency to associate, by default, the liminal with the youthful. I want to unpick something of this default association – not to deny it or to reverse it but to problematize it and to explore the way in which liminality as broad metaphor may also be reappropriated for the in-between-ness of old age.

In what ways might the notion of liminality be applied to ageing? To answer this we may turn to the provocative work of Barbara Myerhoff, the anthropologist, whose studies of the elderly are so brilliantly articulated in her book *Remembered Lives* (1992). Here she draws on Turner and van Gennep in order, suggestively, to equate old age with liminality. Picking up on the notion of liminality in its extended sense, as a state of being identified with 'many varieties of nonbelonging', she goes on to argue that

> Folk wisdom has it that old people 'are the same as they have always been, only more so.' Liminality – being socially in limbo – anomie, rolelessness, neglect and social irrelevance may have the complex advantage of leaving old people alone, to be themselves only more so.
>
> (Myerhoff 1992: 223)

This kind of liminality is a double-edged sword. Myerhoff goes on to talk about the positives of such a state, the resultant 'creativity of desocialized elders … people whose reemerging originality … may be as delightful, surprising and fruitful as anything to be found among the very young' (Myerhoff 1992: 223–24). It may also, however, be terrible and terrifying – as it seems to have been for Oedipus, forced to be 'himself only more so' throughout the period of exile in which the play culminates.

Oedipus at Colonus seems to me to be essentially a play of liminality. Its story hangs between the sacred and the profane; its protagonist, who finds himself between life and death, is himself portrayed as something between a sacred and sacrificial victim, and an angry old man. And even if at the end of the play we imagine Oedipus himself undergoing some sort of offstage transformation that amounts to a 'reaggregation' (Turner 1977: 36), neither we nor his daughters are witness to it, nor can we expect to understand it, much less share it: we, too, are left in a state of incompleteness, in between different understandings of what has happened. Even the theatrical form of the drama seems to be 'in between'. While there are other Greek plays whose climax is a seemingly miraculous transformation, in which the protagonist is carried away to the afterlife or elsewhere, *Oedipus at Colonus* is the

> only work in which the miracle by which the main character is carried away becomes the purpose and the main significance of the whole action. As a consequence, the action on the stage … becomes an enactment of a cult-legend: the visible testimony and perception of a mystery presented as a narrative, celebrated in song and dance, and still potent. Thus in a sense, with the second Oedipus drama Attic tragedy returns to its original significance as mime in the context of cult.
>
> (Reinhardt 1979: 194–95)

To this extent, then, we might say that *Oedipus at Colonus* even sits on some kind of threshold between tragic theatre and cult rite.

Perhaps the strongest statement about the in-between-ness of Sophocles' tragedy belongs to Jacques Lacan. In the seventh book of his Seminars, he had described Sophocles' *Antigone*, as being 'between two deaths'. He goes on to say of all of Sophocles' protagonists (with the possible exception of the earlier Oedipus of *Oedipus Rex*) that

[i]f there is a distinguishing characteristic to everything we ascribe to Sophocles ... it is that for all his heroes the race is run. They are at a limit that is not accounted for by their solitude relative to others. There is something more; they are characters who find themselves right away in a limit zone, find themselves between life and death. The theme of between-life-and-death is, moreover, formulated as such in the text, but it is also manifest in the situations themselves.

(Lacan 1992: 272)

This 'limit zone' is also a liminal zone – a place of in-between-ness. From the beginning of the play the ageing Oedipus is seen to be, like Antigone, 'between two deaths' – the death he died when exiled from Thebes, and the death he seeks, the death he hopes will bring his sufferings to an end. And in this state of being between two deaths, he appears at first to be the embodiment of a 'master narrative of decline': frail, incapacitated, excluded, vulnerable and subject to all the ills of old age that the Chorus laments. The story of the play is the story of Oedipus' eventual resistance to, or transcendence of, this state of helplessness, and while the exact nature of that resistance/transcendence is couched, the reader is left in little doubt that it has taken place. As readers and spectators – especially perhaps as readers and spectators used to the notion that there should be some kind of consolation in tragedy or holiness in ritual – we may seek to complete the rite of passage, to see the reintegration after the period of liminality. Lacan's reading sees something rather different: a play in which the hero 'is shown to be unyielding right to the end, demanding everything, giving up nothing, absolutely unreconciled' (Lacan 1992: 310). The ambiguities of *Oedipus at Colonus*, it seems to me, inhabit the space that lies between these two interpretations, and the tension between them is the tension that is typical of tragedy: by no means triumphantly affirmative, but by no means, either, a straightforward 'narrative of decline'.

Chapter 4

On Negative Stereotypes in Classical and Medieval Drama

Comedy and the genealogy of a stereotype

In a tragedy such as *Oedipus at Colonus* the theme of old age is treated with sympathy and with dignity – and all the more so for not being sentimentalized. As an art form, theatre is not always so respectful of old age. Nor, perhaps, should we expect it to be: the social and communal nature of the theatrical experience and the immediacy of the relationship between the stage and the audience mean that theatrical performance is quick to adopt and recycle the beliefs and attitudes, the codes and the signifiers, the prejudices and stereotypes of everyday life. And since, historically, ageism and respect for the elderly have been culturally intertwined in social life, so too are they in theatre. In this chapter and the two following, I shall be looking at that most blatant negative stereotype of old age: the figure of the *senex*.

The *senex* is the stock figure of the old man in comic plays. In other contexts the word can have quite positive associations (in Jungian psychology, for example, the *senex* may be a figure associated with wisdom) but in theatrical comedy the term usually refers to a foolish old man. And since theatrical comedy so often has a love plot at its centre, the *senex* most often wears one of two faces: the *senex iratus* and the *senex amans*. The former, the angry old man, most usually appears as the domineering father-figure, controlling his children with an iron fist and, in particular, obstructing and seeking to frustrate their erotic desires, insisting that they will marry whomever *he*, rather than they, decides. Money and status is often a major factor: the marriage he seeks for his daughter is likely to be one which will be financially or socially beneficial to him. Sometimes his choice will be more random. When, at the beginning of Shakespeare's *Midsummer Night's Dream*, Egeus storms onto the stage with his daughter Hermia, demanding of Theseus

> the ancient privilege of Athens:
> As she is mine, I may dispose of her;
> Which shall be either to this gentleman,
> Or to her death, according to our law

> (Shakespeare 1974: 223)

the Elizabethan audience would have been very familiar with the stereotype, and would have known broadly what to expect from the ensuing action.

The second type, the *senex amans* is the caricature of the elderly man who falls in love (or in lust) foolishly and inappropriately with a young girl, and who by thus acting against societal expectations makes himself vulnerable to ridicule. The butt of many a joke about impotence, the *senex amans* is frequently portrayed as lecherous and devious, but he is not always driven entirely by sexual desire. His other major motivation is often money, and the true object of his affection might be the young woman's fortune as much as her body. To use another Shakespearean example, when Queen Elizabeth – according to popular legend – commissioned Shakespeare to write a play showing her favourite character Falstaff in love, Shakespeare responded by picking up the innuendo of impotence in Fall-staff's name, and presented the Queen with a play which turned the Vice-figure of the *Henry IV* plays into a *senex amans*, chasing around a small English town in search of sexual and financial relief in *The Merry Wives of Windsor*.

The *senex*, then appears and reappears in various guises throughout cultural history: in the Pantalone of the *commedia dell'arte*, in Shakespeare's tragedies as well as his comedies, in Molière's Harpagon, in the 'heavy fathers' of the nineteenth-century stock companies. His two functions are not mutually exclusive, and some of the best plots arise when the aspects of *iratus* and *amans* are intertwined in the same figure. And while comic love plots are his most natural habitat, he can also exist outside their framework, in which case his miserly and domineering characteristics come to the fore (Mr Burns in *The Simpsons* is a *senex* seen through the eyes of a cartoon child) for the *senex* flourishes best in societies, or in situations, where there is resistance to real or perceived gerontocratic power and authority. I shall be looking both at the 'classical' *senex* and at some variations on the theme.

Origins: The classical *senex*

The origins of the stereotype can be found both in ancient Greek and, more importantly, in Roman comedy. Of the Greek Old Comedy, which flourished during the Peloponnesian War, only some plays of Aristophanes (c. 456–386 BCE) have survived in their entirety. In Aristophanic plays such as *The Acharnians, Peace, The Clouds, The Knights, The Wasps* and *The Birds*, and in the surviving fragments by Aristophanes' contemporary Pherecrates, we find occasional caricatures of foolish and lecherous old men. But Old Comedy, which had earlier developed from phallic rituals, was largely a form of local political satire: heavily dependent upon its immediate cultural context; its characteristics were fantasy, obscenity and *ad hominem* attacks on individual public figures. With the rise of the Greek New Comedy, playwrights turned to something more like a civic comedy, or comedy of manners, with plays such as those of Menander (c. 342–291 BCE) which satirizes more general social foibles, and paints a vivid picture of Athenian social history, foregrounding issues of gender, family and private law. The plot of his *Woman from Samos*, for example, centres around Athenian ideas of legitimate birth and domestic responsibility, and one of its central characters, the aged Demeas (with whom the eponymous Samian woman enters into a relationship), is a very early example of one of the most significant subsets of the stereotype of the old man, the *senex amans* – the old man in love. Menander, too, is known to us only through his fragments, with the exception of one play, *Dyskolos* or *The Bad-Tempered Man*. Knemon, the grouch of the title, is occasionally referred to in the dialogue as 'old', and he fulfils one of the traditional functions of the *senex* in that he attempts to thwart his daughter in her love for the young hero. So perhaps Menander can be said to have provided us with the earliest extant fully developed dramatic portrayals of the *senex*. More interesting examples of the *senex* in the classical theatre, however, are to be found in the comic drama that emerged in Rome a couple of centuries later. (This perhaps, is hardly surprising: the word *senex* itself is Latin, meaning simply 'old man'.)

What we know of Roman comedy comes down to us through the work of just two writers whose work survives: Plautus and Terence. From this sparse evidence an entire tradition has been reconstructed, one in which the use of stock characters – and notably for our purposes the stock character of the *senex* – is a prime source of the comedy. Plautus' comedies are the earliest surviving complete works of literature in Latin. For the most part they are adaptations, direct or indirect, of Greek plays, reframed so as to appeal to a Roman audience. These Roman dramas certainly made great use of comic stereotyped figures of the old man. Along with other stock characters such as the braggart soldier (*miles gloriosus*), the naïve hero (*adulescens*), the clever servant (*servus callidus*) and other comic types which have survived through the ages, the comic figure of the *senex* takes on various manifestations in various plays: sometimes a miserly killjoy, sometimes a helper-figure for the hero, sometimes a cruel domineering figure who stands in the way of true love and sometimes himself a comically inappropriate lover (*senex amans*) in his own right. Between them, characters such as these comprised a stock company of exaggerated two-dimensional figures, and effectively provided a vocabulary of comic stereotypes on which comedy in future centuries would draw repeatedly.

To take examples of this early manifestation of the stage archetype of the old man, Plautus' *Menaechmi*, reckoned by many as his best work, and one of the narrative sources of Shakespeare's *Comedy of Errors* and *Twelfth Night*, has a plot based on a sequence of misunderstandings. The narrative deals with a pair of twins (both named Menaechmus) separated in childhood, who – unknown to each other – find themselves in the same town and in a series of comic situations arising from mistaken identity. Unnamed in the text, the old man is actually the father-in-law of one of the two title characters, Menaechmus of Epidamnus.

It is in Plautus that we first see an elaboration of the central element of the *senex* – that he is a figure who is of some social standing and power within his own world, and whose actions nearly always derive from his desire to increase that social standing and power. And, as Erich Segal points out, it is

surefire comic material when an older and wider *paterfamilias* is overthrown by the lowliest member of his *familia*, especially for the Romans, who, under ordinary circumstances, were renowned for their reverential attitude towards older persons. But in a *deposuit*, the greater the victim, the greater the pleasure. Thus Plautus makes the inversion of status still more meaningful for his countrymen by presenting as comic butts *senes* who are also *senatores*. Almost every old man in his comedies enjoys some sort of social or political rank and is esteemed by the public at large; hence public disgrace is all the more painful.

(Segal 1987: 119)

This status function is more evident in some of Plautus' other plays (such as *Casina*, *Epidicus*, *Captivi*, *Mostellaria*, *Bacchides*) but here in *Menaechmi*, too, the notion of old age as embodying authority is established before it is subverted. This *senex*, who is called into the action at a relatively late stage, is brought on to embody an element of authority: the wife of Menaechmus of Epidamnus turns to him to punish her seemingly callous husband – which is of course really the *other* Menaechmus. At first unsympathetic to his daughter's complaints, he eventually sees her 'husband's' strange behaviour for himself, challenges him, and eventually fetches slaves to arrest him and carry him away. A secondary character in the action of the play as a whole, the old man announces himself as a stereotype on his first entrance, performing by way of self-introduction a set-piece 'aria' on the miseries of old age.

According as my age permits, and as there is occasion to do so, I'll push on my steps and make haste to get along. But how far from easy 'tis for me, I'm not mistaken as to that. For my agility forsakes me, and I am beset with age; I carry my body weighed down; my strength has deserted me. How grievous a pack upon one's back is age. For when it comes, it brings very many and very grievous particulars, were I now to recount all of which, my speech would be too long.

(Plautus [c. 205–184 BCE] 1912: I, 354)

The speech describes what, presumably, the actor playing the part would look like, in however stylized a way: bent, feeble, having difficulty walking. That is the physical presence, embodied by the actor, which the audience would be confronted with throughout the performance of the play. Only after having delivered this set-piece does he turn back to the action of the plot and say

But this matter is a trouble to my mind and heart, what this business can possibly be on account of which my daughter suddenly requires me to come to her, and doesn't first let me know what's the matter, what she wants, or why she sends for me. But pretty nearly do I know now what's the matter; I suspect that some quarrel has arisen with her husband.

(Plautus [c. 205–184 BCE] 1912: I, 354)

The stereotype of enfeebled old age which he presents on his first appearance almost contradicts the authority function that he later embodies in the plot, and this is one of the sources of the play's comedy.

If *Menaechmi* provides us with a good early example of *senex iratus*, it is in another of Plautus' plays that we can see the development of the *senex amans*: Demipho, in Plautus' *Mercator* (*The Merchant*), declares that

> I'll have recourse again to former habits and enjoy myself. In my allotment of existence, almost now run through, the little that there remains of life, I'll cheer up with pleasure, wine, and love. For it's quite proper for this time of life to enjoy itself. When you are young, then, when the blood is fresh, it's right to devote your exertions to acquiring your fortune; and then when at last, you are an old man, you may set yourself at your ease; drink, and be amorous.
>
> (Plautus [c. 205–184 BCE] 1913: II, 258)

Demipho, in the eyes of his audience, condemns himself out of his own mouth, describing a version of the life-course which turns upside down some of the norms of decorum. He is acting – in Roman terms – inappropriately, and inappropriate behaviour among the old is a common source of comedy. Here Plautus makes particular comic capital out of the incongruity between the passionate lover that Demipho would like to be seen as and the grotesque ugliness of his physical appearance:

CHARINUS:	Of what figure, then, did they say he was?
EUTYCHUS:	I'll tell you: grey-headed, bandy-legged, pot-bellied, wide-mouthed, of stunted figure, with darkish eyes, lank jaws, splay-footed rather.
CHARINUS:	You are mentioning to me not a human being, but a whole storehouse, I don't know what, of deformities.

(Plautus [c. 205–184 BCE] 1913: II, 162)

This 'whole storehouse … of deformities' draws on existing Roman satirical tropes of the kind that can also be seen in writers such as Juvenal; and here the speakers' repulsion against the perceived ugliness of old age becomes symbolically charged, and implies an analogy between physical ugliness and defects of character.

The plays of Plautus were highly successful in their own time, but they had an important 'second life' in the sixteenth century, with their rediscovery by humanist scholars. The rise of humanism in late Medieval and Renaissance Europe was accompanied – and to some extent fuelled – by a revival of interest in classical literatures, and in the fifteenth century the Latin plays of Plautus and Terence found renewed popularity, both as texts for reading and study (this being facilitated of course by the invention of printing) and also as scripts for theatrical production: a series of well-received performances of Plautus' plays which were mounted by Pomponius Laetus and others in Rome between 1484 and 1502 established Plautus' popularity – a popularity which continued throughout the sixteenth century (Duckworth 1994: 399). New comedies written in Latin and Italian by fifteenth-century Italian humanists adopted and adapted Plautine techniques, making extensive use of characters and situations drawn from the Roman originals. For example, Lodovico Ariosto, one of the pioneers of the early modern European drama and of this genre of *commedia erudita* ('learned comedy') updated and reworked Plautus' plots to make the *La Cassaria* and *I Suppositi* in 1508 and 1509 respectively – plays which in turn influenced Shakespeare's comedies nearly a century later. The Plautine revival, however, was not the only site for the re-emergence of the comic *senex* in the drama of medieval Europe.

'Ya, ya, all old men to me take tent': Old age and the Middle Ages

However we define 'the Middle Ages' – and in theatre history the phrase often refers loosely to a period which starts with the first recorded 'Quem Quaeritis' liturgical tropes in the tenth century, and ends with the rise of the commercial urban playhouses in the late sixteenth – it seems at first glance not to be a particularly fruitful period for looking at theatrical representations of old age. This is partly an issue of theatre history in the broader sense: looking at any kind of theatrical and dramatic activity in this period – especially in its earlier years – involves dealing with a heterogeneity of activity in different locations, great *lacunae* in our knowledge and problems of categorization. As David Wiles has put it, 'When we pass … into the medieval [world] the writing of a continuous history becomes fraught with difficulty' (1997: 65). Much of the 'new writing' of the early medieval European drama that we know about was connected to the Church and involved the dramatization of Biblical stories or of saints' lives. Alongside these were the allegorical dramas relating to various aspects of the Christian life, allegories which would later be adopted and adapted for use in the polemical debates of the Reformation and post-Reformation. At the same time, improvised folk-dramas and pageants, often comprising a confusing mixture of pagan and Christian elements, were a feature of medieval festivals and games.

Within these traditions it is possible to find treatments of the theme of old age, but not very many. This is neither because there were fewer old people during the Middle Ages, nor because the elderly were of no interest to the culture as a whole: as the work of scholars such as Albrecht Classen has demonstrated, old age was discussed and represented in a wide range of poems, meditations, illustrated homilies, autobiographies and visual sources (Classen 2007). But the stage, for the most part, was looking to other topics and subject matter. In fact, childhood and youth were of far greater interest to theatre-makers, as many of the titles of plays suggest: *The Interlude of Youth*; *Mundus et Infans*; *The Disobedient Child* and *An Interlude called Lusty Juventus, lively describing the Frailty of Youth: of Nature prone to Vice: by Grace and good Counsel trainable to Virtue*. Plays such as these reflected contemporary concerns – in particular the preoccupation of the male nobility with the fashioning of identity and one's place in the social hierarchy. Comedy took on a rather different shape during this period, becoming more didactic within the frame of reference of the Christian church from which the theatre was in the process of separating itself. And while youth, rather than age, was the concern of medieval comedy, these plays inevitably contain their figures of old age (such as Good Counsel in *Lusty Juventus*) since addressing the subject of youth in any detail inevitably involves addressing also its binary opposite. But the comic *senex* tends to disappear behind the scenes for a while in the Middle Ages, to be replaced either by allegorical figures representing wisdom or salvation, or else by a very physical satire on the medical miseries of growing old, such as that in *The Castle of Perseverance* (c. 1425) where the character of Mankind, suddenly affected by old age, cries out

I ginne to waxyn hory and olde;
My bake ginnith to bowe and bende;
I crulle and crepe, and wax al colde.
Age makith Man ful unthende,
Body and bonys, and al unwolde.
My bonys are febyl and sore;
I am arayed in a sloppe;
As a yonge man, I may not hoppe;
My nose is colde, and ginnith to droppe;
Mine her waxith al hore.

(Bevington 1975: 868)

One place, however, where the figure of the stereotypical *senex* does reappear, and perhaps somewhat unexpectedly, is within the Corpus Christi cycle plays: those pageant dramas were based on Biblical stories which were performed in the fourteenth, fifteenth and sixteenth centuries by medieval guilds in towns such as York, Coventry, Wakefield and Lincoln. There are various comic masculine figures in these (Noah, for example, becomes the henpecked husband) and in some of them age plays a part. Some, too, do not have to depart very far from their Biblical sources to find comic routines of which old men are the butts: the medieval author of *The Play of Jacob and Esau* found some darkly comic potential in his Genesis source, in which Jacob tricks his old, blind father Isaac into granting him the birthright that should have belonged to his brother.

But the most interesting old man in the Corpus Christi cycle plays is Joseph. The N-Town cycle, from the English Midlands, contains several plays, added to the cycle at various times, about Joseph and Mary: plays such as *The Betrothal of Mary*, *Joseph's Doubt* and *The Trial of Mary and Joseph*. These plays – which despite their Biblical narratives are effectively domestic comedies, depict Joseph as a version of the stereotypical foolish *senex*. In *The Betrothal of Mary*, for example, Joseph complains self-pityingly about the infirmity of age from his first entrance:

Come? Ya! Ya! God help! Full fain I would,
But I am so aged and so old

That both my legs begin to fold,
I am nigh almost lame!

> (Spector 1991: 10.225–28; my modernization of spelling)

In *The Trial of Mary and Joseph*, Joseph becomes specifically a type of *senex amans* as the onlookers, mocking him for his age, stress the bawdy aspect of the difference in age between Mary and Joseph

A young man may do more cheer in bed
To a young wench than may an old.
That is the cause such law is ledde,
That many a man is a cuckold …
His legs here do fold for age
But with this damsel when he did 'dance',
The old churl had right great courage!

> (Spector 1991: 14.102–05, 267–69)

Joseph's own concerns about the age gap between them is dramatized in *Joseph's Doubt*, where, even before his marriage to Mary, Joseph himself worries that 'An old man may never thrive/With a young wife, so God me save' (Spector 1991: 10.278–79); and when the old man discovers his wife to be pregnant, his immediate assumption is that she has been unfaithful, and that he has been cuckolded.

Ya, ya, all old men to me take tent [pay heed],
And wed no wife in no kynnys wise
That is a young wench …
Alas, alas, my name is shent!
All men may me now despise
And say, 'Old cuckold, thy bow is bent
Newly now after the French guise.

> (Spector 1991: 12.49–56)

This depiction of Joseph as a foolish old man is not confined to the N-Town Cycle. The Biblical cue about the age difference between Joseph and Mary seems to have been taken up ubiquitously across all areas of medieval culture and popular tradition. Certainly all the extant plays from the medieval drama in which Joseph appears portray him 'as the more or less comic old man, no longer capable of the "prevy play", married to a young wife' (Baird and Baird 1973: 159). Thus the early scenes of the Coventry *Pageant of the Shearmen and Tailors*, which deals with the annunciation and nativity, show Joseph confronting Mary with her supposed crime and, again, appealing to the old men in the audience to learn from his mistakes:

Ah! Well-away Joseph, as thou art old!
Like a fool now may I stand …
But in faith, Mary, thou art in sin,
So much as I have cherished thee, dame, and all thy kin
Behind my back to serve me thus!
All old men, example take by me
How I am beguiled here may you see,
To wed so young a child.
Now fare thee well, Mary, I leave thee here alone.

(Craig 1902: 5)

And of course, the scriptural narrative does itself contain the implicit joke that Joseph is ironically quite right on one level: the child is not his.

The Coventry plays are just one example of an almost universal tendency in medieval culture to portray Joseph as a type of *senex amans*; in visual arts and poetry as well as theatre, the age disparity is stressed, and an implicit link is suggested between the figures of Joseph and Mary and the folkloric and fabliau tales of January and May, in which the stereotype of the older man with the young wife is unvaryingly an object of ridicule. The Coventry plays sail quite close to the wind, but they fall short of attributing to Joseph all the negative attributes of a Plautine *senex*. Joseph is foolish, and he is the butt of a predictable ribald humour, but in the end he is treated with a certain degree of sympathy.

The aged body has its symbolic as well as its physiological dimensions, and Joseph's anxiety suggests a crisis of domestic male authority: his belief that he has been supplanted in his wife's affections and cuckolded may refer to an anxiety about the status of male authority in general. But local concerns and contexts might well have been present, too, within the framework of the stereotype (Alakas 2006, Christie 2008). In Coventry, for example, the *Pageant of the Shearsmen and Taylors*, in the version we now have, seems to date from a rewrite by a writer called Robert Croo that took place during the 1530s – a time when Coventry was undergoing a marked economic decline, together with a wholesale restructuring of its social hierarchy. Coventry's affluence during the fifteenth century had been maintained by a social structure which was markedly more gerontocratic than most other contemporary provincial urban centres; the urban crises of late medieval England hit Coventry particularly badly, however, and the resulting economic and demographic downturn in the city's fortunes meant that by the 1530s the power of this ageing elite and its values was rapidly waning, and a younger generation was coming to the fore (Phythian-Adams 2002). The ensuing reorganization of the city's Guilds (the civic bodies that were also responsible for producing the Cycle plays) meant that 'The system of age categorization which served as the organizing principle of the city's social fabric … was severely undermined' (Alakas 2006: 25).

There is insufficient manuscript evidence to tell exactly what changes Robert Croo made to the text of the *Pageant of the Shearsman and Taylors*, but what comparisons can be made between his rewrites and fragments from earlier versions of this and other plays suggest that he intensifies the satire against old age – and that for a contemporary audience at least, Joseph and Mary's relationship would have reflected stresses in contemporary domestic relationships arising from the city's crisis in gerontocracy.

A lean and slippered Pantalone

Local social satire was also a central feature of the *commedia dell'arte*, the 'professional comedy' or 'comedy of the actors' guild' which emerged in Venice at about the same time. Drawing on a range of traditions which included popular street entertainments as well as the Latin comedies of Plautus and Terence, the form flourished throughout Italy in the next couple of centuries and *commedia* companies, often family-based, toured Europe and had an influence on playwrights such as Shakespeare, Jonson, Lope de Vega, Goldoni and Molière. In 1611, Flaminio Scala published *Il Teatro delle Favole Rappresentative* – a collection of *commedia* scenarios, dressed up in rather literary apparel, but from which it has been possible to reconstruct the workings of a *commedia* company. Scala's scenarios are plot summaries and descriptions of episodes, written down without any dialogue but comprising a clear narrative structure around which the company would improvise. Characters were based on exaggerated social stereotypes and the actors who performed them wore thin leather half-masks caricaturing their roles: old men, the young lovers, the comic servants and so on. This comparatively small range of social stereotypes generated a large number of narratives, usually involving love, jealousy, deception, trickery, misunderstandings and happy endings. Titles of these three-act scenarios, such as *The Jealous Old Man*, *The Desperate Doctor*, *The Fake Magician* and *The Just Punishment*, give an accurate idea of their flavour. At the heart of *commedia* improvisation lay the *lazzi* – the company's repertoire of comic routines based on stock situations.

The *senex* reappears as the 'Vecchi', the old men of the stock company: Pantalone, the Venetian merchant, and Graziano (or sometimes simply 'Dottore'), the Bolognese doctor: locality, regional stereotypes and local jokes were an important source of humour for *commedia* players. Long-winded and fussy, Dottore would mince about the stage in black academic dress: the parody of the intellectual. Both he and Pantalone, frequently featured as a father to one of the lovers, or perhaps as the male lover's rival, or even as both. Pantalone was typically dressed in an outdated Venetian costume, with tight-fitting long red trousers or red breeches and a loose long black coat. The Pantalone mask featured a long hooked nose, bushy eyebrows and a pointed beard; the actor's stance would be bent – not only to represent the stoop of age, but to give Pantalone a crabbed and protective gait as he protects his purse – the symbol of his primary characteristic, his avarice. Pantalone is driven by the desire to maintain or increase his wealth; his power, such as it is, derives from his control of the finances. 'He is the employer, giving orders to his servants, and the father dictating to his children, controlling the social structure' (Rudlin 1994: 92).

The world of *commedia* is too varied to make too many generalizations about it. Over the two hundred or so years in which it flourished across Europe, styles varied from troupe to troupe, and the semi-improvised performances varied from place to place, responding to social conditions and local opportunities for jokes. Pantalone, with his greed, his pettiness, his lechery and his self-centredness, seems to have been pretty much a constant: a negative stereotype of old age which spoke to generation after generation in location after location. But even here, we should be cautious: from an analysis of Scala's scenarios, Antony Ellis suggests, in his valuable study of *Old Age, Masculinity and Early Modern Drama*, that Pantalone was a multifaceted figure rather than a 'one-dimensional, derogatory portrayal of old age' and that 'the old man's behaviour is not fixed ... but negotiable' and that the genre's treatment of the caricature of the old merchant 'is consonant with Venetian gerontocratic values' (Ellis 2009: 116).

Ellis' point is a good one, although I believe he overstates his case. With only the plot outlines available, and no improvised dialogue extant from documentations of the performances, it is hard to be certain of tone; and it is true that there are some scenarios in which Pantalone seems to come out with a degree of dignity. More generally, however, his plot function is generally to act as an impediment to the love story which so frequently forms the centre of the *commedia* plot. He is mean to his servants, domineering and manipulative towards his children, and frequently lecherous and exploitative towards the younger women of the plot. He is repeatedly positioned, that is to say, in such a way as to alienate the sympathies of an audience. The satire of the *commedia* companies, moreover, tended to be critical of the social hierarchies of the day – sometimes dangerously so: there are records of *commedia* actors losing their lives as well as their livelihoods for perceived slighting of the rich and powerful. And if, behind this portrait of a vain and mean-spirited old man, there may lurk an implied ideal of what a *good* old man might be, to say this is not to say very much: it is something that is true of nearly all satire. While Ellis is quite right in reminding us that there is variety within the stereotype, what comes across more forcefully, both from the scenarios themselves and from reconstructions of the scenes, is a character who is consistently bullying, mean-minded, aggressive and, in the end, pathetic.

The *commedia* tradition remained popular in Europe until well into the eighteenth century, during which time the figure of Pantalone also turned up, only slightly disguised, in a number of plays by authors outside the strict *commedia dell'arte* genre. He turns up, for example, as the 'lean and slippered pantaloon' in one of drama's most famous speeches about age and ageing: the 'Seven Ages' speech from Shakespeare's *As You Like It*. The speech charts the seven ages of man from birth to death, and the middle-aged 'justice, In fair round belly with good capon lined' is followed by two particularly bleak images of old age as

The sixth age shifts
Into the lean and slippered pantaloon,
With spectacles on nose and pouch on side;
His youthful hose, well saved, a world too wide

For his shrunk shank; and his big manly voice,
Turning again toward childish treble, pipes
And whistles in his sound. Last scene of all,
That ends this strange eventful history,
Is second childishness and mere oblivion,
Sans teeth, sans eyes, sans taste, sans everything.

(Shakespeare 1974: 382)

Vivid as Jaques' speech is, Shakespeare is drawing on a well-established medieval and renaissance motif. Variously given as three, four, seven or more ages, the idea was frequently represented in fifteenth-, sixteenth- and seventeenth-century books, pamphlets and pictures. An anonymous Dutch painting of the 'Ages of Man' in the Museum Kurhause Kleve, for example, depicts time as a set of steps up and down which a man's life is ranged (Thane 2005: 120–21). The picture shows middle age at the apex, and its form states something about a vision of ageing which is less melodramatic than Jaques' and perhaps more generous towards the elderly than Shakespeare's . This artist allows for more stages on the downward slope, more variety within old age. His picture still depicts a master narrative of decline, but less relentlessly than Jacques' pathetic 'shrunk shank … and mere oblivion'. It, too, has the message of consolation to which Shakespeare rarely explicitly resorts: the Dutch artist shows a process of ageing and death followed by resurrection. There is no such redemption in Shakespeare's 'seven ages' speech – a speech whose structure, like that of a sonnet, drives relentlessly towards its own conclusion and its subject's ending. In this – as so often – Shakespeare is both forward- and backward-looking. The modernity of his approach lies in this almost existential secularity, a process ending in an extinction of the personality, and an ending characterized by nothing but 'oblivion … sans everything'. Equally, though, Shakespeare draws on familiar medieval images of the ageing body, drawn from the literature and drama of an era whose moral leaders continually preached that the life of man is vain and transient; that the material world will pass away; that wealth, power and beauty are all ultimately meaningless; and that death eventually makes a mockery of life.

Perhaps Pantalone's most successful transformation was into the tyrannous Harpagon of Molière's *The Miser*. Harpagon rules his children and his servants with a rod of iron, and lives in constant fear of having his wealth stolen; suspicious of all and sundry, he has buried a large sum of money in his garden, and constantly checks it for safety. His daughter Élise is secretly engaged to the mysterious but charming Valère, who is temporarily working as Harpagon's chief steward; meanwhile his son Cléante is in love with the beautiful but poor Marianne. But Harpagon has designs on Marianne himself, and intends to wed Élise to the wealthy but equally elderly Seigneur Anselme. The action revolves around the various intrigues which this love tangle set in motion, and is brought to a head when Harpagon's secret hoard of treasure, buried in the backyard, is stolen.

The debt which Molière owes to the *commedia* tradition, both in *The Miser* and in other plays, is well-documented. His plot structures and stereotyped characters can be traced back to the scenarios of the Italian comedy, as can the *lazzi*, the comic verbal and physical routines, which drive the scenes and the dialogue. Molière makes good use of the stock characters which had been the mainstay of the Italian comedy: the parasite, the pedant, the seducer, the hypocrite and the miser; and 'the motifs, the techniques, the stagecraft of the Italian theatre were part of Molière's accumulated cultural and professional experience' (Wadsworth 1977: 24). It has been argued that in his characterization of Harpagon, Molière 'departs from the stock character of the *senex amans* [because] Harpagon's narcissism, reverse ageism and avarice – rather than his absolute age – cause his downfall' (Wood 2010: 152). But there are few examples of the *senex* – or of Pantalone – in which this is not true. 'Absolute age' is rarely the point: more significant are the social and moral failings which social stereotyping in various epochs conventionally attributes to old age.

Chapter 5

On Sex and the *Senex*: English Restoration Comedy

Old age in a culture of youth

The term 'Restoration comedy' conventionally refers to a sub-genre of the comedy of manners, whose golden age on the English stage began a few years into the reign of Charles II, and waned by the end of the first decade of the eighteenth century. Molière was one of the models to whom the writers of English Restoration comedy looked for inspiration: *The Miser* itself was adapted for the English stage by Thomas Shadwell, in an extended version with additional characters and subplots. Typically, though, English Restoration comedies are less domestic in their settings and their concerns than are Molière's plays. They are urban and urbane comedies of erotic pursuit and intrigue, set among rich young men and women of marriageable age – the wits, gulls, rakes and heiresses of the smart set of late seventeenth-century London. The most well-known of these plays have plots that are driven by the machinations of their witty, promiscuous libertine heroes, such as Dorimant in George Etherege's *The Man of Mode* or Mirabell in William Congreve's *The Way of the World*.

These plays – in which sex comedy meets comedy of manners – theatricalize the relationship between erotic desire and social organization. In exploring the boundaries of acceptable sexual relations and the force of individual desire, they also implicitly challenge traditional authoritarian structures in general. They dramatize the social and political tensions of a period when, following disillusion with royal restoration as well as with commonwealth/revolutionary rule, a profound scepticism about the foundation of royal authority 'generated parallel skepticism about traditional forms of familial authority. Both comedies and heroic plays thus often explore the possibility of marriage, like government, as contractual rather than patriarchal' (Rosenthal 2008: 7).

The consequent emphasis on the values of an emerging generation means that the older man or woman in Restoration comedy is generally a secondary character. This is ground, too, in which ageist stereotypes are likely to flourish, and the typical attitude of Restoration comedy towards the older man might be found in Otway's *Soldier's Fortune*, where Sylvia bewails the fate of her friend Lady Dunce, a young woman married to an elderly husband:

Tis an unspeakable blessing to lie all night by a Horse-load of diseases, – a beastly, unsavoury, old, groaning, grinting, wheezing Wretch, that smells of the Grave he's going to already. From such a curse and Hair-Cloth next my skin, good Heaven deliver me.

(Otway [c. 1670–80] 1968: 107)

Lady Dunce agrees bitterly:

> Bless us, to be yok'd in Wedlock with a paralitick, coughing, decrepid Dotrell, to be a dry Nurse all one's life time to an old Child of sixty five, to lie by the Image of Death a whole night, a dull immoveable, that has no sense of life but through its pains; the Pidgeon's as happy that's laid to a sick man's feet, when the world has given him over; for my part this shall henceforth be my prayer:
> *Curst be the memory: nay, double curst,*
> *Of her that wedded Age for interest first.*
>
> (Otway [c. 1670–80] 1968: 111)

The first lines of her 'prayer', though, sum up succinctly the gender politics and the economic imperatives of her situation. As so often in Restoration comedy, Lady Dunce had been forced to make a marital choice based on financial considerations. Having 'wedded Age for interest', she is now faced with the consequences of her choice. Even so, these speeches have something in them which goes beyond the familiar dichotomy between love and money: in the exuberant unpleasantness of the imagery, it is made clear that in Otway's world the elderly lover is fair game for any amount of vituperation.

Occasionally, a playwright will relent, and by way of variation offer a somewhat more forgiving picture of the *senex amans*. William Congreve's first play was *The Old Bachelor* (1693), a play whose eponymous hero, Heartwell, is 'a surly old bachelor, pretending to slight women; secretly in love with Silvia' (Congreve [c. 1690–1700] 1982: 8). Heartwell, then, combines the stereotype of the *senex amans* with two other favourite seventeenth-century comic types: firstly, the apparently misogynistic love-refuser (or at least the reluctant lover), who will, in the end succumb to love – the sort of character that Shakespeare made much of in comedies such as *Much Ado about Nothing* and *Love's Labour's Lost*. And secondly, Heartwell is a version of the 'plain dealer', another well-established stereotype which Restoration audiences found particularly interesting, and which William Wycherley had made famous in his 1676 play of the same name. And so, Heartwell's refusal of love and all its games is presented – by both him and his companions – as a subset of his refusal of social hypocrisy of all kinds:

BELLMOUR:	How now George, where hast thou been snarling odious truths, and entertaining company like a physician, with discourse of their diseases and infirmities? What fine lady hast thou been putting out of conceit with herself and persuading that the face she had been making all the morning was none of her own? For I know that thou art as unmannerly and as unwelcome to a woman, as a looking-glass after the small-pox.
HEARTWELL:	I confess I have not been sneering fulsome lies and nauseous flattery, fawning upon a little tawdry whore, that will fawn upon

me again, and entertain any puppy that comes, like a tumbler with the same tricks over and over.

(Congreve [c. 1690–1700] 1982: 14–15)

Congreve complicates his stereotype, and thus also the audience expectations which the stereotype generates. If the comedy of the *senex amans* most usually involves the frustration of his erotic aims, the comic plot which focuses on the reluctant lover generally depends on bringing him round to an acceptance of his more sentimental side – and is thus more likely to resolve in a conventional happy ending in which 'Jack shall have Jill'. It is the tension between these two sets of expectations which generates the comedy of *The Old Bachelor*. And in fact, Heartwell (whose name also predisposes the audience to think well of him) is subjected to a more generous kind of comedy than we might expect from the title. Throughout the play he can keep up with the young wits, who treat him with a degree of affection, and his credentials as a plain-speaker, cutting through the evident social hypocrisy of much of the world that surrounds him, gives him a credibility with the audience; and he is eventually rewarded with a happy ending – although not the one he originally wanted.

But Congreve seems unable to leave alone the theme of the *senex amans*. While Heartwell gets off comparatively lightly, another character in the same play is the subject of the traditional mockery. Isaac Fondlewife, an elderly banker and member of a dissenting sect, is married to a young wife Laetitia; their discourse is peppered with baby-talk ('dealous' for 'jealous') and pet names ('Nykin' and 'Cocky')

LAETITIA:	*Nykin*—if you don't go, *I*'le think you been dealous of me still.
FONDLEWIFE:	He, he, he, wilt thou poor Fool? Then *I* will go, *I* wont be dealous— Poor Cocky, Kiss *Nykin*, Kiss *Nykin*, ee, ee, ee,—Here will be the good Man anon, to talk to Cocky and teach her how a Wife ought to behave her self.

(Congreve [c. 1690–1700] 1982: 54; original emphasis)

Predictably, Fondlewife is suspicious and jealous.

I will reason with my self—Tell me *Isaac*, why art thee jealous? Why art thee distrustful of the Wife of thy Bosom?—Because she is young and vigorous, and I am old and impotent—Then why didst thee marry, Isaac?— Because she was beautiful and Tempting, and because I was obstinate and doating; so that my Inclination was (and still is) greater than my Power—And will not that which tempted thee, also tempt others, who will tempt her, Isaac?—I fear it much—But does not thy Wife love thee, nay doat upon thee?—Yes—Why then!—Ay, but to say truth, she's fonder of me, than she has reason to be; and in the way of Trade, we still suspect the smoothest Dealers of the deepest Designs—And she has some Designs deeper than thou canst reach, thou hast experimented, Isaac—But Mum.

(Congreve [c. 1690–1700] 1982: 52; original emphasis)

Predictably, too, Laetitia *is* unfaithful to him.

In *The Old Bachelor*, then, we get two different perspectives on the traditional figure. Even in a play which takes pains to show some respect towards the older lover, Restoration comic conventions demand that the *senex amans* be shown to be ridiculous. But if old men may sometimes get away with their follies in Restoration comedy, the same is rarely true for older women.

'The pretty foibles of superannuated beauties': The female *senex* on the Restoration stage

Parts for older actresses in Restoration comedy tend to be supporting roles; they play characters whose old age becomes a foil for the values of youth. One of the best of these roles is that of Lady Wishfort in *The Way of the World* (1699–1700).

At the level of the play's highly convoluted narrative, 'Old Lady Wishfort', as she is described when first mentioned in the play, fulfils the traditional function of older 'parental' characters in romantic comedies: she is the guardian of Millamant, the play's heroine and principal object of desire. Lady Wishfort also holds the purse-strings to the bulk of Millamant's fortune, and since (predictably) she also disapproves of the main male protagonist, Mirabell, she is an obstacle to the consummation of that primary love narrative. More than that, however, she is also herself a player in *The Way of the World*'s game of erotic pursuit; her dislike of Mirabell stems not just from a protective attitude towards her ward, but from the fact that she had previously misinterpreted his flattery towards her as sexual interest, and now feels insulted.

The incongruity of such an old woman being in a love-plot is a source of unending comedy in the play. Being, as Mirabell ironically describes her in the opening scene, 'full of the Vigour of Fifty five' (Congreve [c. 1690–1700] 1982: 316) she should in theory be out of the erotic game, if not out of the marriage market: marriage in Restoration comedy is invariably a financial proposition as much as a romantic one. But Lady Wishfort is portrayed as a creature who still seeks both reassurance about her own physical attractiveness, and also sexual gratification on her own part: her name ('Wish for 't' – a pun which Congreve makes sure his audience does not miss) connotes both sexual desire and also its lack of gratification. As such, Lady Wishfort is a recognizable and durable comic type on at least two counts.

As a fifty-five-year-old she would only just count as 'old' in most contexts, but it is clear that in this youth-obsessed world of Restoration comedy she is old indeed. In seventeenth-century England, the upper classes tended to age less early than the lower, but in all sectors of society women tended to be defined as 'old' earlier than men. The comedy of manners which was so popular on the Restoration stage magnified this tendency even further. Lady Wishfort is post-menopausal, and it seems that she has accepted that she is past bearing an heir (inheritance being a crucial financial consideration in Restoration love-plots). She should, according to the rules, no longer be a player in the courtship game that drives

Restoration comedies. By continuing to play the game beyond her appropriate age she opens herself to the ridicule which ensues throughout the play.

Old age, as we have already noted, is relative; what counts as old in one culture is seen as the prime of life in another. The borderlands between the two are misty and uncertain, the maps continually being redrawn. In Restoration comedy we come across some of the 'youngest old' in the drama that we are looking at. Because Restoration comedy is so repeatedly concerned with erotic pursuit, old age sets in as sexual allure diminishes. But because erotic pursuit in Restoration comedy is also repeatedly concerned with money and status, the picture becomes a little more complicated. There are, in general, two criteria for success in the game of Restoration comedy: sexual attractiveness, and a fortune or title. If the two can be combined, so much the better. And if they can be woven together with that most elusive but highly prized of Restoration qualities, wit, then better yet! However, while sexual attractiveness, according to conventional judgement, declines with advancing years, money and status need not: indeed, as mere expectations of inheritance turn into actual assets, or as family and personal fortunes increase through sound investments or alliances, older players of both genders may find themselves with significant investment power in the game. Both women and men can play by these rules, although advancing age affects the two differently: the older man of wealth or property whose erotic attractions have waned is generally in a stronger position than his female equivalent. Even so, the older woman is not entirely ruled out of the game. And while the 'sentimental' elements of the genre stack the deck (just about) in favour of love over money, the material world of late seventeenth- and early eighteenth-century London society, in which Restoration comedy and the attitudes of its audience was so firmly rooted, had plenty of respect for money as well.

This, then, is the social and generic logic of the world of Restoration comedy which produces a female *senex* such as Lady Wishfort. (There is no separate word for the female of the species, although the Latin noun itself is masculine both grammatically and referentially.) Lady Wishfort does not make her entrance until quite late in the play, but her part, while a supporting role, is not a small one: from that point she holds centre stage, she has the greatest number of lines of anyone in the play from her entrance onwards, and she is a driving force of the play's humour. Her desire for revenge against Mirabell leads her to have a particular interest in obstructing his pursuit of Millamant. However, her own self-delusion and sexual appetite are used against her by Mirabell in a counterplot: he arranges for a supposed suitor (actually his valet) to woo her – with a view to obtaining a hold over her once the deception is brought to light.

The first glimpse we have of Lady Wishfort is in her room, as she tries desperately to hide the signs of her own ageing – both from others through make-up, and from herself through alcohol, in the form of the fashionable drinks of cherry brandy and ratafia.

LADY: I have no more patience. If I have not fretted myself till I am pale again, there's no veracity in me. Fetch me the Red—the Red, do you hear, Sweetheart? An errant Ash colour, as I'm a Person. Look

	you how this Wench stirs! Why dost thou not fetch me a little Red? Didst thou not hear me, Mopus?
PEG:	The red Ratafia, does your ladyship mean, or the Cherry Brandy?
LADY:	Ratafia, Fool? No, Fool. Not the Ratafia, Fool—grant me patience!—I mean the Spanish Paper, Idiot; Complexion, Darling. Paint, Paint, Paint, dost thou understand that, Changeling, dangling thy Hands like Bobbins before thee? Why dost thou not stir, Puppet? Thou wooden Thing upon Wires!
PEG:	Lord, madam, your Ladyship is so impatient—I cannot come at the Paint, Madam: Mrs. Foible has locked it up, and carried the Key with her.
LADY:	A Pox take you both.—Fetch me the Cherry Brandy then.

(Congreve [c. 1690–1700] 1982: 347–48)

Much has been written about the 'two bodies' of the Restoration actress: that is, about the relationship between the real-life women and the characters they played (Maus 1979, Howe 1992, Pullen 2005). Theatre historians have tended to stress the erotic element of these bodies: the Restoration period saw women on the English professional stage for the first time in any numbers; the plots of Restoration comedies were erotically charged; and contemporary seventeenth-century belief held that acting was akin to prostitution. The Restoration stage, it is frequently asserted, repeatedly exploited the sexuality of the actress and subjected her to a 'male gaze' which both objectified her and confirmed the society's dominant gender ideology (see, for example, Howe 1992: 37–65). For the most part, however, scholars have concentrated on the younger actresses and their roles. To look at older women on the Restoration stage we need to squint a bit, since both the material with which the plays typically dealt, and the conditions of playing, tend to direct our attention to those younger actresses and their characters. In the case of *The Way of the World*, this means Millamant and Marwood, the two women at the fulcrum of the comic plot; in the original production they were played by Anne Bracegirdle and Elizabeth Barry respectively: these two stars of the Restoration stage translated their well-established pairing as tragic heroines (the dark, powerful Barry complementing the sweet and innocent Bracegirdle) into the comic pairing of the bright attractive Millamant and the intense, almost tragic, Marwood (Howe 1992: 162–70). Just behind these two, though, came Lady Wishfort, played by Elinor (or Ellen, or Elizabeth) Leigh, who specialized in the broader comedy of old age.

We do not know a great deal about Mrs Leigh. When she first played Lady Wishfort during the 1699–1700 season, she, like her character, may have been in her mid-fifties. Her earliest known stage appearances had been in association with the Dukes Company, about thirty years earlier in 1672 (see Milhous 1979: 247). But even in her younger days she specialized in older female characters. By 1676 she was certainly playing Lady Woodvil – another matriarchal character like Lady Wishfort – in *The Man of Mode*, and it may be that even in 1672 she was specializing in elderly comic roles such as Mrs Caution in Wycherley's

The Gentleman Dancing-Master; and other similar roles which she is known to have played include Lady Fantast in *Bury-Fair*, Lady Maggot in *The Scowrers*, Moretta in *The Rover*, Part I, and Prue's Nurse in *Love for Love* (see Mignon 1947: 34–35, Wycherley 1996: 417).

In her prime, Elinor Leigh was clearly a significant figure on the Restoration stage, being for a time a co-sharer in the management of Lincoln's Inn Fields with Barry, Bracegirdle and Betterton. Colley Cibber had this to say of her:

> Mrs. Leigh, the wife of Leigh already mentioned, had a very droll way of dressing the pretty Foibles of superannuated Beauties. She had, in herself, a good deal of Humour, and knew how to infuse it into the affected Mother, Aunts and modest stale Maids, that had missed their Market; of this sort were the Modish Mother in the *Chances*, affecting to be politely commode, for her own Daughter; the Coquette Prude of an Aunt, in *Sir Courtly Nice*, who prides herself in being chaste, and cruel, at Fifty; and the languishing Lady Wishfort, in *The Way of the World*: In all these, with many others, she was extremely entertaining and painted, in a lively manner, the blind Side of Nature.
>
> (Cibber 1756: 121)

Mrs Leigh's particular skill had nothing to do with the 'male gaze' – or rather, it subverted that gaze for comic purposes. She seems to have been particularly adept at exploiting the incongruity between self-image and popular stereotype. Old women in Restoration comedies of manners are not represented as objects of desire; indeed, the conventions of the genre mean that any older woman who presents herself as such must be inherently ridiculous – and Lady Wishfort's misapprehension that she *is* such an object delivers her up to the laughter of the playhouse audience.

That laughter is cruel and the comedy painful. In a later scene in the play we see Lady Wishfort worrying about how best to present herself to a supposed wooer, and trying out various 'alluring' postures:

> Well, and how shall I receive him? … I'll lie—ay, I'll lie down—I'll receive him in my little dressing-Room; there's a Couch—yes, yes, I'll give the first Impression on the Couch— I won't lie neither, but loll and lean upon one Elbow, with one Foot a little dangling off, jogging in a thoughtful way— yes—and then as soon as he appears, start, ay, start and be surprised, and rise to meet him in a pretty disorder—yes—oh, nothing is more alluring than a Levee from a Couch in some Confusion. It shows the foot to advantage, and furnished with Blushes, and recomposing Airs beyond Comparison.
>
> (Congreve [c. 1690–1700] 1982: 369)

Lady Wishfort, too, is a 'performer', but her performance of the Flirtatious Coquette is presented as a comic failure. Further, her self-consciousness about her own body as an object of the gaze operates, ironically, as one the markers of her old age. The 'art' by which in the earlier scene she had attempted to look young again by means of make-up, is here recapitulated in her attempts to manipulate her own body image to enhance its desirability. It is an age-old comic *lazzi* ('Preparing for the One you Want to Impress') that still works today as a stock routine of the comedy scriptwriter's trade. Even so, in this most artificial society of Restoration London as seen through the eyes of its comic dramatists, this world in which appearance and surface are paramount, it is cruelly ironic that in these scenes Lady Wishfort's artificiality is used as an image of 'unnatural' old age attempting to ape the natural attractiveness of the young.

The laughter that Congreve extracts from the Lady Wishfort scenes frequently depends upon the contrast between her public 'performance' of the flirtatious coquette, and the behind-the-scenes activity on which the construction of that performance depends. Congreve dramatizes quite perfectly some of the insights of Erving Goffman's influential analysis of *The Presentation of Self in Everyday Life* ([1959] 1990). One of the central aspects of Goffman's explanation of social dramaturgy is his insistence on a distinction between 'front' and 'back' regions. The 'front region', in Goffman's terms, is the equivalent of the stage: the place where the carefully structured and choreographed performance takes place. (Obvious examples are the teacher performing in the classroom, or the salesperson on the sales floor.) And if

> accentuated facts make their appearance in what I have called a front region; it should be equally clear that there may be another region – a 'back region' or 'backstage' – where the suppressed facts make an appearance.
>
> A back region may be defined as a place, relative to a given performance, where the impression fostered by the performance is knowingly contradicted as a matter of course … It is here that the capacity of a performance to express something beyond itself may be painstakingly fabricated; it is here that illusions and impressions are openly constructed. Here stage props and items of personal front can be stored in a kind of compact collapsing of whole repertoires of actions and characters … Here the performer can relax; he can drop his front, forgo speaking his lines, and step out of character.
>
> (Goffman [1959] 1990: 114–15)

Although this back region may be thought of as metaphorical, in Goffman's model it is usually literally a separate place: the theatrical backstage and green room, the salesperson's back office, the teacher's staffroom, the craftsman's workshop, the lady's dressing room. Goffman argues that for successful dramaturgy to take place, the back and front regions need to be kept quite separate.

> Since the vital secrets of a show are visible backstage and since performers behave out of character while there, it is natural to expect that the passage from the back region to the front region will be kept closed to members of the audience, or that the entire back region will be hidden from them. This is a widely practised technique of impression management.
>
> (Goffman [1959] 1990: 116)

In *The Way of the World*, Congreve leads the real-life theatre audience into the 'backstage' region of Lady Wishfort's performance – that region to which Lady Wishfort's fictional audience (her potential lover) may not be admitted. The laughs – cruel, sexist and ageist – arise from the disparity between the performance and its construction, as Congreve demonstrates how the performance of the 'front region' is being so 'painstakingly fabricated'.

Mrs Leigh retired from the stage in 1707, according to her contemporary John Downes, whose *Roscius Anglicanus* is one of the earliest histories of English theatre (Downes [1708] 1929: 203). The kinds of characters she had specialized in creating did not long outlive her. A new kind of 'sentimental' comedy was on the rise, pioneered by playwrights such as Richard Steele:

> [D]ramatist, essayist, and self-appointed 'Censor of Great Britain,' the appellation he gave himself in *The Tatler*, Steele aspired both to regulate and reform English morals through English drama. His earliest dramatic works, *The Funeral* (1701), *The Lying Lover* (1704), and *The Tender Husband* (1705), show gentle humor and a tolerance of folly as they model gentlemanly conduct.
>
> (Wilson 2011: 497)

Steele's continual campaign to demonstrate the moral and political power of the stage led to a mode of comedy in which bourgeois values triumphed and virtue was rewarded – often by domestic bliss. Whereas Mrs Leigh had portrayed characters such as Lady Wishfort and Lady Woodvil in *The Man of Mode* as figures of fun, Steele reads these characters in a very different way. Commenting in 1711 on *The Man of Mode*, for example, he is appalled at the way in which the heroine, Harriet, treats her aged mother:

> She laughs at Obedience to an absent Mother, whose Tenderness Busie describes to be very exquisite, for *that she is so pleased with finding* Harriot *again, that she cannot chide her for being out of the way.* This Witty Daughter and fine Lady, has so little Respect for this good Woman, that she Ridicules her Air in taking Leave, and cries, *In what Struggle is my poor Mother yonder? See, see, her Head tottering, her Eyes staring, and her under Lip trembling.*
>
> (Steele 1711 [1891]: 107; original emphasis)

Theatre continually produces new works – but it also continually feeds off its own past, reviving and revisiting its own previous triumphs and disasters. In doing so, it allows us a particularly privileged insight into revolutions in the history of sensibilities. A play that means one thing in its original production can be revived with subtly – or radically – different meanings. In the case of Steele's spectatorship of *The Man of Mode* we can see that an audience which is responsive to the conventions of the comedy of manners is being replaced by one imbued with the conventions of sentimental comedy. And in the process, we can also see the way in which a figure who appears in the former as a ridiculous old woman is being proposed by a proponent of the latter as a tender mother who deserves respect. It is a valuable reminder of the plasticity and the pliability of the stereotypes of old age. What was created as a negative stereotype can, within a few years, be seen as a positive one, and vice versa. The stereotypes of old age are enduring – but their meanings are repeatedly up for debate and negotiation.

Chapter 6

On Dirty Old Men and Trickster Figures

The *senex* and generational conflict in another culture of youth

Traditionally, comedy provides aesthetic structure for dealing with those things we find aberrant or threatening. Sometimes this happens through the reassurance of a happy ending, sometimes by other means: most often, comic form requires that some kind of order should be restored at the end – a formal demand most commonly typified by the marriage at the end of the romantic comedy. But to say that comedies 'deal with' things we find threatening does not necessarily mean that they do so in a way that is reassuring or optimistic. In fact, the extent to which a comedy might be regarded as optimistic, liberating or reassuring depends upon the attitude that one has towards that restoration of order.

Television situation comedy (sitcom) is an extreme example of this. Because of the nature of the cultural production and reception of television itself, the dramatic logic of many TV series, in whatever genre, depends upon a tension between repetition and variation: the continuity from week to week of character and situation. This is particularly true in the case of sitcom. It is this limitation that generates the comedy: the characters are stuck with each other, and stuck in the house or flat they live in, or the office in which they work. And if each new episode provides a new angle on this 'stuckness', nothing must happen to fracture the basic situation which dominates and controls them. As Mick Eaton has put it, these 'formal necessities ... provide the existential circle from which the characters cannot escape' (Eaton 1978: 74). These kinds of structural determinants were an inherent part of the success of Ray Galton and Alan Simpson's classic series *Steptoe and Son*.

Galton and Simpson were two of the most successful writers that British television sitcom has seen. In the late 1950s and early 1960s their partnership did much to define the paradigms of British sitcom – not least because in their work the formal constraints of sitcom, with its endless cycle of return to the norm and the mood of claustrophobia which this frequently generated, worked superbly well with the content of Galton and Simpson's stories, and the themes of their social commentary. In their best work of this period, both with Tony Hancock in *Hancock's Half-Hour* (which began on radio and transferred to TV in 1956) and with Wilfred Brambell and Harry H. Corbett in *Steptoe and Son* (which ran for eight series from 1962) they were telling stories of protagonists – Hancock and Harold – who dreamed continually of bettering themselves, of escaping from the mundane repressiveness of their everyday lives. They were stories that had a particular poignancy, in a Britain that was moving out of a period of post-war austerity (following the disappointments of Attlee's

New Jerusalem), and looking for a way to reinvent for itself a more cosmopolitan, liberal and 'swinging' identity. Galton and Simpson's protagonists were men who sensed that a change was in the air, longed and desired to be part of it, and were justifiably fearful that they were going to be left out. For Tony Hancock's eponymous character, the obstacles to self-improvement lay both in himself and in the generalized bourgeois suburbia to which he so clearly belonged. For Harold Steptoe, however, these obstacles became externalized: they were continually represented by the figure of his father Albert, the 'dirty old man' who represented, not only the miseries of the past and everything from which he sought to escape, but also everything which prevented him from doing so. In *Steptoe and Son* the social tensions of an era were personified, like a medieval allegory, in the combat between Youth and Age, played out with extraordinary intensity in the Steptoes' rag-and-bone yard in Oil Drum Lane.

Steptoe and Son did not begin as a sitcom series, but as a stand-alone television drama in the BBC's 'Comedy Playhouse' slot. *The Offer*, as the original 1962 script was known, introduced the old rag-and-bone man, Albert Steptoe, and his son, Harold. The original drama had many of the *lazzi* between the two characters which later became familiar to audiences of the series:

ALBERT: What's all this then? Have you been scouring the streets all day just for this? All day just to collect this load of old rubbish? Didn't anybody know you were coming? Has the clapper in your bell gone or something? Did you put slippers on the horse? So nobody'll hear you? Eight hours you've been out. I used to get more than this out of one hour's …

HAROLD: There isn't so much junk about these days … I was shouting. I've got a sore throat shouting. And I'm so cold – just don't start.

ALBERT: Well we can't retire on this.

(Galton and Simpson 1962: n.p.)

The play's opening exchange establishes the situation and the relationships which the rest of the play, and eventually the series, would develop. Albert – old, selfish and manipulative – complains continually about Harold's shortcomings as a rag-and-bone man. Harold – middle-aged, socially aspirational and utterly frustrated – is full of barely suppressed anger, fuelled by his resentment at being dominated by the father from whom it is clear he will never break away.

The 'offer' of the title is an unspecified offer of a glamorous job which Harold claims to have had from a successful businessman. It is made clear to the audience that Harold's offer is an imaginary one; he has made it up in order to provide himself with some ammunition in his perennial battle with his father. At times Albert seems to share the audience's confidence that the offer is fictional; but he is obviously haunted by the possibility that it may just be real. The play is built around the bickering routines of the two of them as they unload and reload the rag-and-bone cart. The various items they handle are used to illustrate the details of their lives, but the central conflict of the play involves Harold's threats to leave, and Albert's stratagems to keep him at home and to maintain the *status quo* of their mutual dependence.

And this is the conflict which underlies both this play and all the episodes of the later series. Harold, the son, is desperate to break out of the dreary shabbiness of the rag-and-bone lifestyle in which he is trapped with his ageing father, Albert. He yearns for a life less ordinary, more intellectual, more cultured, more stylish and more cosmopolitan. The tone of *The Offer* is rather more downbeat than most of the episodes in the later series. There are laughs, it is true, but the overall feel of the play owes much to the social realism which was the dominant mode of British 'serious' theatre in the 1950s and early 1960s. When *The Offer* was first aired, in fact, reviewers made comparisons with Ibsen, Dickens, Beckett and Strindberg; the *Times* reviewer referred to its 'almost Chekhovian ambience' (Wiggin 1962), while Galton and Simpson have been quoted as saying about their initial reluctance to turn the one-off play into a series, 'We think we've written a little piece of Pinter here, and we can't repeat it' (Cornell, Day and Topping 1996: 75).

They did repeat it, however, and it developed over twelve years into a landmark television series. In the process it repeated and elaborated the basic conflict between Albert and Harold against the background of the social and cultural upheavals of the 1960s and early 1970s, playing out the politics of class and gender in the restricted ideological space of a London junkyard. Class and gender, indeed, are the terms in which *Steptoe and Son* is most usually analysed (see Rolinson [2002] 2012, Neale and Krutnik 1990, Williams 1989), and both are certainly thematically central to the comedy. But the battleground on which these matters are fought is that of the conflict between generations, between age and (comparative) youth.

HAROLD: You frustrate me in everything I do. You are a dyed-in-the-wool, fascist, reactionary, squalid, little know-yer-place, don't-rise-above-yerself, don't-get-out-of-yer-hole complacent little turd …
I HAVEN'T FINISHED YET! You are morally, spiritually and physically a festering flyblown heap of accumulated filth!

ALBERT: What do you want for yer tea?

(Galton and Simpson 1972: n.p.; original emphasis)

Harold's sense of frustration erupts into a superb, angry rant against the old man who is continually standing in his way. The vicious rhetoric builds rhythmically to a devastating climax ('festering flyblown heap of accumulated filth!') a climax of resentment which must surely shatter their relationship forever – only to be punctured by Albert's laconic 'What do you want for yer tea?' Nothing, clearly, is going to change. 'You frustrate me in everything I do!' Harold cries out in anguish – and that is exactly Albert's dramaturgical function: continually to frustrate Harold's attempts to achieve his objectives, be they social, cultural or sexual. Sometimes, then, in episodes such as 'Loathe Story' and 'And so to Bed', Albert acts the part of the traditional *senex* of classical and Renaissance comedy, standing in the way of the younger generation's pursuit of love – and nothing is more threatening to the stasis of this father–son relationship than the possibility that a woman might enter into their world. At other times it is Harold's more general ambitions of self-improvement that he thwarts. As Harold recognizes, '[I]t's everything. I mean, every idea I have for improvement – I mean, improvements to the house, improvements to the business – you're agin' it' (Galton and Simpson 1972: n.p.).

Sixty-nine-year-old Albert Steptoe was played by Wilfred Brambell, who, throughout his career, had specialized in playing old men. He was fifty when he first created the role of Steptoe senior (and had not quite caught up with his character's fictional age by the time the series finished in 1974). If Harold's vituperative rhetoric pulls no punches in creating a picture of domestic gerontocratic oppression, then Brambell's portrayal of Albert is equally ruthless in its stereotyping of the physical decrepitude of old age. It owes much to traditional popular-theatre depictions of cunning, miserly old men, and the tradition of *commedia dell' arte* is visible in Brambell's performance. Like Pantalone, Albert's body language is closed and pinched; he holds himself in defensively and suspiciously, peering around to protect himself and his possessions from any intruder. Even Brambell's face has something of the *commedia* mask about it; naturally a rather refined-looking man, he screwed up his face for the part, and limited his facial vocabulary to a few key comic expressions: cunning, fear, delight, anger. It was a risk to use on television (whose default language is surface naturalism) a form of acting which owed so much to the traditions of popular live performance, but it worked.

And if Brambell's performance places Albert Steptoe firmly within the age-old tradition of the comic *senex* of popular theatre forms, he could also use the particular and contemporary qualities of television itself to great effect, as he demonstrates in one glorious comic moment in 'Divided We Stand', the episode quoted previously: the increasingly frustrated Harold starts to go through some of the dirt and rubbish which is lying around their living room. He sifts through newspapers dating back thirty years, dust so thick it's 'more like topsoil', ancient cups stuck to their saucers. To his disgust he opens a forgotten tea caddy and discovers an old set of Albert's false teeth – lost in an air raid in 1941. Albert's delight at finding them again ('the best teeth I ever had!') turns to dismay as he tries them on only to discover that they no longer fit: 'My gums have shrunk,' he wails in an image played in semi-close-up straight to camera, as the teeth flap around in his gummy mouth and Harold looks on in horror (Galton and Simpson 1972: n.p.). It is a moment of brilliant, disturbing and very televisual comedy.

Steve Neale has compared the father–son relationship in *Steptoe and Son* to the story in *Arabian Nights* of 'The Old Man of the Sea' (Neale and Krutnik 1990: 256). In this tale a young man agrees, out of pity, to carry on his back an elderly and infirm man, only to find that he cannot shake him off, and that he has become the perpetual slave of the cunning, selfish old rascal. And, as Neale has also pointed out, there is more at stake in the constant competition between Albert and Harold than simply a battle of comic stereotypes. Neale defines this stake as being *masculine authority*: in this all-male family unit father and son battle for dominance, and Harold attempts unsuccessfully to establish his own independence. It is a neurotic pattern, familiar to psychoanalysis.

But gender authority is only a part of the game; also involved is another narrative of authority – the authority of age in relation to youth. The actual physical and economic power of Harold – past his prime but still visibly powerful and vigorous – is set against Albert's physical frailty and his economic dependence on Harold as sole breadwinner. But Albert is also another elderly trickster-figure, and he manages to keep Harold equally dependent on him; through cunning, deception and manipulation, he endeavours to maintain the parental authority which he established in his younger and stronger days. The emotional power which he wields over Harold derives from the fact that Harold himself is unsure about his own filial obligations and duties. There is little affection on which to base them – their relationship is one of mutual distrust, frequently bordering on contempt.

The tension between father and son is a political as well as a personal one, and the stakes for which they play are high in a number of ways. For Harold, personally, they are to do with self-actualization, and his ability to become his own person, to achieve the independence for which he longs. For Albert, the stakes are even higher: he is perfectly aware 'that Harold could, if ever he took it into his head push him into an old home or just walk out and leave him helpless' (Nathan 1971: 129). On the cultural and political level, then, the conflicts between the two characters are about the values of 1960s Britain, including questions of social responsibility and care for the elderly.

But what makes *Steptoe and Son* such a classic of its kind is that its comedy of age and youth plays out on several levels. On the structural, mythical and stereotypical levels, it is about generational conflict, and more specifically about the conflict of two particular generations: broadly speaking, a pre-war generation and a post-war one that identifies with a new social order. On an emotional and personal level, it is about authority and resistance or rebellion: the Oedipal conflict between father and son being given a particular twist by the absence of the dead mother, and by the fact that the son's rebellion is taking place so late in both their lives. On a socio-political level it is about individual aspiration in an age of increasing social mobility versus the demands of social responsibility for the old. And here, too, the conflict is multidimensional, since two different models of social responsibility are in operation: Albert holds to the traditional kinship model that demands that his son care personally for him; Harold is dimly aware that the provisions for the elderly of the post-war welfare state might offer him a way out of his familial prison.

Frank Randle's mask of anarchy

The figure of the *senex*, from Plautus to Galton and Simpson, then, articulates tension and resistance to the perceived power and/or authority of an older generation – a power or authority which might in reality be minimal, or even illusory, but which generates a reaction and a challenge. This is why the *senex* is so typically a character who has some degree of social power and authority, but whose grip on that authority is increasingly fragile. His attempts to impose that authority, and to hang on to his power, generally result in his becoming the butt of the play's humour. Mean, obstructive, self-centred, inappropriately lustful – these are all traits which make the classic *senex* a target of comedy and alienate him (or her) from the sympathies of the audience. In the history and the genealogy of the *senex* we see theatrical performances which repeatedly reaffirm negative stereotypes of old age in order to mock them.

But the *senex* has a 'flip side', too, and on occasion the negative stereotype can be reversed into something much more positive: in these cases the *senex* mutates into something very much like the folkloric figure of the 'trickster' – one of the

> lords of in-between. A trickster does not live near the hearth; he does not live in the halls of justice, the soldier's tent, the monastery. He passes through each of these when there is a moment of silence and he enlivens each with mischief, but he is not their guiding spirit. He is the spirit of the doorway leading out, and of the crossroad at the edge of town ... In short, trickster is a boundary-crosser. Every group has its edge, its sense of in and out, and trickster is always there, at the gates of the city and the gates of life, making sure there is commerce. He also attends the internal boundaries by which groups articulate their social life. We constantly distinguish – right and wrong, sacred and profane, clean and dirty, male and female, young and old, living and dead – and in every case trickster will cross the line and confuse the distinction. Trickster is the creative idiot, therefore, the wise fool, the gray-haired baby, the cross-dresser, the speaker of sacred profanities.
>
> (Hyde 2008: 6–7)

Trickster figures in folklore may be young or old, but one of his or her attributes is that he or she is lacking in social power or authority. In societies, cultures and situations where the old are generally without power, where the ideology is already *anti*-gerontocratic, a special affinity may arise between the trickster and the older person. Social anthropologist Barbara Myerhoff talks of the trickster function of the elderly in certain societies, arguing that while the marginalization of the elderly often creates anomie and isolation, at the same time it offers to resourceful elders

> occasions in which they may innovate and exploit the rolelessness, a set of fruitful possibilities. Often freed from heavy social obligations and prohibitions for the first time, the elderly may become deft manipulators and entrepreneurs, justifying stereotypes concerning their unconventionality, originality and wisdom. The wily old man, the truly frightening powerful old witch, the curmudgeon recluse in the hills, the mysterious, unpredictable old crone, are types of exploiters of cultural freedom and confusion ... [I]n this light the relative normlessness surrounding the aged and old age holds promise as well as penalties.
>
> (Myerhoff 1992: 221)

The elder as trickster is not so much the opposite of the comic *senex* as his obverse. This is a figure that Shakespeare explored when he created Falstaff – that elderly bag of appetites; the selfish, cowardly, manipulative, greedy, deceitful old rogue who, in *Henry IV Parts One and Two* attains an almost heroic stature – and then in *The Merry Wives of Windsor* collapses back into the traditional *senex amans*.

A more recent manifestation of the elder as trickster can be found in another well-known British television sitcom. Roy Clarke's *The Last of the Summer Wine* is perhaps the programme which, for British viewers, comes to mind most easily as one which is 'about' old age. The series became (fittingly enough) the most long-lived of all British television sitcoms, running for eighteen series and several 'specials' over a quarter of a century, and in the process outliving several of the veteran character actors who made it so successful. Its continuing presence on British TV screens is now assured by channels such as GOLD, whose schedules include a high percentage of repeats. And it shows no sign of diminishing in popularity – not least among the older viewers who are its key demographic. The show's characters and storylines tend to display a calculatedly British eccentricity and the general tone of the series – greatly helped by its small-town semi-rural Yorkshire setting – is that of a gentle nostalgia which when it first appeared was endearingly refreshing, but which had started to wear a little thin by the end of its one-hundred-and-sixty-two episodes. Despite this and a kind of humour which cannot help patronising both the elderly and the working classes, even as it champions the anarchic energy of which they are capable, *The Last of the Summer Wine* strikes a blow for the elderly. Its three central male protagonists are ageing as positively as they can, and in the process they are repeatedly subverting expectations about what old age 'should' be like.

It is not merely that they represent old age as a rather blissful second childhood. There is, indeed, something of this about their world, and it is true that the mishaps and misadventures of Clegg, Compo and their various companions are the result of no longer having to act responsibly. More importantly, though, their irresponsibility and their continual search for new ways to fill their time or to satiate their various appetites, means that they operate in a way that resembles the tricksters of traditional folklore: going about their business, looking for food or fun – and in the process causing chaos, subverting societal norms and upsetting expectations.

Myerhoff's description of the trickster function of the elderly is very close in spirit to the world of *The Last of the Summer Wine*. The 'rolelessness' that the old pals enjoy and the confusion that they cause in their otherwise orderly Yorkshire community are to some extent both creative and subversive. The creative subversiveness of *The Last of the Summer Wine* is, however, greatly tempered by its gentle but insistent nostalgia. More genuinely anarchic examples of the old person as trickster can be found in that tradition of British popular entertainment of which British sitcoms are the indirect heirs. The middle years of the twentieth century saw the migration of the 'stars' of popular entertainment from the music halls and live variety shows to the television and cinema screens. This migration began in the 1930s, and was clearly irreversible by the 1960s. Live variety shows continued to survive in working men's clubs and seaside summer seasons and later in the revival of the comedy club circuit but as a secondary force.

Meanwhile, generations of entertainers, from George Formby to Morecambe and Wise, reworked their material to appeal to a mediatized national audience. Many successful live performers never made the transition, and their names have begun to fade. One such is Frank Randle.

Born in Manchester in 1902, Randle was a stand-up comic who – after a relatively unsuccessful early career under the name of 'Arthur Twist' – reinvented himself in the mid-1930s as a character-based comedian, specializing in monologues and sketches. His primary audience base was in the flourishing Northern variety circuit, his comedy was rooted in issues of class and regional identity, and his most successful characters were mischievously aggressive old men. During the 1940s he was earning over £1000 per week: a staggering sum. By the end of that decade he was Britain's best-paid comedian.

He was an anarchic figure in real life, a man who

burned down a hotel where he'd received bad service, fired a loaded revolver at a recalcitrant extra on a film set, hired a plane to bombard Blackpool with toilet rolls after an obscenity conviction. A man who was truly mad, bad and dangerous to know and yet adored by his audience … [a] man who, if heckled, would hurl his false teeth at the offending miscreant.

(Lee 1996: 34)

A typical anecdote, which tells of one occasion when Randle was invited as guest of honour to a Lord Mayor's banquet, gives us a glimpse of the sense of danger which surrounded him:

The mayor steps forward to greet him.

'Mr Randle, may I say how honoured I am to extend a heartfelt welcome to you, our most distinguished citizen.' People are relaxing now. The smiles become real. He is sober and collected. There will be no scene.

'Thank you, Mr Mayor. However, I must insist the pleasure is mine entirely. It is an honour indeed for a troupe of humble players to enjoy the full panoply of civic hospitality. Shall we move into the banqueting chamber?'

'One moment, Mr Randle. This is my wife.'

'Well that's your fucking fault, owd pal.'

(Nuttall 1978: 99)

The sudden collapse from compliment to insult, from the formal to the vernacular, encapsulates Randle's characteristic comedy, puncturing as it does middle-class pomposity in the language of the industrial working classes.

Both in real life and in his comic personae there was something of the grotesque – both funny and frightening – about Randle; something which is reminiscent of the trickster figure of folklore (Fisher 1973). It can be seen in the extant visual documentation of his performances; in the publicity photographs and in the films which he made for Mancunian Studios between 1940 and 1953, which included 'live' extracts from his stage shows. Like Clive Dunn (familiar to later viewers as Corporal Jones in *Dad's Army*), Randle specialized from a comparatively early age in playing extremely old men. In order to create these geriatric stereotypes, the then thirty-something Randle had all his own teeth extracted, and he then used various sets of exaggerated and distorted dentures – or sometimes a gummy smile – as a basis for his characterizations. As the previous extract from *Steptoe and Son* reminds us, the British find something enduringly humorous about false teeth.

But unlike Dunn (whose 'Grandad [We love you]' became a number one hit record in 1971) there was nothing cosy or loveable about Randle or the lecherous, drunken, sparky old men that he made his speciality. Characters such as 'The Old Boatman' and 'The Old Hiker' broke the taboos of their time. Much of Randle's material may seem comparatively tame by the standards of modern comic iconoclasm, but in an age when the stage was still vigorously policed at both national and local levels, his act was dangerously near the edge.

Sometimes, indeed, it was over the edge: throughout the 1940s and 1950s, Randle had numerous brushes with the law on obscenity charges, and was subjected to arrests, fines and cancellations of shows by local magistrates. His response was to appeal to the shared sense of the realities of life which he and his audience, primarily drawn from the industrial working classes of Northern England, held in common.

> Ladies and gentlemen, you have seen that the little show we have presented for you this season has been under a great deal of criticism. You have seen that certain citizens, some of them quite eminent have seen fit to call our performance, 'filthy', 'obscene', 'offensive', and that may well be their opinion, but I come to you ladies and gentlemen and ask you to be my final judges. I am, like you, a simple man, born of simple folk, a man of the industrial north of England. My pleasures are simple: my packet of Woodbines, my glass of Guinness. The simple joys of the seasons. Simple people of our kind understand the facts of life in a way that many of our critics don't. You will know that my little bits of fun are founded upon the facts of life and because you understand life and the realities of life – I ask you to be my judges.
>
> (Nuttall 1978: 84)

The 'realities of life' as Randle saw them are articulated, for the most part, through the eyes of a series of old men who are aggressive, sexually predatory, and always chasing the next drink. In one sketch, known as 'Wanted a Housekeeper' he plays the octogenarian Sebastian, advertising for a housekeeper with a view to matrimony, having had four wives already ('If the lord keeps providing 'em I'll keep burying 'em'). The arrival of his intended betrothed prompts a series of puns and sexual innuendos that seem to bridge the gap between the Marx Brothers and the *Carry On* films:

SEBASTIAN:	Eee, I'll bet you're a hot 'un.
GLORIA:	I'm afraid I don't understand what you mean.
SEBASTIAN:	Well, in your letter you said you're young and vivacious.
GLORIA:	Well. Am I not?
SEBASTIAN:	Eh, I'd like to see your vivacity …
GLORIA:	I dare say you would, but not here … I've come here for an interview, not an operation … How old are you?
SEBASTIAN:	That's nowt to do with it, a man's as old as he feels.
GLORIA:	(*Removing his hand*) Well, you're feeling pretty well.

(Randle 1942a)

If Randle's lewd double entendres would not raise many eyebrows among liberal audiences today, the sexual politics of sketches might. In 'Putting up the Banns', he plays Jeremiah Clutterbuck, another geriatric lover, who enters with the line 'Eee darling, my sweetie pie – I'll knock spots off thee' (Randle 1942b) and then immediately wrestles his fiancée to the couch. At the vicarage to arrange their wedding, he spends much of his time fondling his fiancée's knee, but also picks a fight with the vicar (whom he offers at one point to headbutt) and threatens his girlfriend with physical abuse ('I'll soon knock that silly giggle off thy dial'). The anarchic violence of Randle's octogenarians may trouble our own sense of the propriety of comedy as well as that of our grandparents' and great-grandparents' generation.

Randle's most famous character creation was 'The Old Hiker'. As well as a later film version of the monologue, there is an extant sound recording which Randle made in 1938. The old hiker tells the audience.

I'm the daddy of all hikers. I'll be eighty-two in a few more days, eighty-two and I'm as full of vim as a butchers dog … Why, I'll take anybody on of my age and weight. Dead or alive. And I'll run 'em, walk 'em, jump 'em fight 'em … Ay, or I'll play 'em dominoes … eighty-two and just look at these for a pair of legs. I tossed a sparrow for these and lost … eighty-two and straight as a bulrush! I just passed a couple of tarts on the road – heehee, they were a couple of hot 'uns. Ay! One o' them went like this to me. I took no notice. Much. I said to 'er 'Not today, love, I'd rather have a Kensitas' … Think I'll have a sup'.

(Randle 1938b)

Fighting, sex and alcohol again dominate the monologue, which is punctuated by exaggerated belches, and delivered in front of a scantily clad female chorus of hikers who are there largely to decorate the stage. It finishes with one of Randle's best-known gags:

Its only t'other day I were going to a funeral. I was coming away from graveside, a chap looked at me, he says 'How old are you?' I said 'I'm eighty-two.' He said 'Ay, I don't think it's much use thee goin' home at all!'

(Randle 1938b)

116

Frank Randle died at the age of fifty-five; he was always a younger man playing old. Why, then, were these masks of old age so important to his comedy?

On the level of sheer technique, they were the equivalent of clown-faces, comic signifiers in themselves. Moreover, the convention of young-playing-old offered Randle the traditional advantage of incongruity that other kinds of comic theatrical cross-dressing (pantomime dames, Shakespearean cross-dressed heroines) also afford: the audience's knowledge that what it sees is not what it gets provides an immediate ironic distance which is fertile ground for laughter. In addition, the stereotype of the drunken old man, with all the loss of bodily control that that implies, is another kind of comic gift to the skilled physical performer: to play such an apparent lack of control needs a great degree of actual control.

Randle's act is, of course, open to the charge that he was perpetuating negative stereotypes of old age – and on a superficial level that may be true. But what was important was the use he made of the stereotype: old age *per se* was never really his *subject*. The roots of his humour were twofold. They lay, first and foremost, in the regional and class identity which the popular culture of the day largely affirmed, and to which Randle appealed in his defence against the censors. The elderly figures which he played represented to his audience a sense of history and continuity in this regional identity – a sense of history and continuity which, paradoxically, had its own dignity.

Secondly, the roots of Frank Randle's humour lay in a genuine and aggressive delight in taboo-breaking for its own sake. And here the mask of old age seems to have offered Randle – and his audience – a kind of licence and a kind of protection. As suggested earlier, Randle the man was 'truly mad, bad and dangerous to know' (Lee 1996: 34); and while his elderly characters were far from the cosy Grandad stereotypes of a Clive Dunn, the very fact of their old age made more palatable a vision of 'life and the realities of life' which released both Randle and his audience into the realms of the surreal. This is Myerhoff's identification of the elder as trickster writ large: the funny old man can be the subversive trickster figure *because* of the marginalization, the rolelessness of the elderly in mid-twentieth-century British society. 'The wily old man … [as] exploiter of cultural freedom and confusion' (Myerhoff 1992: 221) sums up Randle's appeal perfectly. The old hiker seems to give the game away with his exit line: 'Don't take any notice of me, I'm just an old fool, that's all'. But the line is disingenuous: we – and Randle's audiences of the time – *do* take notice.

PART III

Memories

Chapter 7

On Memory and Its Modes

A creative act in the present

As we get older, memory changes shape. One of the classic symptoms of ageing is the impairment of short-term memory, which depends upon sustained neural activity. Sensory memory and working memory fail to convert new information into longer-term memory, which relies on structural changes in the brain. Memories that were established a long time ago, however, are recalled more easily and become proportionally more vivid and more important.

Memory pervades and colours our consciousness, not only as we think about our history but also as we are aware of the present and as we consider the future, since we understand the world through the knowledge structures which we formed in the past. Issues of memory also involve questions of narrative. Memory is both itself constituted of narratives, and is also one of the building blocks of the stories by which we constitute our identities. And while memory is usually broadly considered in terms of the three stages of encoding, storage and retrieval, this should not deceive us into thinking of it as being like a computer or a photograph album. It is not the case that all we have to do is sort through the neural files to recover an exact image or movie clip of what happened in the past. Memory is reconstructive; it depends upon nerve pathways that fire anew each time we recall the original event. Memories are affected by later events, they get mixed up with other memories, they contain gaps which the mind rushes to fill up, they are dependent upon the language in which they are recalled. To remember the past is, whether we like it or not, to perform a creative act in the present (see Manns and Eichenbaum 2010, Loftus and Palmer 1974).

It is only comparatively recently that this 'creative act in the present' has been seen as something which may have a therapeutic value, or which may improve the quality of life for older people. In many care homes for the elderly in the mid-twentieth century, for example, residents were positively discouraged from 'indulging' in reminiscences, this being seen as a sign of senility and an indication that they were so obsessed with the past as to be unable to engage with the present (Coleman 1986, 1994).

The first fully theorized account of the positive value of memories was articulated by Robert Butler in his theory of the 'life review' – a systematic argument for the value of an elderly person's reviewing their past (Butler 1963). In common with certain types of traditional wisdom, Butler saw the life review as a mature preparation for death: a process by which a person comes to value his or her own past, accepting both their achievements and their disappointments and so grows to great self-understanding.

> Some of the positive effects of reviewing one's life can be a righting of old wrongs, making up with enemies, coming to acceptance of mortal life, a sense of serenity, pride in accomplishment, and a feeling of having done one's best. It gives people an opportunity to decide what to do with the time left to them and work out emotional and material legacies. People become ready but are in no hurry to die. Possibly the qualities of serenity, philosophical development, and wisdom observable in some older people reflect a sense of resolution of their life conflicts. A lively capacity to live in the present is usually associated, including the direct enjoyment of elemental pleasures such as nature, children, forms, colors, warmth, love, and humor. One may become more capable of mutuality with a comfortable acceptance of the life cycle, the universe, and the generations. Creative works may result, such as memoirs, art, and music. People may put together family albums and scrapbooks and study their genealogies.
>
> (Butler, quoted in Merrill 2001: n.p.)

The term has become used with different degrees of precision, according to context: at one extreme 'life review' is used only to refer to a limited set of self-contained and clearly defined techniques, which are practised within the context of formal care structures, and whose proper implementation can only be carried out by a certified life-review trainer. At the other end of the spectrum, 'life review' becomes an umbrella term for a variety of narrative modes by which the individual may access, structure and represent themselves and the relationship between their past and their present.

And in fact the potential benefits of narrative as a tool for healing are now being recognized in medical fields other than that of ageing. While Freud's 'talking cure' was applied largely to the diseases of the mind, practitioners of 'narrative medicine' are now exploring ways in which our human propensity to make stories out of our lives might also help in healing the body. Arthur W. Frank suggests both the potential strengths and also the limitations of such an approach.

> When I speak with groups of ill people or clinicians, they want to know whether and how stories can heal. Sometimes they expect stories to be a form of alternative/ complementary therapy, and healing is supposed to be remission from disease. I find it impossible to affirm that kind of desire. What I can affirm is how stories can bring existential or spiritual healing, and crucial to that healing is the capacity of stories to open a distance between the patient living in a diseased body and the ill person who is able to narrate illness.
>
> (Frank 2009: 193)

The larger questions of narrative medicine and its efficacy in relation to disease and physical injury lie beyond the scope of this book. But the capacity of stories to 'open a distance' between different modes of experiencing illness – or ageing – clearly has relevance for our present concerns.

The value of self-narrativization in successful ageing, and the extent to which it contributes to enhanced well-being, reduced isolation and a greater sense of self, has become an important topic in social gerontology. Life-history discussions, life writing, life reviews, narrative and reminiscence of various kinds have become increasingly embedded in therapeutic and interventional care for the elderly. At the same time, academic gerontologists have analysed, theorized and evaluated the practice in various ways: from Butler's original formulation of the life review (Butler 1963) to the revaluation of reminiscence in clinical work with the elderly (Kaminsky 1984, Sherman 1991), to narrative study of development (Cohler 1982), to the articulation of narrative gerontology (Kenyon, Clark and De Vries 2001) to the explosion of life-story writing among elders (Kenyon and Randall 1997, Birren and Cochrane 2001) – to name but a few important areas (Cole and Sierpina 2007: 253). Most studies have reported positive findings, although 'minority reports' also emerged, with some early studies in particular finding reminiscence and the process of self-narrativization to be of little or no use in successful ageing (Perotta and Meacham 1981–82, Revere and Tobin 1980–81).

Part of the problem in analysing activities such as 'narrative' and 'reminiscence' is that the terms themselves are too generalized. Just as narrative in literary and dramatic forms may be subdivided into a whole range of sub-genres and sub-sub-genres (epic, romance, realist novel, fantasy, picaresque, satire, mock-epic, detective fiction, 'chick lit' and so on) so narrative in these real-life situations among the elderly also has its genres and its sub-genres. And, like literary and dramatic forms, too, the genres of real-life narrative have their built-in discourses and emotional flavours: the epic offers a different emotional journey from the detective story, 'chick-lit' places its reader in a different position from the mock-epic – and part of the task of becoming an 'educated' reader or spectator of literary/dramatic fictions involves mastering the subject positioning involved in each of these various genres. To generalize about the effects of 'narrative' in successful ageing is as nebulous as trying to generalize about the effects of narrative in literature: there is no one 'effect'.

Recognizing this, various researchers have sought to develop a taxonomy of the genres of life narrative. For example, one approach – developed separately and with slightly separate emphases by Lieberman and Tobin (1983) and by Coleman (1986) – suggested categorizing narratives in terms of the subject's attitudes towards reminiscence (e.g. positive, negative, avoidance of review, successful completion of review, etc.) rather than on the contents of the narratives themselves. While addressing issues of emotional 'flavour', this is a rather blunt instrument, and risks ending up saying very little. A more sophisticated taxonomy is needed, and one which allows not just for authorial attitude but also for content analysis. Wong and Watt (1991) suggested the following broad kinds of narrative reminiscence which are particularly relevant to the elderly:

1. *Integrative reminiscence* functions as an attempt on the part of the subject to achieve a sense of self-worth, coherence and reconciliation with regard to his or her past.

This category is the most similar to Butler's life-review model, and while it may not always *succeed* in achieving integration, that is its primary drive. Even in cases where integration is not fully achieved, this kind of life review may contribute to successful ageing in terms of increased self-understanding, personal meaning, self-esteem and life satisfaction.

2. *Instrumental reminiscence* involves remembering past plans and projects: the ambitions of earlier life and the achievement of those ambitions, the attainment of past goals, and attempts to overcome difficulties in order to achieve those goals. It contributes to a subject's perception of his or her own continuity (Lieberman and Tobin, 1983) and a sense of internal control, and may enable him or her to draw on past experience in order to solve present problems.

3. *Transmissive reminiscence* has a very different purpose: its primary function is the passing on of one's cultural heritage and personal legacy. Closely linked to oral history, this kind of reminiscence involves talking about the culture, values, experiences and practices of an earlier era, and passing on the lessons of experience. The importance of this transmission of knowledge and experience to well-being in later life should not be underestimated: Jung (1933) suggested that it is a major provider of meaning and purpose in the second half of life. This kind of reminiscence is most closely connected with the old age as a *locus* of wisdom, and through transmissive reminiscence the elderly person not only offers a positive contribution to a younger generation, but in doing so they validate their own sense of worth.

4. *Escapist reminiscence* (also sometimes referred to as *defensive reminiscence*) is the other side of the same coin, but is characterized by the glorification of the past – often at the expense of the present, and sometimes with an exaggerated view both of the past itself and of the subject's own past status and achievements. This is essentially a narrative of decline, based on notions such as 'things ain't what they used to be' and nostalgia for 'the good old days' – although for the reminiscing subject it may also provide an imaginative compensation for the dissatisfactions of the present. Wong and Watt point out that '[e]mpirical studies have yielded some evidence in support of the benefits of escapist reminiscence … [However], like any form of fantasy, escapist reminiscence may provide instant relief from a painful present, but it becomes unadaptive when it is prolonged and excessive' (1991: 273).

5. *Obsessive reminiscence* is the dark side of *integrative reminiscence* – or perhaps more precisely it is what might happen when integrative reminiscence fails and a subject is unable to come to terms with the failures and/or problems of the past. It is characterized by guilt about the past, and by obsessive rumination on these events and on the sense of guilt, bitterness, failure or despair which they engender. These in turn can lead to depression, panic attacks and even suicide.

To these five main categories, Wong and Watt added a sixth, catch-all category which they called simply *narrative reminiscence* – somewhat confusingly, since all their reminiscence types actually involve narrative. By this they mean reminiscence which mainly involves a description of the past: 'statements of autobiographical facts, simple accounts of past events without interpretation or evaluation, and statements that do not belong to the integrative, instrumental, transmissive, escapist, or obsessive categories. In other words, simple narrative can also be defined by excluding other types of reminiscence' (Wong and Watt 1991: 274).

This study in the typology of reminiscence was conducted with a specific clinical end in mind: 'to resolve the controversy regarding the adaptive benefits of reminiscence … [and] to investigate what types of reminiscence are associated with successful aging' (Wong and Watt 1991: 272). (Unsurprisingly, perhaps, the researchers concluded that 'only certain types of reminiscence are beneficial' (Wong and Watt 1991: 272).) Wong and Watt's typology offers a useful framework for considering plays which address issues of coming to terms with the past in old age. In the rest of this chapter I will be looking at a series of plays, some of which fit comparatively easily into this sort of typology, others of which extend or challenge it.

Integration: *Mr Jones Goes Driving* (2011)

Theatre, like memory, is also a 'creative act in the present' which draws upon the past. In fact, one of the most archetypal and most frequently repeated dramatic stories is just this: the story about the impact which the past has upon the present. And so Oedipus, in *Oedipus Rex*, looks into the past only to find it crashing into the present to destroy him; Hamlet encounters a ghost, who burdens him with the details of his family's murderous history, and the prince has to decide how to deal with it in the here-and-now; Ibsen's eponymous Master Builder finds the past knocking on his door in the figure of a young woman whom he met ten years earlier, and who brings with her the hopes and expectations of that first encounter. Marvin Carlson opens his book *The Haunted Stage* by citing the familiar observation that all Ibsen plays could be called *Ghosts* because they all involve the past coming back to haunt the present – and then suggests that this could be extended to theatre as a whole. Perhaps, he suggests, all plays might be called *Ghosts* since they repeatedly involve

> the images of the dead continuing to work their power on the living, of the past reappearing unexpectedly and uncannily in the midst of the present … All theatrical cultures have recognized, in some form or another, this ghostly quality, this sense of something coming back in the theatre, and so the relationships between theatre and cultural memory are deep and complex … one might argue that every play is a memory play.
>
> (Carlson 2003: 1–2)

Of course, some plays are more directly about memory than others: Shelley Silas' Afternoon Play for BBC Radio 4, *Mr Jones Goes Driving* (2011) takes the concept of life review and turns it into a dramaturgical principle.

The Afternoon Play slot – typically between 2.15 p.m. and 3.00 p.m. on weekday afternoons – is an interesting one in terms of plays dealing with ageing. Its target audience, those who are likely to be at home at that time, includes a large number of elderly people. Moreover, in general, the typical Radio 4 audience is frequently characterized (not least by Radio 4 comedians) as being middle-aged to elderly, and middle-class; and while this does not tell the whole story, it is broadly accurate. The BBC's own most recent report on Radio 4 demographics, carried out in compliance with its regulatory framework as a public broadcaster and based on RAJAR (Radio Audience Joint Research) figures from 2009–10, concluded that while 'there are audiences across all demographic groups who have an interest in intelligent speech radio' and while Radio 4 does attract listeners from a range of these groups, listening is significantly higher among certain audience groups (BBC 2011: n.p.). Not only is Radio 4's reach much lower among audiences from black and minority ethnic backgrounds, but the station also

> has much higher reach amongst older audiences and those from better-off households. These groups also listen to Radio 4 for much longer periods – on average, a Radio 4 listener aged over 55 will hear 15 hours of Radio 4 programming each week compared with 7 hours for a listener aged between 25 and 34.
>
> (BBC 2011: n.p.)

The report suggests that these demographic differences are due to 'various social and cultural reasons', although it does not get much further than the somewhat circular explanation that 'Primarily, speech content tends to appeal to older and better-off audiences, while popular music radio tends to be far more attractive to younger audiences' (BBC 2011: n.p.). Both in terms of its station, then, and in terms of its broadcast slot, *Mr Jones Goes Driving* might be said to be playing squarely to an audience who are likely to be particularly responsive to plays about retirement, reminiscence and coming to terms with getting older. And, as its promotional material explains, *Mr Jones Goes Driving* is 'about growing old but not always gracefully. It's about facing up to things in life we don't want to. It's the story of a man giving up the one thing that he has always loved' (BBC Radio 4 2011: n.p.).

We soon discover that in this 'story of a man giving up the one thing that he has always loved', the thing is a car – a Rover P6 with a V8 engine, which its owner, Johnny Jones, affectionately calls 'Zelda'. A stereotypical masculine/feminine relationship between man (*sic*) and machine is thus immediately established. Moreover, while the car has a deliberately memorable and individualistic name, the protagonist has a name which, if not deliberately generic and anonymizing, certainly has the suggestion of an 'Everyman' function about it. Johnny is giving up the car because he is having to give up driving: at the age of sixty-seven he has started to suffer from occasional seizures and he has been told by a medical consultant that while his condition is not life threatening, he will no longer be able to drive.

This, of course, is not a uniquely masculine life crisis. For many people in the modern world, men and women alike, the moment when we give up driving has become a hugely significant marker of transition. And, as anthropologist Barbara Myerhoff points out, while we have rites which demarcate *some* of the phases of old age (fiftieth wedding anniversaries, special birthdays, etc.), we

> have no comparable rites for losses: giving up the family home, transferring property and privilege to children, completing menopause, relinquishing one's driver's license, moving into an institution, accepting a wheelchair or hearing aid, and the many large and small events that are usually thought of as failures and signposts indicating that the end is near.
>
> (Myerhoff 1992: 224)

In the absence of these social rituals, many old people develop 'their own private rituals with enthusiasm, even obsessiveness' (Myerhoff 1997: 225) and *Mr Jones Goes Driving* depicts a man who has certainly developed a ritualized – and indeed, a fetishized – relationship with his car. Not only does he take systematic and devout care of her; he also observes a seasonal pattern whereby 'she' is put carefully away for the winter, then brought back to life in spring; and he attaches dietary rules and prohibitions to her: sweets are allowed, any other kinds of food and drink are not. Although Johnny is now in his late sixties, these are rituals which have developed over a period of years: we are encouraged to believe that he was as obsessive when in his thirties or forties as he is now. They add up to a recognizable caricature of automotive-obsessed masculinity – perhaps one with a specifically generational dimension. Both Zelda and Johnny date from an era when a detailed understanding of technologies such as car engines and how to maintain them was one of the recognized markers of a successfully achieved masculinity – a time before the development of computer-regulated engines and sealed units made such understanding unnecessary, even useless. Johnny, we are told, had been a toolmaker before he took early retirement: he is not only an accomplished *user* of tools, but a craftsman who is able to *make* them – although nowadays, as he wistfully admits, nobody wants handmade tools any more. His former trade establishes him as an extreme exemplar of a kind of masculinity which has now effectively become redundant.

Attitudes towards technology, in fact, are used as indexes of ways of ageing in the play. Both Johnny and his wife Alice have ambivalent relationships with technology. Alice is excluded from Johnny's intimate relationship with Zelda (she refuses to drive her – in part at least – because Zelda is an automatic) but she has a bright new car of her own, equipped with a satellite navigation system, and she is very much at home with digital technology. She makes good use of her mobile phone and hands-free set, both for calls and text messages, while Johnny (who claims to be 'no Luddite' and is interested in computers) resents both the mobile phone and the satnav: 'What's all that about, then?' he grumbles, 'I like a good old-fashioned map.'

It is worth making brief reference, by way of contrast, to Alfred Uhry's Pulitzer Prize-winning *Driving Miss Daisy* (1986), which had been regarded as one of the iconic modern plays 'about' old age long before it was made into a successful movie: like *Mr Jones Goes Driving*, Uhry's play uses the relinquishing of the driver's licence as a signpost of ageing, and explores its consequences. *Driving Miss Daisy*, though, has more to say about race and class than it does about old age. Its central dramatic conflict is between two sparky individuals: the rich Jewish white woman, 'Miss Daisy', and the poor black man who is hired as her driver, Hoke Colburn. Both are quite old at the beginning of the play and both age considerably more over the span of the dramatic action. But old age is not the play's real subject. *Driving Miss Daisy* is an American social issue drama, which charts and celebrates changes in attitudes towards race in the Southern states between 1948 and 1973, touching on some of the similarities and differences between the Jewish experience and black experience of racism and oppression. A key scene is the one in which news comes to 'Miss Daisy' that her synagogue has been bombed by racists:

DAISY: Well, it's a mistake. I'm sure they meant to bomb one of the
                conservative synagogues or the orthodox one. The temple is
                reform. Everybody knows that.
HOKE: It doan' matter to them people. A Jew is a Jew to them folks. Jes'
                like light or dark we all the same nigger.

(Uhry [1986] 2010: 38)

Old age is portrayed sympathetically and sensitively in Uhry's play – but its main function is one of dramatic structure: old age is the site, not the central concern, of the play's action. The two central characters are given a particular point of view by their shared age, a point of view which is both engaged in and also at some distance from the societal changes that are taking place. Moreover, because both start out as recognizably 'old', this gives them a kind of stability throughout the play: society changes between 1948 and 1973, and Daisy and Hoke change, too, both bodily and in terms of their ideas and social attitudes. Daisy, in particular, mellows as she becomes one of the 'oldest old'. But they do not, for the most part, go through the series of life changes that younger protagonists would have gone through in a similar twenty-five-year period. Old age, in this play, offers a kind of stasis. That said, *Driving Miss Daisy* offers a rare theatrical opportunity for actors to play not just 'old age' as a single state, but old age as an ongoing process – to play, in fact, a range of old ages. In the recent London revival of the play (at Wyndham's Theatre in 2011) James Earl Jones and Vanessa Redgrave both grabbed this opportunity with aplomb, with Redgrave, in particular, imbuing the part of Miss Daisy with a physicality and sensuous presence that was very different from Jessica Tandy's film interpretation of the role.

In *Mr Jones Goes Driving*, Silas, unlike Uhry, concentrates the action of the play into a single day, and indeed into a single action: Johnny's final ritualistic drive in Zelda. And while many of the smaller daily and seasonal rituals which Johnny has constructed around his relationship with the car are not specifically related to his age or to growing older, this central ritual is clearly designed to mark the passing of one phase of life and the entering of another.

The opening of *Mr Jones Goes Driving* offers us a stereotyped image of an ageing couple. As Johnny prepares to set out on his journey, his wife Alice looks fussily and fondly after him, making sure he takes the snack and the pills and the flask she has prepared for him, and admonishing him to drive carefully and keep his phone on so that she can contact him – which she does, even as he drives away, texting him to scold him mildly for forgetting his apple. The opening raises a series of questions about where Johnny is going and why, and these only get answered later. But it establishes a sense of occasion: this is somehow a special day, and Johnny is going for a special drive. This sense of occasion is played off against a contrasting sense of the mundane, as the couple bicker familiarly: Johnny had asked for white bread and coffee 'today', Alice had provided brown multigrain bread because it is better for him. This underlying sense of tension, even of conflict between them, is brought into sharp focus by Alice's unexpected question as Johnny makes to leave: 'You will come back?' And as it turns out, that is the question that the action of the play asks – whether Johnny will indeed come back. Alice's insecurity about Johnny beats through the play and through Johnny's memories: his treasured *A–Z* has a message from Alice inscribed in it: 'For Johnny, so you'll always know how to return to me'.

As the action unfolds, the audience begins to understand the reason for this last drive – discarding along the way some of the red herrings offered by the narrative: might Johnny be preparing to commit suicide? It is Johnny's consciousness that dominates the story: the whole play takes the form of an internal monologue by Johnny, a monologue consisting largely of his own thoughts about the present and his reminiscences of the past. Many of the former tend to reaffirm a common stereotype of the grumpy old man, complaining about: 'Bloody mobile phones … I preferred it when you couldn't be contacted twenty-four hours a day. When receiving a phone call was exciting.'

In the original broadcast of the play, Johnny is played by Richard Briers, whose actual age at the time was seventy-seven: ten years older than the character he was playing. As such he certainly had no need to stress the old age of the character in his performance; and indeed Johnny's voice does not sound particularly 'old'. It is, however, a voice which is very recognizable to viewers and listeners who have known Briers for many years as a staple actor of British situation comedy, and it quickly established the 'Richard Briers presence' – drily witty but reassuringly familiar – as one of the component pleasures of the play. The part of Alice was played by Ann Davies, Briers' wife in real life. (Ironically, Alice sounds rather older than Johnny, even though she is described as younger than her husband.)

Johnny's monologue is occasionally intercut with fragments of other people's speech: Alice, their children and grandchildren, the consultant who examines Johnny, Imran who serves at the petrol station. Usually these are limited to single lines, although they sometimes amount to short scenes. But all the scenes are about Johnny and they rarely contain more than one other voice: the play's form emphasizes the dominance of Johnny's point of view, and we are asked to see things through his eyes – though not always uncritically. Radio drama is particularly adept at placing the listener 'inside' the consciousness of a single character, offering the illusion of shared subjectivity, and Silas makes full use of this capacity in this play.

It soon becomes clear that Johnny's final drive is a ritual through which he is trying to come to terms not only with the loss of his driving licence and hence his car, but also with his life as a whole. And if we soon realize that nothing as melodramatic as suicide is on the cards, it also becomes clear that more is involved than a sentimental farewell to a much-loved automobile. Johnny's journey involves revisiting some of the key sites of his own life, and re-encountering the emotional charges that they hold. The first of these involves yet another ritual, which starts as Johnny buys some flowers at his local petrol station: 'They're not for Alice', he tells Imran, and we are led to suspect that perhaps he is having an affair. But in fact the flowers are to place on the grave of his and Alice's first son, stillborn many years earlier and still haunting their memories. What might have been quite a conventional scene is given a harsh edge by its setting: it does not take place in a cemetery but in an anonymous piece of waste land 'in the middle of nowhere, with the motorway raging behind us', where they had secretly and ashamedly buried the child. The background roar of the cars behind his visit to the child's burial place continues the presence of the automobile which is so important to this play.

It seems at first as if this will be the dark secret at which the uneasy opening moments of the play hinted. In fact, though, it is merely the first stage on Johnny's journey through his own memories. The development of this journey is accompanied by a development of the familiar trope of the car-as-woman. Zelda is treated as an eroticized object, and also as an object of intimacy: Johnny talks to her constantly and describes her as his 'confidante'. 'Sometimes I think you love Zelda more than you love me', says Alice, and Johnny quietly adds, 'And sometimes Alice is right'. It is a common enough cliché of masculine attitudes towards cars, but unusually it is matched by the suggestion that Alice is not above anthropomorphizing, and even eroticizing automobiles in her own way: she has her own bright red French car, with its satnav set to a seductive French male voice ('Philippe makes me feel like I'm driving in Paris') and Johnny suspects she has a crush on James May, whom she also, oddly, imagines as being French. But *Top Gear* is a decidedly masculine television show, and it is Johnny's masculinity that is really at stake, defined as it is by his relationship with Zelda. It is this – his masculine identity and an important part of his sense of self – that he is faced with relinquishing along with his driving licence.

It is fitting, then, that it is the erotic aspect of that masculinity that forms the climax of the play's narrative. Johnny Jones' journey in Zelda, the car that is also a love object, takes him back to the house of Elizabeth, his former lover, twenty years younger than him – another classic male fantasy! There is, then, a sexual affair in Johnny's past history after all. It was a relationship which began six years ago when he was a year into early retirement. It was occasioned by his and Elizabeth's mutual enthusiasm for classic cars, and it continued for several months. Now, without quite knowing why, Johnny knocks on Elizabeth's door to confront both his memories of desire and his own guilt at the abrupt way in which he ended the affair several years earlier. On the surface, this scene would seem to be the least satisfactory of the play in terms of the apparent psychology of the individuals. The initially uncertain Johnny finds his desire reignited at the sight of Elizabeth, and finds himself suddenly on the verge of leaving Alice for his former lover. Elizabeth, on the other hand, seems to have no such plans; nor does she have much reason to feel excited at the prospect of resuming a relationship with a man who let her down badly once before. How realistic is the dramatic crisis of this play? How seriously can we take the possibility that Johnny might not, after all, go back to Alice; that he might leave her for Elizabeth?

In fact, he does return to Alice – bequeathing Zelda to Imran at the petrol station on the way, and working against stereotype, or possibly updating a stereotype, by making plans to reclaim something of his youth in a different way by buying some marijuana – 'Ganja' – from a street dealer ('They say it's good for seizures!'). The play ends with Johnny saying to Alice, 'I'm coming home', and on that level it works perfectly well as a sentimental meditation on old age, reminiscence and the possibility of positive ageing.

Mr Jones Goes Driving, then, does pretty much what its advertising blurb says it will: it dramatizes – predominantly through an internal monologue whose terms the listener is broadly encouraged to accept – a man facing up to loss, and through that process coming to terms with his past, with his relationship to that past, and with his present.

Part of the dramatic tension of *Mr Jones Goes Driving* involves the question as to what sort of reminiscence this will turn out to be. It moves through what Wong and Watt would call the *instrumental* (remembering past plans and projects) and at another point it touches on the *nostalgic* (glorifying the past). But in the end, Johnny's act of ritualistic reminiscence turns out to be *integrative*, enabling him 'to achieve a sense of self-worth, coherence, and reconciliation with regard to his or her past'. In the fictions of old age this kind of integration becomes the archetypal comic ending. We see it dramatized (though with reservations) in the late plays of Shakespeare and we see it problematized in the last plays of Ibsen. We frequently see it, implicitly or explicitly, in the conventions of reminiscence theatre, one of whose functions is to find ways of socially valuing and celebrating the memories and experiences of older people.

It may be, too, that sometimes we see it because we *expect* to see it – influenced, perhaps, by cultural expectations that the narratives of self *should* be integrative. A taxonomy such as Wong and Watt provide is useful insofar as it reminds us forcibly that the narrative of integration is only one *kind* of reminiscence, that the act of reviewing one's life has a range of generic affiliations and a range of potential outcomes. But in life narratives, as with literary and dramatic genres, drawing up an initial taxonomy can only provide a starting point, since genres are both fixed and fluid, offering points of stability but also subject to development, transformation and cross-fertilization. Moreover, any one narrative is unlikely to remain entirely within a single generic boundary.

In the case of *Mr Jones Goes Driving*, some listeners, to be sure, may feel that there is something a little too neat, a little too schematic, about the way in which the play fulfils this integrative function – especially given the dominance of the masculine point of view throughout the play. Because Johnny's voice is so utterly dominant in the structure of the radio drama, and because events are seen so much from his point of view, it may seem that we as audience are expected to see things only in the way he does. But that is not the whole story: dominant though Johnny's voice is in the play, there is another level, albeit one which we glimpse only occasionally, which begins to prise this unity open a little and allows the listener a perspective beyond that of Johnny himself. It is there in the slightly discordant note that emerges in the scene between Johnny and Elizabeth. We begin, perhaps, to discover that there may be other points of view involved: Alice's and Elizabeth's in particular. And while we are never asked by the play to reject Johnny's take on the narrative, on his relationship with Alice, Elizabeth and Zelda, or on coming to terms with his own ageing, we may be asked to respond not entirely uncritically to his fantasies and his memories.

Obsession: *Krapp's Last Tape* (1958)

A play which presents a much more intense challenge to an audience in terms of knowing how to respond to a character's fantasies and memories is Samuel Beckett's *Krapp's Last Tape* – one of the author's many works (like *Molloy*, *Malone Dies*, *Rockaby* and *All that Fall*) in which old age seems to be both subject and setting. The plot is simple: on his sixty-ninth birthday, Krapp – a 'wearish old man' (Beckett 1986: 215) – eats bananas, listens to tape recordings of his middle-aged self, and records a new tape (his last?). Like reminiscence therapy and life review, the play seems to ask questions about the 'sense of self-worth, coherence, and reconciliation with regard to his … past' (Wong and Watt 1991: 273) that can be achieved by Krapp in the process of remembering and reviewing.

The process, though, becomes a multi-layered one, as fallible human memory is set against the 'objectivity' of technology in the form of the tape recorder. It turns out that this ritual of recording a new tape – and of listening to old tapes from his past – is one that Krapp carries out annually: piles of boxes, spools of tapes and notebooks indexing their contents testify to the accumulation of recordings. And so we listen with him to the voice of the thirty-nine-year-old Krapp (a voice which is both similar to and different from that of the present, older Krapp) as he reviews his own past year of thirty years ago. It was the year in which his mother died, but that event merges with other trivia of his middle-aged life: a new light for his den, his own physical ailments, a woman neighbour singing and not singing. And, like his older counterpart, the middle-aged Krapp has been listening to his younger self on tape:

> Just been listening to an old year, passages at random. I did not check in the book, but it must be at least ten or twelve years ago. At that time I think I was still living on and off with Bianca in Kedar Street. Well out of that, Jesus yes! Hopeless business. (*Pause*) Not much about her, apart from a tribute to her eyes. Very warm. I suddenly saw them again.

(*Pause*) Incomparable! (*Pause*) Ah well … Hard to believe I was ever that young whelp. The voice! Jesus! And the aspirations! (*Brief laugh in which the older KRAPP joins*) And the resolutions!

(Beckett 1986: 218)

The narratives return frequently to the theme of love and the possibility of tenderness, warmth or intimacy – and time after time Krapp (past or present) seems to reject any such possibility. Time after time, too, Krapp (past or present) rejects his past selves, repeatedly seeking to distance himself from the voice, the aspirations and the attitudes of 'that young whelp'.

The play continually explores the relationship between the older self and the younger. It plays with an age-old conundrum: the extent to which the 'self' is best conceived of as singular or plural. Are we, as many of us feel ourselves to be most of the time, a single continuous 'self' – complex and sometimes contradictory, perhaps, but essentially a unity? Or is the unity of selfhood simply an illusion, and are we actually continually and irrevocably reinventing ourselves (or being reinvented) moment by moment? Susan Blackmore puts the issue clearly:

The central question is why it seems as though I am a single, continuous self who has experiences. Possible answers can be divided into two major types. The first answers the question by claiming that it is true – there really is some kind of continuous self that is the subject of my experiences, that makes my decisions, and so on. The second accepts that it *seems* this way but claims that this is misleading. Really, there is no underlying continuous and unitary self. The illusion that there is has to be explained some other way. Oxford philosopher Derek Parfit (1987) has aptly described these two types as 'ego theories' and 'bundle theories'.

(Blackmore 2003: 95)

At one level these two ways of thinking about the self involve crucial arguments about the fundamental nature of consciousness. At another level, though, they are meditations on two sides of the same coin: a testimony to the fact that the 'self' plays itself out in time, and that as a result we both are and are not the same person that we were either a decade or a week or a millisecond ago. *Krapp's Last Tape* depicts a man exploring both the continuity and discontinuity of his own past and present selves, and Beckett's dramaturgical ingenuity enables three of Krapp's 'selves' to be present to the audience: the sixty-nine-year-old, the thirty-nine-year-old and the (approximately) twenty-nine-year-old. We never hear the youngest of these three directly, but it is reported that he, too, looks back on his former adolescent self with the same sort of contempt as that with which middle-aged Krapp looks back on the young man – and the same contempt with which the near-septuagenarian, when he makes his own recording, looks back on his thirty-nine-year-old self.

KRAPP:	Just been listening to that stupid bastard I took myself for thirty years ago, hard to believe I was ever as bad as that. Thank God that's all done with anyway.

(Beckett 1986: 222)

The image is one of multiple regressions as each successive Krapp looks back and rejects – but also repeats – the characteristics of his earlier self. Krapp at sixty-nine is contemptuous of Krapp at thirty-nine, but joins in with him in his scornful laughter at Krapp at twenty-nine/twenty-seven. The various versions of Krapp are 'united with each other by certain continuities, principally a continuous egoism, which ironically also isolates them from one another by the mutual lack of sympathy it engenders. Each despises the others' (Webb 1972: 70).

Krapp's Last Tape does not answer the question which consciousness studies raises, the question of whether we are 'a single continuous self or a collection of multiple selves' (answering philosophical questions of this kind is rarely what art does best). What Beckett's play *does* do is to dramatize the possibility of both these choices simultaneously. In the same way, the question about Krapp himself is not really, as some have suggested, 'how far do we take him as a particularized character, a lonely old eccentric, and how far as Everyman?' (Hayman 1968: 48). He is presented as both: as a quirky, individual with a particular history and unique mannerisms, and also as a grotesquely tragicomic archetype of old age, whose repetitive cycle of confrontations with his other selves represents something of the human condition: what Robert Brustein described, in his review of the New York performance of the play, as 'Beckett's latest and very possibly his best dramatic poem about the old age of the world' (Brustein 1960: 21).

This ambiguity is expressed in the very style of the piece. On the one hand, the play text gestures towards a detailed, even relentless, theatrical realism: the wordless action of the first few minutes of the play describe activities so banal that it appears to take realism to an extreme. And while Beckett, in his stage directions, explains that he has set the piece in '*[a] late evening in the future*', this was done not to undercut the logic of realism, but to enhance it by answering the possible realist objection that 'as the magnetic tape recorder is a relatively recent invention, it was not possible in 1958 for an old man to listen to tapes recorded in his youth' (Fletcher and Fletcher 1978: 124). On the other hand, the setting which Beckett specifies – which stipulates nothing but a '*[t]able and immediately adjacent area in strong white light. Rest of stage in darkness*' (Beckett 1986: 215) suggests that the theatrical rules and conventions by which we are to read the play might have more to do with Expressionism than with Naturalism. Yet again, the description of Krapp himself ('*White face. Purple nose. Disordered grey hair*' (Beckett 1986: 215)) has something of the clown about it. In the same way, Krapp's banal actions of listening, recording, eating and searching are performed repetitively, deliberately and obsessively in such a way that they are eventually elevated into a clown-like comic routine. Beckett plays different kinds of theatrical conventions off against each other in order to create the uncertain world of the old man in his den.

Ambivalence and ambiguity, I would argue, are at the heart of *Krapp's Last Tape*. Not all critics have seen it this way. With only a few dissenting voices (e.g. Alvarez 1974: 100–01) the consensus seems to read the play in terms that could adequately be summed up by phrases describing the negative end of Wong and Watt's typology. And certainly Krapp's mode of reminiscence appears to be what they would call 'obsessive': a mode in which a subject is unable to come to terms with the failures and/or problems of the past; a mode which is characterized by guilt about the past, and by obsessive rumination on these events and on the sense of guilt, bitterness, failure or despair which they engender (see Wong and Watt 1991: 273).

For example, Eugene Webb talks of Krapp having changed and grown a little bit by confronting his past but adds 'this growth has not carried him very far … He is not healed at the end but paralyzed' (Webb 1972: 71), while Andrew Gibson agrees with Alain Badiou that 'Beckett finds no salvation in memory' (Gibson 2006: 243).

My own reading is slightly different. The play does not seem to me to be about healing versus paralysis, nor about salvation and damnation. More useful is James Knowlson's account of the way in which the symbolism of light and dark in the play articulates Beckett's fascination at the time with ideas drawn from Manichaean philosophy and theology (Knowlson 1972). Manichaean doctrine sees human experience as being constituted by a continual battle between opposing forces (light and dark, good and evil, positive and negative) in the world. It is in the interplay between such conflicting forces that the power of the play resides; the way in which it both utterly resists sentimentality, and yet at the same time bears witness to what Alain Badiou called 'the other life of which we are all bearers' (Gibson 2006: 243). Beckett's understanding of old age is shaped by such oppositions.

These oppositions can be seen clearly in the performance of Krapp by Patrick Magee, the actor for whom the part was first written. Magee played Krapp in the first production of the play, when it was presented at the Royal Court Theatre, London on 28 October 1958 in a double bill with *Endgame* – a pairing which makes Brustein's phrase, 'dramatic poem about the old age of the world', seem particularly apposite. Beckett wrote the script for Magee because he had been so impressed by Magee's reading of extracts from some of his prose works. Magee's rasping voice was one of Beckett's stimuli (Knowlson 1992: 46) and the manuscript for the first draft, dated '20-2-58', was titled simply 'Magee monologue'. While we do not have direct access to the 1958 performance, we do have access to one of its 'echoes'. In 1972 its director, Donald McWhinnie, restaged the production for a BBC television broadcast (*30-minute Theatre*, BBC2, 29 November 1972), in which Magee, in an ironically Krapp-like way, reprised his own performance of fourteen years earlier.

At the time of the BBC performance Magee was fifty years old: still nearly twenty years younger than the character he was playing – and whom he would originally have played at the age of thirty-eight! His representation of Krapp's old age is totally convincing, however, and deeply painful to witness. The close-ups available to the television camera make the experience of watching Krapp listening to his younger self particularly intense. In the passage quoted previously (in which Krapp listens to his middle-aged self remembering the time when he was living 'on and off with Bianca in Kedar Street') Magee's face took on a gentle, almost childlike wistfulness as Krapp strained to listen to his past life. This, though, immediately turned into scornful sneers as the taped voice lapsed into its customary harshness: 'Jesus yes! Hopeless business … Hard to believe I was ever that young whelp. The voice! Jesus!' In the contrast between the two expressions was articulated a world of loss.

To what extent should we think of Magee's performance of Krapp as 'definitive'? This is a difficult question – and an important one, given Beckett's well-known insistence on the details of the live performance of his work. At first sight, Magee's Krapp *looks* definitive: the play was written specifically for him, and Beckett was in rehearsals throughout for the original Royal Court production and made many suggestions and interventions regarding staging (Knowlson 1992: xiii). On the other hand, the Magee that most of us have seen – the one in circulation both commercially and on YouTube – is the Magee of the later televised BBC revival, and Beckett had no such direct input into this. Moreover, there were other productions with which Beckett himself *was* more closely concerned, such as the French production at the Petite Orsay Theatre in Paris in 1975, and the German production with Martin Held as Krapp, at the Schiller-Theater Werkstatt, Berlin in 1969. Both of these were directed by Beckett himself, and some Beckett scholars see the latter in particular as authoritative (e.g. Fletcher and Fletcher 1978: 120). No public-domain video documentation of these performances exist; and the Magee version has attained a level of authority (in the Anglophone world at least) in part because of its sheer availability. But there is nothing to suggest that in these German and French productions Beckett made any move to lessen that complexity of tone which is so evident in Magee's performance. Magee embodies with extraordinary power the 'conflicting forces' which drive *Krapp's Last Tape*. On the one hand there is the rasping voice which sneers and scoffs at the Krapps of the past – and by extension at the Krapp of the present too. On the other hand there are his reactions to the play's brief moments of lost lyricism which are never quite extinguished by that harsh voice.

The most poignant of these comes at the very end of the play, as present-day Krapp goes back to one of the rare lyrical moments in his tape. We have heard it before: it is an account of a moment of eroticism, in which he and a girl are described, drifting in a punt. We revisit the scene with him:

> I lay down across her with my face in her breasts and my hand on her. We lay there without moving. But under us all moved, and moved us, gently, up and down, and from side to side.
> (*Pause. KRAPP's lips move. No sound.*)
> Past midnight. Never knew.

(Beckett 1986: 221)

That was where the passage had ended the first time Krapp had played it. Now we listen to it with him once more, and this time he lets the tape play a little longer.

Never knew such silence. The earth might be uninhabited.

(*Pause*)
Here I end this reel. Box – (*Pause*) – three, spool – (*Pause*) five. (*Pause*) Perhaps my best years are gone. When there was a chance of happiness. But I wouldn't want them back. Not with the fire in me now. No, I wouldn't want them back.
(*KRAPP motionless staring before him. The tape runs on in silence.*)

(Beckett 1986: 223)

The additional lines seem to undercut the poignancy of the memory, dismissing it and rejecting it with a finality that seems to be Krapp's own last word on the subject. 'I wouldn't want them back' – the line resonates bleakly as the play finishes.

But that bleakness is not all that we are left with. I began my discussion of *Krapp's Last Tape* by saying that its narrative drive seems to be structured around the question of whether Krapp's reminiscences will enable him to achieve any sense of self-worth, coherence, and reconciliation with regard to his past. But the play's answer to this question is ambivalent – much more so than Krapp's final words make it seem. Those words, 'I wouldn't want them back', with their stark rejection of the memory or the possibility of happiness, belong, still, to that younger Krapp. What we are left with, as 'the tape runs on in silence', is the sixty-nine-year-old listener, motionless and silent. We suspect that if he *does* speak he will do so in his usual harsh tones, and will say something equally harsh. But while that silence continues (and it continues until the play ends) it holds open a space in which opposites can still exist. It enables a space which acknowledges both the presence and the absence of his fleeting moments of past happiness, its existence and its loss.

Dislocation: Abi Morgan, *Lovesong* (2011)

Abi Morgan's *Lovesong*, written for Frantic Assembly (with whom she has collaborated on several previous occasions) is another play which presents simultaneous versions of the old and young self. But whereas in Beckett's *Krapp's Last Tape* young and old were represented by one live actor and a series of taped voices playing against each other, *Lovesong* uses four actors to play two characters. Billy and Maggie, a couple in their seventies in the present day (played by Sam Cox and Siân Phillips in the Frantic Assembly production), are seen also as their younger selves (called, perhaps just for the sake of textual clarity, William and Margaret, played by Edward Bennett and Lianne Rowe).

We follow Billy and Maggie over a period of a few crucial days, while William and Margaret are tracked over a period of years, through their twenties and thirties: as newlyweds, as a struggling young professional couple, as a couple in marital crisis. In a mid-rehearsal video interview, director Scott Graham described the play as being 'about two characters at a certain point in their life where their relationship is coming to an end, and they're starting to be haunted by these memories' (Hoggett and Graham 2011a: n.p.). The description rather undersells the play, in fact: by making it sound as if it is really 'about' the older couple and their memories, it does not do justice to the fragile ambiguity which made the play such a powerful theatrical experience, and such a subtle and nuanced look at love and ageing.

The technique of double-casting, young and old, gives us a particular kind of perspective on this married couple, but it is a complex one, which takes some teasing out. Double-casting in itself, of course, is hardly unique or revolutionary. Cinema uses this kind of technique more than theatre, perhaps: at a very early stage it borrowed *analepsis* from literary prose narratives and epics (which had never had to worry about the exigencies of casting) and rebranded it as 'flashback' – or, as D. W. Griffith termed it, 'switchback'. (Griffith's *Intolerance* (1916) was the film that effectively pioneered the technique, while the one that elevated it to one of the most familiar of cinematic conventions was Welles's *Citizen Kane* (1941), a film which turned flashback into a central structuring principle.) Now, whether used for short backstory expositions or as a framing device for an entire film, the flashback is part of the basic vocabulary of cinematic narrative. But theatrical narrative also enjoys playing games with time; and the technique of double-casting, in which a character is shown at different stages of their life, allows both for that sort of playfulness, and also for a degree of ironic distance or narrative detachment that mid-twentieth-century British dramaturgy liked to think of as Brechtian. Thus, to take a simple and fairly well-known example, Peter Shaffer's *Royal Hunt of the Sun* (1964) made use of it, telling the story of Pizarro's conquest of the Incas through the eyes of an old man, Martin, looking back on his youth, remembering and watching himself as a naïve young boy (played by an appropriately young actor) as he gets caught up in the events that led to the genocide in fifteenth-century South America.

But although at first sight the use of double-casting in *Lovesong* seems to be akin to the extended flashback or the dramatic narrator, it actually works rather differently from either cinematic *analepsis* or Brechtian alienation. In fact, it works in a way which owes more to the brilliantly structured bourgeois comedies of Alan Ayckbourn, in which several annual family gatherings all happen at once before the eyes of an audience, and comic gags play across entrances and exits in time in the way that Feydeau's nineteenth-century French farces had played their gags across entrances and exits in space. Thus Morgan's two couples both inhabit the stage simultaneously: Billy passes in front of William's path, or Maggie picks up a bowl that Margaret has just put down.

The action takes place in a single house: the one they moved to when first married, and that house is represented by a deliberately simple set: a table, a couple of chairs, a window, some garden. This scenographic minimalism was combined with a playfulness of design which allowed characters to enter and exit through unexpected places – closets, refrigerators – breaking up the apparent surface realism of the setting, and dislocating the space, enabling the action to shift seamlessly and wittily back and forth, both between the present day and the 1960s or 1970s, with neither of these eras being more real or more 'present' than the other. The play shifts, too, between a naturalistic environment and a dream-like one – a home that both has and has not changed over the years, that has grown comfortably old together with Billy and Maggie, their daily lives and their dreams.

The overall effect is one of a delicately poised double perspective on life, love and the process of ageing. For ageing is certainly at the centre of *Lovesong*, both as a theme and as a process. Frantic Assembly are known primarily as a devising company (directors Hoggett and Graham have co-authored the *Frantic Assembly Handbook of Devising*) but they work closely with writers, giving the writer freedom to *be* the writer, but developing the work in a collaborative framework. In their collaboration with Abi Morgan, the issue of age, in its broadest sense, was a driving force right from the beginning. In an interview conducted halfway through rehearsals, director Scott Graham explained that in their previous shows

we have worked with either people of our own age or people of a similar age, and somehow the shows were based around our experiences and what we wanted to say about our lives at that particular time. With *Lovesong*, through a series of various events, we'd come to the conclusion that we wanted to make a show about an age group older and an age group younger, so they're the people we might become and the people we forgot we once were, because we feel that there's a fascinating gap between those two generations.

(Hoggett and Graham 2011b: n.p.)

Abi Morgan agrees:

[The idea for the play] really came from Steven and, in particular, Scott, who was very attached to the work of T. S. Eliot, and in particular *The Love Song of J. Alfred Prufrock*. That was the starting point ... We talked about now, all coming together ten years on [from their previous collaboration], we were all entering our early 40s, and how different that was, and where we were at – individually, but also within the context of our age. That made all three of us talk about the notion of aging and getting older ... What intrigued me is that suddenly at this pivotal moment of 40, I know what it's like to be a 20-year-old and I'm getting an inkling of what it is to be older. What I love is that there will be two sides of the audience self-reflecting and looking at each other.

(Morgan interview with Clair Chamberlain 2011)

Morgan's script is beautifully understated and works extremely well in conjunction with Frantic Assembly's characteristic physical theatre. In *Lovesong*, the dialogue scenes between Billy and Maggie, William and Margaret are intercut with choreographed dance sequences: not fast and explosive like some of Frantic's earlier work, but slow, graceful and very beautiful. And while, on the whole, the younger pair of actors perform the more physically demanding movements, both generations of performers contribute equally to the beauty of the choreography, with Phillips and Cox both performing lifts, kicks and carries which demonstrate extraordinary strength, athleticism and physical control. The directors' programme notes that 'if you have not seen Siân Phillips doing press-ups at the end of a gruelling warm-up you have not lived' (in Morgan 2011: 20) is clearly written in all seriousness.

But the dance sequences do more than simply subvert expectations of the physical capabilities of 'old people'. Just as the scenography is ambiguous as to the 'reality' of their setting, so these dance sequences play against the dialogue in such a way as to disrupt any tendency to default purely to the logic of naturalism. And so, while during the dialogue sequences, characters brush past each other without either couple ever quite *seeing* the other, the choreography allows them moments when they meet. Most of these choreographed sequences are not represented in the written text, but a couple of them are, and Morgan's stage directions for one of them in particular gives a sense of how they work. Towards the end of the play, Maggie and Billy have gone to bed; then

> (*MAGGIE's hand reaches up, catching* BILLY's *hand, lying restless in bed.* BILLY *turns as* MAGGIE *sinks back into the bed, to be replaced by* MARGARET *now sitting up.*)
>
> MARGARET: Sleep ... sleep.
>
> (*MARGARET and* BILLY *caught in an embrace in the bed, the twist and turn of the sheets until at once* BILLY *is now* WILLIAM, *lost in lovemaking with* MARGARET *and then with another twist* MARGARET *is now* MAGGIE *and then* WILLIAM *and then* BILLY *until ...*)

(Morgan 2011: 87)

The prose of the stage directions can only suggest the fugue-like, dream-like interplay between memory and desire which the audience experiences. And the point is that during these sequences these generations of lovers do not merge into one, nor does one pair ever seem more 'real' than the other. Graham and Hoggett, joint directors of Frantic Assembly, acknowledged, 'We are the generation between our couples. This meant placing ourselves between the ages of the cast' (in Morgan 2011: 20). This sense of 'in-between-ness' (and once more we are back to the notion of liminality, this time in its more familiar sense) permeates the play and the production: just as Graham and Hoggett are in between the ages of their cast, so the audiences experience the world of a play which is poised somewhere *between*. The reality of old love and the reality of young love are in equilibrium: we are not being asked to choose between one and the other, but being allowed the privilege of experiencing *both/and*. And if, perhaps at the end of the play, we are pulled towards the narrative of the older couple more powerfully than that of the younger one, it is not because it is more real, but because it is about to end: as the play develops we come to understand, through a series of increasingly less oblique remarks, that Maggie is terminally ill, in frequent intense pain, and about to end her own life.

The affirmative tone of *Lovesong* is as far as can be imagined from even the most optimistic reading of *Krapp's Last Tape*, and if (to my mind) it never falls into sentimentality, it does seems to teeter on the edge of it, just as *Krapp* sometimes seems to teeter on the edge of nihilism. Yet what the two plays share is as important as what separates them, for, like *Krapp's Last Tape*, *Lovesong* plays with multiple versions of the ageing self. Abi Morgan talks of how one of the aims of the play is to help the audience

> to realise that inherently you are still the same person. Although life circumstances might change, you still at times feel like a 17-year-old and I feel very acutely that that's probably the way I'll feel when I'm 70. I like the idea that it might be a piece that brings an audience together. That stops them looking at age and makes them realise that we make time linear, but in fact it doesn't necessarily have to divide us in the way it does.
>
> (Interview with Clair Chamberlain 2011)

Attractive though Morgan's idea is, again, I think this slightly oversimplifies a complex theatrical experience. As for 'bringing an audience together', it certainly did that at the performance I attended: the experience was an emotional one and many members of the audience were in tears at the end of the play. But as well as being intensely moving, the play kept the audience intellectually engaged. 'Theatre', says Morgan, 'is the place of language and ideas' (Interview with CC). My own experience of seeing *Lovesong* was not simply to 'realize that inherently [I am] still the same person': rather it was to be made aware of my own sense of continuity and discontinuity, and of the interplay of sameness and difference between youth and age. Like *Krapp's Last Tape*, *Lovesong* asked questions rather than answering them: a strange, lyrical counterpoint to Beckett.

Disintegration: Theatre without memory

The American theatre director Charles Marowitz gave a memorable definition of an actor in his book, *The Act of Being,* one that is worth quoting at length. An actor, says Marowitz,

> is someone who remembers.
>
> On the simplest level, someone who remembers his lines, his cues, his moves, his notes, to do up his fly-buttons, to tie his shoelaces, to carry his props, to enter, to exit. Simple things, complex things. An actor is someone who remembers.
>
> On another level, an actor is someone who remembers what it felt like to be spurned, to be proud, to be angry, to be tender – all of the manifestations of emotion he experienced as a child, as an adolescent, in early manhood and maturity. An actor remembers the 'feel' of all the feelings he ever felt or sensed in others. He remembers what happened to other people through all periods of recorded time – through what he has read and what he has been taught. In tracing lineaments of his own sensibility, he has the key to understanding everyone else.
>
> On a deeper level, an actor is someone who remembers the primordial impulses that inhabited his body before he was 'civilized' and 'educated'. He remembers what it feels

like to experience intense hunger and profound thirst, irrational loathing and sublime contentment. He recalls the earliest sensations of light and heat, the invasion of infernal forces and the comings of celestial light. He remembers the anguish of disapproval and the comforting sense of guardians ...

To be without memory and to be an actor is inconceivable. An actor is someone who remembers.

(Marowitz 1978: 26–27)

And – to carry Marowitz's idea to its logical conclusion – through the things that he or she remembers, an actor also makes the audience remember 'what it felt like to be spurned, to be proud, to be angry, to be tender'. Memory seems to be utterly central to acting, to drama, to theatrical performance itself. Which makes dementia a particularly difficult, and a particularly fascinating, subject for theatre. 'To be without memory and to be an actor is inconceivable'.

And yet as we become more aware of our ageing population, dementia becomes a subject that demands attention, from the theatre as from other art forms. And over the past few years the theatre has responded. It has responded, certainly, with several plays about the experience of living with someone who has dementia. Plays such as Bruce Graham's *The Outgoing Tide*, Tamsin Oglesby's *Really Old Like Forty-Five* and Bryony Lavery's *A Wedding Story* contain sympathetic portrayals of those suffering from dementia, but their real interest lies with those who have to cope with the loss of the person they once knew. Somewhat unexpectedly, perhaps, BBC Radio soap opera *The Archers*, came up with one of the most successful and thoughtful portrayals of dementia in contemporary drama: the onset of dementia in long-standing *Archers* character Jack Woolley was a storyline which elicited an extraordinary rich response from listeners. The long-time scale over which the soap-opera format structures its narratives allowed for a more subtle development of the portrayal of the condition than is usually possible in theatre.

Radio, in fact, has frequently dealt rather well with the issue of dementia. Perhaps this is because the great tradition of radio drama, a tradition established by writers such as Dylan Thomas and Giles Cooper, has always worked outside the box of naturalism, has always had an ear for the absurd and the surreal.

The comedian and novelist Charlie Higson (who first came to public attention in the UK as one of the creators of BBC2's *The Fast Show*) came across a book called *Ancient Mysteries* by David Clegg, who for several years had been collecting and transcribing the surviving memories of Alzheimer's sufferers. *Ancient Mysteries* 'adds up to a very skewed oral history of the 20th century because, intriguingly, you never quite know what is real. Mixed in with actual memories are fantasies, and bits and pieces borrowed from films and books and television programmes' (Higson in Clegg 2007: n.p.). Higson 'immediately thought how powerful these pieces would be if spoken by actors. We're used to hearing about Alzheimer's from medical experts or family members, from the outside, as it were' (Higson in Clegg 2007: n.p.). Working with his writing partner, Paul Whitehouse, Higson created a powerful and moving piece of radio drama, which was broadcast serially in the drama slot on Radio 4's *Woman's Hour*. It gave listeners 'a chance to hear about what it was like to have dementia from the other side of the wall. To give a voice to people who usually have no voice' (Higson in Clegg 2007: n.p.). Voices like that of Pauline, who qualified as a nurse in 1939 and who now tells the listener,

I must be someone else now. I've been dusting around here a long time … yeah … lovely here … dusty … very nice … all the people are nice … I don't know what I was doing … tidying the wardrobe? I think I was tidying the wardrobe. (*A bell rings in the corridor*) They're ringing a … I don't know. It must be near the seaside. I was born in a little place called Churchtown in Ireland … that could be right … a country place. Born in Farnham … No … not born in Farnham … I was evacuated to Farnham … one sister, two brothers and me. Two dogs and one cat and … I'm a little piggy wiggly. Two brothers … oh, I'm trying to think … dark hair … I can't remember … brown hair … that's funny … funny I can't remember … I was the youngest … you were the oldest.

(Clegg 2007: n.p.)

The pieces were performed by actors of various ages; they included Kathy Burke, Anne Reid, Richard Briers (again) and Siân Phillips (again):

We decided early on that we didn't want to hire only older actors. The fascinating, touching thing the monologues reveal is that most of the patients live in the past and believe themselves to be young. We didn't want to impersonate extremely elderly, frail and confused people, we wanted to bring out their true characters, and show how they had once been. The final pieces are, I think, very moving, unusual and yes, now and then, funny.

(Higson in Clegg 2007: n.p.)

Apart, though, from a few outstanding experiments such as those of Higson and Clegg, drama – and live theatre in particular – has tended to fight somewhat shy of the representation of dementia; ever since *King Lear*, certainly, comparatively few plays have attempted to portray dementia 'from the inside', from what Higson calls 'the other side of the wall'. One recent play that does attempt this, however, is Melanie Wilson's *Autobiographer*, a work which approaches the issue in a way which offers an interesting comparison to Abi Morgan's *Lovesong*.

In *Autobiographer* four actresses plus a small child, a voice-over, and an immersive soundscape create a poetic portrait of the life and the internal world of a woman called Flora who is suffering from dementia. The four actresses, including Wilson herself, are costumed identically but are of different ages; they portray Flora – the play's only visible 'character' – in her teens, thirties, fifties and seventies, and as a child. And as Flora talks both to herself and to the audience, her words are woven together into a shared monologue.

Autobiographer picks up the theme which we have already seen in Beckett and Morgan – that of the multiplicity of the self. The form of the play, with the differently aged Floras all simultaneously present, sharing their lines and their dress sense, embodies that. It is, nonetheless, stated in the text as well:

FLORA 1:	… Because sometimes you'll ask.
FLORA 2:	And I really think you'll mean it. You'll say 'How are you feeling?' And I'll think … I am a 76-year-old woman, but inside I feel like I'm 33. Just to let you know. Before you forget.

(Wilson 2012a: 18–19)

But whereas for Beckett that multiplicity was a function of memory, here it is a function of forgetfulness. And whereas the double-casting of *Lovesong* represented integration, this in *Autobiographer* represents fragmentation.

Like Frantic Assembly, Melanie Wilson and Fuel Theatre (the production company with whom she created the show) are usually associated with the contemporary British theatrical avant-garde. Subjectivity, consciousness, perception and interiority are long-standing themes of Wilson's theatre-making, and she was drawn to the subject of dementia because of the 'very particular devolution of perception of the self and the world around' which it entails (Wilson 2012b: n.p.). Whereas much verbatim and reminiscence theatre emerges from work with specific elderly communities, Wilson's was based on initial research at the British Library; she also worked with the Alzheimer's Society, the Wellcome Trust and the Croydon Memory Service. Wilson has described the process of working on the play as 'A game changing experience for me', adding,

Autobiographer … seeks to challenge and engage with the vivid possibilities of contemporary theatre. As such, I hope the audience will feel that they have for a very brief moment, brushed up against a state of being lived out by many thousands of people in this country at this moment, but told in a highly engaging, singular and thought provoking way.

(Wilson 2012b: n.p.)

The play is certainly very 'contemporary' in its theatrical style, and, on the night I saw it, was playing at a studio venue which was very clearly part of the contemporary theatre scene, to a small audience (mainly in their twenties and thirties) who were obviously well-versed in the conventions of contemporary performance. Lighting (by Ben Pacey) and sound design (by Wilson herself) carried much of the effect of *Autobiographer*: above the audience hung hundreds of light bulbs of different sizes and brightness, switching on and off at varying speeds like the synapses in a brain. The immersive sound design played with piano phrases and vocal whispers, echoes and naturalistic weather sounds, synthesized sounds, notes and tones, silences and ambient noises that built towards a disorientating crescendo at the climax of the play.

The language of the play is important, too, however, and the listener/reader is asked to follow the characters' linguistic leaps and unexpected juxtapositions and repetitions. At times this simply appears to replicate the mental processes of the very confused:

FLORA 4:	can I …
FLORA 3:	can I …
FLORA 2:	can I …
FLORA 1:	can I …
FLORA 4:	canulai
FLORA 2:	can I …
FLORA 3:	ah …
FLORA 1:	I
FLORA 2:	speaking now
FLORA 4:	ah …
FLORA 3:	I'm speaking now
FLORA 1:	sorry

(Wilson 2012a: 54)

At other times, however, it becomes a lyrical monologue which both on the page and in performance overtly takes on the quality of poetry:

FLORA 1:	I have this story.
	I was told this story
	Of a boy … a small boy.
	And a yearning so profound that it entered his heart like a clanging bell …
	… making it struggle and resist the walls of his chest.
FLORA 3:	A small boy … shaped his heart into a bird
	with the sound of a bell
	his heart into a bird of green
FLORA 1:	brilliant green
FLORA 3:	with eyes, shining.

(Wilson 2012a: 32–33)

In passages such as this, the fragmentation of the thoughts of the dementia sufferer becomes a poetic principle in its own right, one which generates its own images and rhythms and thus its own unique meanings.

The play was a critical success, with many reviewers echoing the sentiments of *Time Out*'s Andrzej Lukowski:

> Melanie Wilson's gorgeous, harrowing *Autobiographer* is an absorbing performance poem ... Wilson's language is dazzling ... The crisp, immersive sound design is astonishing, *Autobiographer* is above all a work of vivid poetry about memory, its loss and the beauty that lives on in the ashes of a failing mind.
>
> (Lukowski 2012: n.p.)

A few, though, expressed disappointment. Jake Orr, for example, reviewed the production for a website whose implicit stance on the politics of ageing might be deduced from its name: *A Younger Theatre: Theatre through the Eyes of the Younger Generations*. Orr considered that

> Wilson's piece deals with dementia with such fragility that the piece feels *too fragile* for its audience to handle; it's too disjointed and too unwilling to let us in. The pace of the piece is very melodic and whimsical, and even during a heightened moment of tension we never quite rise with it ... Wilson's fragmented text and performers work well to represent the lost connections of the mind, but *Autobiographer* misses the emotional and heartbreaking nature of such a disease. It misses the nightmare that it inflicts upon the tormented sufferer, and whilst Wilson has created a tender piece she misses the theatrical scope to really show her audience what it means, what it *feels* like ... *Autobiographer* deals with some challenging notions, and presents a poem of much lyrical beauty, but never stirs us from just being observers, observing and not caring, and this just *doesn't feel right*.
>
> (Orr 2012: n.p.)

The Guardian's Lynn Gardner concurred: '[W]e simply never get to know Flora well enough to care about what has been lost, and the lack of tonal variety becomes wearisome. The piece is so busy being poetic that it sells Flora and her fragmented story short' (Gardner 2012: n.p.). Even the more enthusiastic reviewers conceded that the play 'leaves only a vague, wispy residue behind ... *Autobiographer* can feel like an entrancing mobile to be gawped at unthinkingly. The piece is passed through without significant lasting impact or transformation' (Trueman 2012: n.p.).

I have some sympathy with Orr, Gardner and Trueman: I understand what they mean by the play's 'fragility'; I shared the frustration at the lack of tonal variety within the performance. (And by depicting the dominant tone of senile dementia as being one of wistful lyricism, are we not sentimentalizing it?) And I, too, felt detached from the action, not knowing the character 'well enough to care about what has been lost'. And yet, perhaps there is a paradox here? Earlier, I quoted Wilson's hope that an audience 'will feel that they have for a very brief moment, brushed up against' the state of dementia. Those critics who like the play least do so because they recognize in it a sense of fragility and emotional detachment, a monotonic (or even monotonous) quality, and experience the play as being 'without significant lasting impact', something that 'leaves only a vague, wispy residue behind'. These attributes, fixed upon as negative theatrical qualities, are also the attributes of the dementia sufferer's experience. It may be that even for those whose responses to the play were comparatively negative, *Autobiographer* was communicating something of what Wilson intended.

This sort of argument can only be taken so far. Intentionalism is not the sole criteria by which artistic effect can be judged. And while emotional content and theatrical form may inform each other, they do not usually replicate each other: if you are going to write a play about unhappiness (according to the traditional wisdom of playwriting) then make it a funny one. If you are going to write about the disintegration of the memory, then make it memorable. But the truth is that the art of the theatre is only just beginning to pluck up the courage to engage with some of the more extreme implications of our increasing scientific understanding of old age; work such as Melanie Wilson's *Autobiographer*, seeking as it does to find theatrical ways to express the experience of the dementia sufferer, makes a valuable contribution.

Chapter 8

On Reminiscence, Interaction and Intervention

'Material to create shows': The dramaturgy of reminiscence

The simple idea underlying reminiscence theatre was that reminiscences collected from old people could be used as material to create shows which could then be toured back to the people who had provided them in the first place.

(Kershaw 1993: 345)

In the field of elderly care, the term 'reminiscence' has a particular kind of meaning: the work done on modes of reminiscing by researchers such as Wong and Watt underpins a whole area of therapeutic activity, in which carers work with the elderly in order to use reminiscence, in its most positive aspects, as an aid to well-being. In theatre, too, 'reminiscence' has taken on a specific meaning in the last few decades. Reminiscence theatre is a mode of documentary theatre-making which takes the memories and experiences of older people as a basis for a theatre script or performance. It was influenced in its early years by developments in reminiscence therapy, although reminiscence theatre itself need not have a therapeutic dimension.

In fact, some of the earliest precursors of reminiscence theatre were driven by political rather than therapeutic aims. Foremost among these were the series of Radio Ballads that Ewan MacColl and Charles Parker produced for the BBC during the late 1950s and early 1960s. These programmes, such as *Singing the Fishing* (1960) and *The Travelling People* (1964), were described by producer Charles Parker as

a form of narrative documentary in which the story is told entirely in the words of the actual participants themselves as recorded in real life; in sound effects which are also recorded on the spot, and in songs which are based upon these recordings, and which utilise traditional or 'folk-song' modes of expression.

(BBC 2006: n.p.)

MacColl's background was in agitprop and political theatre, with groups such as Red Megaphones, Theatre of Action and Theatre Workshop – companies with a socialist agenda and a documentary approach to theatre-making, often involving local workers in both the scripting and performance of their plays. The MacColl/Parker Radio Ballads were not specifically *about* old age, but they foregrounded the memories, experiences and perspectives of older people because the majority of them were about working-class communities – fishermen, road-builders, railwaymen and miners – whose ways of life were rapidly changing and in some cases vanishing with the changing times. The final verse of MacColl's song 'The Travelling People' sums up something of the tone

> All you freeborn men of the travelling people
> Every tinker rolling stone and gypsy rover
> Winds of change are blowing, old ways are going
> Your travelling days will soon be over

(MacColl 1964)

MacColl's project, then, was part of his broader socialist cultural and political agenda, an agenda which was concerned with the state of the nation and in particular of its industrial working classes. Many early reminiscence theatre practitioners shared those politics to some degree, but the live reminiscence theatre companies which emerged in and after the late 1970s worked on a more local and individual basis, and were explicitly or indirectly inspired by therapeutic practices.

The term itself seems to have been used first by the Devon-based community theatre group Medium Fair when they established, in 1978, 'Fair Old Times', a subsidiary group specializing in theatre with and for older communities in Devon. Performing for the most part in local authority care homes for the elderly, the group developed documentary techniques which had already been used successfully in other contexts by the parent company. Part-funded by the Manpower Services Commission and Devon Social Services, Fair Old Times worked with Gordon and Dorothy Langley – a psychiatrist and a dramatherapist, respectively – in order to create a theatre which was explicitly rooted in the emerging practice of reminiscence therapy with the elderly. One of the company members of Fair Old Times was Baz Kershaw, who later described the theoretical basis of the company's work as follows:

> Reminiscence theatre is based on a therapeutic practice, reminiscence therapy, which aims to improve the psychological and social health of the elderly. Reminiscence by the elderly is held to be appropriate to this objective because the long-term memory improves with the aging process: thus memory increasingly becomes a powerful tool for the enhancement of identity, self-esteem, and self-confidence in the present. In Britain such enhancement is a much-needed compensation for the culture's treatment of many old people, who are ghettoized, through dependency, in residential homes.

(Kershaw 1993: 345)

The result was a series of fifteen shows between 1978 and 1982 which combined presentational and participatory techniques: dramatic scenes were interspersed with, and sometimes interrupted by audience members' reminiscences. Another company member Nick Sales described shows in which

> [d]iscussions and scenes and songs and slides follow each other in what appears to be no logical sequence at all. Sometimes songs and sketches are announced, sometimes they just emerge from the general discussion and take off, but always one or other of the performers is acting as coordinator, picking up comments from the audience and relaying them back into the discussion.
>
> (Langley and Kershaw 1981–82: 15)

But while Fair Old Times was working within a therapeutic framework, the company, like Ewan MacColl, was simultaneously looking for ways in which the dramaturgy of reminiscence could be combined with an alternative social vision, one which envisaged the possibility that the empowerment which reminiscence theatre could offer the elderly might also operate as a form of resistance to the ghettoization of old people in the very care homes in which they performed.

A rather different vision fuelled the work of the practitioner and the company whose names are now most firmly associated with reminiscence theatre. Age Exchange was set up as a professional company in London in 1983 by Pam Schweitzer. Schweitzer had experimented with intergenerational theatre work as the Education Officer for a voluntary organization working with pensioners. Her first project brought together a group of elderly people in a sheltered accommodation unit, and a group of sixteen- and seventeen-year-old school students who

> had prepared some questions and came equipped with tape recorders. They asked the older people about what life was like when they were their age, what they had worn, where they had gone for entertainment, how they had met boys, how they learned to dance and what music they liked to dance to, how they got their job and what they were paid. Because the young people knew they were going to perform these memories they listened intently and their questioning had a certain urgency.
>
> (Schweitzer 2007: 25)

After a careful process, which involved checking with the older people and valuing their expertise, the resulting scenes were played, both to the residents of the sheltered housing unit and also as part of an assessed A-level drama project. Schweitzer herself

> found this whole experience enlightening and encouraging. I had seen the power of reminiscence to revitalise older people, to put them in touch with their own past and with one another. From the work with the students I also saw that the young people had gained artistically, educationally and socially.
>
> (Schweitzer 2007: 25)

For Pam Schweitzer, however, working within a school curriculum also imposed a serious limitation: it meant that there was no scope for developing a production beyond a very few performances. In 1983 she set up Age Exchange theatre company on a professional basis in order that the memories of older people could be dramatized and toured by a company who 'could do 30 or 40 performances of the finished product, taking the show to thousands of other older people who had not been involved in the original creative process' (Schweitzer 2007: 25). The company has produced reminiscence theatre in a variety of forms and on a variety of topics: productions have included work with elders in London's Jewish, Indian and Irish communities; work which focused on particular areas or features of London, such as Blackheath; and, exceptionally, work based on the memories of a single person. *On the River* (1989) recorded the vanishing past of Thames river-workers in a way reminiscent of MacColl's Radio Ballads; and in 2000 was reworked in conjunction with writer Noel Greig, who developed a new and very different play, *In Full Flow*, from the original research material. Pam Schweitzer retired as Artistic Director of Age Exchange in 2005, but the company continues to produce a rich programme of intergenerational work, educational work, and work with and for the elderly.

The work of companies such as Age Exchange and Fair Old Times has been inspirational to many, and several other practitioners and companies have followed in their footsteps, both professionally and within community and educational contexts. A good indication of the interest that exists in pursuing and developing this kind of work is provided by the publications page of Age Exchange's website at http://www.age-exchange.org.uk/our_work/publications/index.html, which showcases a large number of reports, guides, handbooks and 'how-to' books, offering advice on reminiscence work.

Reminiscence theatre often works by subverting the unspoken 'rules' of conventional dramatic theatre: the rule that dramatic dialogue should be well-crafted, for example, may be subverted by the dialogue being 'verbatim' – told in the actual words of the remembering subjects. Much reminiscence theatre uses the dramaturgical methods of verbatim theatre – a process which, at its purest, involves the use of the precise words of the interviewed subject as the dialogue of a play, which is then performed (usually) by actors who take the parts of the real-life protagonists. In practice, the extent to which the writers or devisers intervene in editing and crafting subjects' interview responses into dramatic dialogue varies from one company to another. For some, absolute adherence to the subjects' actual words, speech patterns, accents and physical mannerisms is of the essence; others feel free to take a more liberal approach.

As with all verbatim theatre, the aesthetic and ethical issues that this kind of reminiscence work raises are by no means straightforward. Questions relating to respect for the subjects and their experiences are continually interwoven with questions about both 'authenticity' and dramatic form. A particularly important question concerns the slant which reminiscence theatre puts on the relationship between past and present: while reminiscence is inevitably about recalling the past, another of the unspoken rules of theatre as an art form is that it usually works best in the present tense. 'Presence' is one of the key attributes of a successful performer; 'don't *tell* me, *show* me' is a mantra of performer trainers of all sorts of traditions; and the theatrical 'ghosts' that Marvin Carlson talks about (Carlson 2003) are ghosts that are experienced in the present moment – in fact it is the present experience of them that constitutes the drama. Schweitzer herself was perfectly aware of this: it was her observation that older people, when reminiscing, would often 'almost perform their stories as though they were happening in the present' (Schweitzer 2007: 24) that alerted her to the theatrical possibilities of reminiscence as a form. Even so, the basic refrain of reminiscence theatre is 'I remember ...' – and plays that consist of people who sit on stage and talk about the past usually struggle to engage or excite. Subverting the unspoken rules of an art form has its risks, and one of the 'traps' of reminiscence theatre is that it can all too easily become all reminiscence and no theatre: and part of the skill of a good production lies in the effectiveness in which it translates the one into the other.

Not that aesthetic and artistic values are necessarily paramount in reminiscence theatre work. As with reminiscence therapy, or with dramatherapy with the elderly in which life-story work may play a prominent part (Wilder 1996, 1997), the greatest value of a theatre project, for those involved in it, may reside in the simple act of listening. That early phase in which older people are asked about the past by people who value what they have to say, may be the most important aspect of the project.

But theatre is something both more and less than therapy. A therapy session is primarily for the benefit of the clients; it may also benefit the therapist, who may learn from the process, but this is secondary. Some reminiscence theatre companies operate in just this way, but even Pam Schweitzer's early, intimate explorations with that first group of students and pensioners involved a slightly different 'contract' from this. That project had a dual aim: not only to facilitate the reminiscences and celebrate the experiences of the older generation, but also to enable the students to benefit from hearing the stories of the elders. Reminiscence theatre work may stay within this intimate compass, and often does so successfully, but even on this scale, other considerations are likely to creep in. In this case, it was the students' need to translate the stories of the elders into a theatrical performance that would get them good marks according to the criteria of their A-level assessment. Sometimes, then, the aesthetic values do not matter; but sometimes they do!

They begin to matter more urgently at the point where a reminiscence theatre group may see the need – as Schweitzer saw the need – to address a wider audience, 'taking the show to thousands of other older people who had not been involved in the original creative process' (Schweitzer 2007: 25). And at this point the intimacy of the initial shared memory work changes its nature; it becomes 'research' for a 'finished product' which will be a show playing to audiences who have a different, and less personal, stake in the narrative. As this happens, 'aesthetic' considerations – in the sense of decisions about how to tell the story most effectively for a wider audience – become increasingly important; and the wider that audience is the more important these considerations become. Schweitzer set up Age Exchange to take shows 'to thousands of older people' – but older people may not be the only audience that a reminiscence theatre production decides to address. If its aims include raising awareness of age-related issues among the wider population, it will need to find theatrical ways of engaging with an audience who have no initial stake in the narrative at all. The intimate sharing of a memory, perhaps between a few people, done primarily for the benefit of the sharer, is one thing. To tell a story to thousands of people so that it will make sense to them and enrich *their* lives is something else. (And, by definition, most of the reminiscence theatre work that is known about and written about is of this latter kind.) Reminiscence theatre constantly engages with the tensions between real-life experience in all its richness and formlessness, and the aesthetics of performance, with its own conventions and forms. These tensions may at times be greatly creative; at times they may lead to frustration or an artistic and/or ethical impasse. The following three brief examples demonstrate some of the strategies which different productions have used to negotiate these tensions.

Three reminiscence plays

a) The Exeter Blitz Project

I should preface my discussion of *The Exeter Blitz Project* by acknowledging that it is not one about which I am writing impartially, since it had links to my own AHRC *Staging Ageing* project. Directed by Helena Enright and Jessica Beck for the theatre group Viva Voce, the project commemorated the seventieth anniversary of the Exeter Blitz of May 1942, when the German Luftwaffe carried out bombing raids which reduced whole streets to piles of rubble, and changed the landscape of the city forever. The company interviewed twenty or so survivors who had been between the ages of six and twenty-five in 1942, and from their stories created a narrative featuring sixteen characters played by five professional actors. The theatre shows were supplemented by intergenerational schools workshops, and many of the participants and their families talked about the profound and lasting impact that their involvement in the project had had on them

Viva Voce – as the name suggests – bases its dramaturgy very firmly on verbatim techniques, not only in its processes but also in its performance aesthetic. Accordingly, each of the characters introduced themselves by name and by telling the audience the age that they were in 1942. The production design also evoked the 1940s in terms of costume, set and musical soundscape, an effect which was enhanced by the physical characteristics of the venue in which the production was staged: Exeter's Bike Shed Theatre is an intimate bare-brick cellar space which, as at least one reviewer noted, was 'an ideal location for this project, evoking, with pitch perfect sound effects, well-chosen music and props, the Morrison shelters and the blackouts, the austerity and simplicity of war-time Britain' (Silk 2012).

The dialogue did not shirk the issue of the repeated 'I remember...' refrain. Here, for example is a monologue by one of the characters, Roger Free, '11 years old in 1942':

> I can remember going to
> some sort of gang show in the,
> I don't know where it might've been,
> in a school somewhere.
> But um, there was a song
> in those days called
> 'Run Rabbit Run',
> have you ever heard of it?
> Well, there was a rabbit, well obviously,
> a human being dressed up as a rabbit,
> but with Hitler's unfailing, you know,
> quiff and moustache and so on,
> being chased across the stage.
> I can remember that so ...
> I can almost see that now.
> Just as ... again, taking the mickey out of him,
> cause I think, a lot of the time
> it was just taking the mickey out of this,
> he was supposed to be a wallpaper hanger,
> I think, and he was known for chewing carpets
> when he was in a rage, I mean these kind of,
> just folk things that probably weren't true at all,
> But we just saw him more or less
> as a figure of fun, really, more than anything,
> and Mussolini was just another ridiculous Eyetie.
> The Japanese were just sort of ferocious people
> that we didn't understand a' all.
> Other songs ... well, there was a song called
> 'Roll me over in the clover',
> which I think I probably missed
> the underlying implications of ... *(Laughs)*
> *(Female drags him up on the dance floor ... he protests does a little*
> *bit then breaks away.)*

The rhythms and patterns of everyday language do not always translate well to the stage, but in this case the language has been chosen and edited with a sense of playfulness, and as a result it becomes one of the theatrical pleasures of the production. Delivered by trained actors, the linguistic textures of everyday speech ('I can remember that so.../I can almost see that now / Just as ... again') alternated between the ordinary, the comic ('well, obviously, a human being dressed up as a rabbit') and the poetic.

The characters' narratives themselves, as might be expected, had an inherently dramatic quality; they were about life and death, as the comparatively peaceful events of everyday life built towards the devastation of the nights of the bombings. The characters were sharply delineated by the cast, enabling the audience to follow individual narratives; and characters moved easily between their past 'experiencing' selves (dancing, showing embarrassment, etc.) and also as their present-day, remembering selves, rethinking their experiences and commenting on them from a new perspective: '"Roll me over in the clover"/which I think I probably missed the underlying implications of'. Together these techniques created a vivid 'dramatic present', one which was completed by an audience whose common point of reference was not that of age, but of *locale*. The play did powerful intergenerational work, bringing together and offering a sense of community to people of different ages who already shared a sense of belonging to a place: a place whose present landscape is rooted in the events of the past.

b) Gay and Gray

A different kind of community, and a different kind of audience engagement, was envisaged by *Gay and Gray* – a play which I saw in 2010 in Chicago, performed by three older gay men to a small audience of the Senior Theatre Focus Group at the conference of the Association for Theatre in Higher Education. This was not the play's primary target audience, although it *was* an audience of people interested in theatre and ageing, and who were consequently predisposed to be sympathetic towards it. This performance was a restaging of part of a longer piece which had toured in the north-western United States, largely to audiences of gay men in community and educational contexts, and it comprised personal true-life stories drawn from interviews and condensed and woven into three interweaving monologues. The script was the product of a larger archival research project, documenting the lives of older members of the broadly defined gay community, and was based on interviews with fifty LGBTQ (Lesbian, Gay, Bisexual, Transgendered and Queer) elders: thirty men and twenty women. The actors themselves, though themselves both gay and gray, and working here on a not-for-profit basis, were all accomplished and professionally trained.

Through the stories of the three central characters the play charted the sexual and emotional histories of a generation of gay men: stories of coming out, of fears, of coming to terms with themselves, of having trouble coming to terms with themselves, and of the two major milestones in the life of the gay community: the Stonewall demonstrations of 1969, and the inception of the AIDS epidemic which decimated the gay community with appalling speed in the 1980s. In one of the narratives, for example, a man called Tom talks about how he had experienced the liberation of coming out as a gay man, but then was pressurized into moving back home to look after his homophobic father – a move that was meant to be for a few weeks but which lasted fifteen years:

So I moved in with him: and went back into the closet. Even after all that time living together, he'd say to me, 'You know, Tom, I really can't deal with your lifestyle …' He'd monitor my phone calls. 'Some guy called. Who are all these guys calling? I don't want any guys calling on my phone!' I moved in with him, lived with him, because I loved him. But I didn't like it. I couldn't be myself outside of the house, for fear of embarrassing him.

(Pennell et al. 2010: n.p.)

His father's eventual death, sad though it was for Tom, seemed to offer him once more some kind of freedom:

So, now he's gone. I thought – I've got to be me now … I drove down to Provincetown and I bought myself a rainbow flag, and I put it right up out front of the house my father left me. The next-door-neighbour said to me, 'It's about time you came out!' So I've got the house to myself. I thought to myself: 'I'm forty-six years old. I've got to be me now' … The mortgage is paid off. And I'm drinking. Heavily. Because my father just died. But those were also my salad days. Drinking. Going to bars. Going to bathhouses, rest areas … I was having the time of my life. Living large. Then it all came to a crashing halt. November 29th 1993. The day I was diagnosed with HIV.

(Pennell et al. 2010: n.p.)

The staging of *Gay and Gray* was deliberately minimalistic, consisting simply of bar stools (bars are an important environment for the gay community) and a piano. This simplicity was designed to facilitate touring to schools and community centres, and was effective enough in those terms. This did mean, however, that the play had none of the advantages of *mise-en-scène* which gave *The Exeter Blitz Project* its sense of theatricality and indeed of entertainment. Nor did *Gay and Gray* have that offbeat playfulness of language which enriched the *Blitz Project*. In fact, it seemed to have all the disadvantages of a form which can revert to the stasis of having people sitting on stage and soliloquizing about the past.

And on one level, indeed, this is what it was. But against that must be set the sense of urgency which enabled the play to embrace the potential limitations of reminiscence as a format, and then turn them into virtues. The play articulated a strong, campaigning element – a sense that these characters' life experiences mattered, and that it was important to pass them on to a new audience; and that since the mainstream media were unlikely to do that, it was up to theatre workers to do it in whatever way they could. And so its directness, and the painful honesty of the stories that were being told, made it so effective as documentary theatre.

As director, researcher and deviser Steven Pennell put it: 'The stories of the elder gay community aren't being told. How can you ask your grandparents about their life and experience? We don't have a history.' In the discussion after the show (a post-show discussion is often an integral element of this kind of applied theatre) this sense of urgency was reiterated and elaborated. The fact that the stories of the elder gay community are *not* being told has led to the younger gay community suffering from a lack of understanding of the journey that their parents' and grandparents' generation went through. And while it is not uncommon for a younger generation to ignore the lessons of its forebears, there is a particularly dangerous outcome of this particular silence. 'It is setting up another generation for another AIDS crisis,' explained one audience member. 'When I think of young people of this generation who have grown up with AIDS and still don't care if they are infected … and they don't have a sense of wanting a future. Or rather they can't see that future because they can't see beyond age thirty' (Pennell et al. 2010: n.p.).

Theatre has frequently been effective in giving a voice to those 'without histories': women's theatre, black theatre, queer theatre have all validated the experiences and the histories of 'minorities'. Reminiscence theatre has become an important way of giving a voice to the elderly – but once more we are reminded that the elderly are never *just* the elderly, but are also men, women, black, white, rich, poor, gay, straight and so on. The lessons that the gay community learned during the last few decades of the twentieth century were particularly painful ones, and the intensity of the belief that they must not be forgotten by the next generation is particularly urgent. The painfulness and the urgency of this community offer timely reminders that, in other communities, too, the 'reminiscences' of the older generation will contain things that should not be forgotten.

c) On Ageing

Both *Gay and Gray* and *The Exeter Blitz Project* were comparatively low-profile productions, playing for the most part to existing audience 'communities'. London's Young Vic Theatre is not exactly a free-market commercial venue, although it is effectively in competition, both for funds and for audiences, with the major subsidized London theatres and with the West End. It has a reputation for both progressive and educational work, and its audience demographic is composed predominantly of young people. Fevered Sleep is a theatre company that more usually specializes in site-specific performances and installations, and is broadly associated with the contemporary avant-garde theatre scene. The company and the venue seem at first to be an unlikely combination to stage a piece of verbatim theatre about old age and the experience of the elderly.

As it turned out, *On Ageing* was staged in 2010 by Fevered Sleep at the Young Vic to almost unanimous critical acclaim. The play was effectively a 'cross-over' piece, which took the verbatim techniques which had been well-known in applied and community theatre for many years and placed them on a mainstream London stage. The dialogue contained a mixture of memories and present impressions, and – as in Schweitzer's initial intergenerational experiment – schoolchildren articulated the thoughts and memories of the elderly. In this case the young actors were *very* young, aged between seven and thirteen, and they made little or no attempt to pretend to be anything other than their actual ages. They presented themselves as children even as they spoke the words of eighty-year-olds; both were 'present' simultaneously, and the play was sustained by the tension between 'two basic notions: children live in the immediate present while ageing is a process of accumulation of memories and objects' (Billington 2010: n.p.).

Occasionally, the theatrical device of having children speaking the scripted words of their elders became, as one dissenting critic described it, 'distressingly cute' (Coveney 2010: n.p.), but for the most part the disjunction between the thoughts of the old and the bodies of the young generated a theatrical energy that kept the audience slightly off-balance. This disequilibrium was intensified by a series of interspersed moments when the children talked about their 'own' lives, experiences and memories: about birthday parties and losing their milk teeth, for example. When a speaker began to talk, there was no way of knowing whether you were meant to be listening to the voice of the child you could see, or of the older person she might be impersonating. Most effectively, though, a great deal of the dialogue was very much in the present tense: the past and its memories were brought onto the stage more through the set than through the words. An initially nearly bare stage – consisting of a long conference-style table with microphones and glasses of water at which the children sat – was transformed during the course of the performance into a cluttered attic full of furniture, toys, books, ornaments, telephones, televisions: the memorabilia of a life. The production played to 98 per cent capacity, and its coverage in the national press enabled it to make a significant contribution to raising awareness of issues relating to the representation of ageing in contemporary culture.

Reminiscence theatre, then, comes in many forms and it can perform various functions. It can be undertaken as a therapeutic intervention, primarily for the benefit of the participants. It can be sourcework for social history or a rules-based method of devising a dramaturgical procedure in its own right. It can be a form of social activism and even, potentially, offer a framework for socio-political analysis. As Baz Kershaw puts it:

> the micro-level of oral history (through reminiscence) is a potential analytical scalpel for opening up the ingrained ideological assumptions about the construction of history and its significance for the present. In this way reminiscence theatre contains the possibility of a radical approach to the socio-political status quo.
>
> (Kershaw 1993: 346)

But reminiscence – and thus reminiscence theatre – can also quickly slide into nostalgia: a rose-tinted reaffirmation of the 'good old days' which produces immediate pleasure but which in the long run, far from empowering the subject in the present, can simply increase his or her sense of alienation. And while there is clearly great social value in taking performances into the care homes and sheltered housing units in which much reminiscence theatre takes place, the context of institutionalized care bears its own price: a limited range of opinions and discourses are encouraged and validated; others (such as dissent or expressions of dissatisfaction) are discouraged or even prohibited. For a group such as Fair Old Times, who saw the societal ghettoization of the elderly in local authority care homes as a major problem in itself, the contradictions between empowerment and accommodation, between subversion and the constraints of existing social reality were particularly sharply experienced. And even for those who approach reminiscence theatre with less of a radical intent, these conflicts and tensions are continually present.

Nonetheless, reminiscence theatre, at its best, is a powerful way of validating, celebrating and empowering the elderly and their life experiences. It is, by its nature, interactive – although the nature of that interactivity will vary. Sometimes the memories of older people become the research base from which a playwright or a company develops a script for professional or amateur performance by younger actors. Sometimes, as with Fair Old Times, the performance is participatory, with spontaneous contributions from the audience becoming part of the show. Sometimes the older performers themselves take centre stage, and the presence of their ageing bodies on the stage is an integral part of the performance: again, this can take place on an amateur or professional basis. But in all these cases, by making art out of memory, reminiscence theatre can assist positive ageing for the participants, and extend understanding of age-related issues to others. It may contain elements of what Wong and Watt call 'instrumental', 'transmissive' or even 'escapist/defensive' reminiscence, but its aesthetic and its implicit ideology tend to gravitate most strongly towards Wong and Watt's 'integrative reminiscence': reminiscence which helps the subject (which may by extension include the audience) to achieve a sense of self-worth and coherence with regard to his or her past. And in terms of dramatic and literary genres, this vision is essentially a 'comic' one, one which tends towards reconciliation and integration.

'An engaged lifestyle': The uses of theatre

Reminiscence theatre, then, amounts to more than a dramaturgical technique for writing and devising particular kinds of documentary- or verbatim-style shows. It is an activity which promises – and frequently delivers – benefits to the elderly themselves; and some of these benefits are directly related to the acknowledged value of reminiscence as a tool for positive ageing. But theatre, too, has its benefits for the elderly, some of which go beyond the scope of 'reminiscence'.

First of all, it is generally agreed that 'an engaged lifestyle is seen as an important component of successful ageing. Many older adults with high participation in social and leisure activities report positive wellbeing' (Adams, Leibrandt and Moon 2011: 683). This so-called activity theory of successful ageing is based on positive results which have been seen in a range of 'social, leisure, productive, physical, intellectual, service and solitary activities'

(Adams, Leibrandt and Moon 2011: 683). Participating in drama, theatre and performance is just one of many ways in which an older person might choose to embrace a more 'engaged lifestyle'.

There are reasons to believe, however, that as an essentially social activity which involves both mind and body, it may be a particularly valuable one. In fact, during the course of the last half-century or so, the potential of drama, theatre and performance for enhancing well-being among individuals and communities of all ages has been increasingly recognized. During this period there have been two key developments. Firstly, there was an increasing recognition that drama, as a participatory activity, was itself of individual and communal benefit: amateur and community drama, which started to flourish in the years between the wars, was increasingly seen as valuable cultural and educational activity, one which in its own right could contribute to people's well-being. As one of the earliest chroniclers and critics of the amateur dramatic movement, Norman Marshall, put it in 1947:

> There are tens of thousands of people whose lives are much fuller and happier because of the amateur societies. Acting gives them a chance of escape from their everyday environment; it stimulates them; it probably rids them of a number of inhibitions; it gives them confidence and poise and teaches them to speak and move with a certain amount of grace.
>
> (Marshall 1947: 85)

He goes on to add (with all the lofty condescension of the true theatre professional towards the amateur), 'Such is the glamour of the stage that it shines even on the amateur actor, giving him a new importance among his friends, and increased confidence in himself' (Marshall 1947: 85). Undeterred by such patronizing tones, the amateur theatre movement in the United Kingdom flourished in the mid-century years, and continues to do so.

Secondly, there was the growing belief that theatre could also offer techniques, ideas and methods which can be applied, outside the boundaries of theatre buildings and traditional places of performance, in a variety of ways in order to benefit individuals and groups. Of course, throughout history theatre has frequently been used to teach, or to address social issues. However, what we now think of as 'Applied Drama' or 'Applied Theatre' really emerged in the last three decades of the twentieth century. This ranges from the closely defined procedures of psychodrama, sociodrama or Boal's Forum Theatre, through a variety of forms of dramatherapy, educational theatre, 'playback theatre', theatre in institutions, community performances; what these forms and practices have in common is that they are explicitly designed to achieve change – 'often premeditated, change in a given societal circumstance' (Somers 2009: 194). As a comparative newcomer, the term 'Applied Drama/Theatre' is itself complex, and the limits of its reference are to some extent controversial precisely because of the very diversity of forms to which it can refer. It does, however, raise questions about 'to what or whom drama and theatre might be applied, and for what reasons, and whose values the application of theatre-making serves and represents' (Nicholson 2005: 5).

In the case of 'applying drama and theatre' to the elderly, whether through applied, participatory or social drama work, many of the benefits are those which are true of other groups and populations as well. There are particular social, emotional and even physical problems to which elderly people are especially prone, however, and which drama can address: these problems include isolation, boredom, lack of energy and depression. Participating in drama, whether the village pantomime or a Boalian Forum, can offer experiences which can ameliorate such issues. Typical benefits from such theatre work may include: relaxation, fun, pleasure, a sense of community and communal effort, making connections, taking control, legitimizing feelings, working through feelings, gaining insight into self and others, validating experience and making connections between past and present.

As a result there has been a growing interest in theatre work with the elderly, ranging from targeted Senior Theatre and Intergenerational Theatre work with specially constituted groups, through to initiatives by mainstream civic theatres which involve taking a more positive interest in their older audiences. The latter, to some extent, goes against the grain of much contemporary arts policy, which tends to focus on the younger audience. For several years, Arts Council England, for example, have been insistent that their strategy for 'increasing opportunities and broadening the range of theatre-related activity in which young people can participate ... is a priority within Arts Council England's national policy for theatre' (from the executive summary document of ACE 2007 *Paving the Way: Mapping of Young People's Participatory Theatre*). So it is cheering to discover the range of theatre-based activities for older people that is quietly developing.

As well as numerous voluntary groups and organizations working theatrically in various ways with senior citizens, there are professional companies who make work with the elderly an important part of their programmes. A good example of one such group, and how its work with the elderly came about, is Ladder to the Moon (http://www.laddertothemoon. co.uk/), a London-based theatre company which

> began as a street arts group working with young people and noticed that older people were often in a similar situation with nothing to do. This led them to specialise over the last five years in working with older people in care homes and hospitals in London. Professional actors, trained in interactive theatre, come into the health care setting as 'key characters'. The actors treat patients or residents, staff and visitors as part of the same 'virtual world' they are creating in their piece and respond in character. A piece is created through prior research and consultation with the members of the organisation and produced to operate at different levels so that it is accessible to someone with dementia. Examples of pieces have included retellings of the film *Casablanca* and plays by Shakespeare.
>
> (Cutler 2009: 48)

Other examples include The Clod Ensemble (London), a radical performance and theatre group which uses a wide range of media and maintains a strong emphasis on music and movement. In its early days it shared premises with a day centre for older people; as a result it developed a strand of work with and for the elderly: 'Extravagant Acts for Mature People' is a series of free lunchtime arts events and performances for people over sixty. The Ensemble has also run interactive projects with groups of senior citizens in Islington, including a range of drama workshops, as well as a large intergenerational project which resulted in a Swing Night, first performed at Battersea Town Hall in 2006, and recently revived as part of the London Creativity and Wellbeing Week 2006. The Liverpool-based Collective Encounters employs theatre as a tool for social change and runs a variety of participatory programmes. Their Third Age Acting Company, which meets weekly, is in its fifth year at the time of writing, with members of the company 'developing their acting skills, devising performances and undertaking local and national tours of their work' (Collective Encounters 2012: n.p.), including Forum Theatre performances for the National Pensioners' Convention and local NHS workers.

The charity and pressure group Age Concern (now part of Age UK) has been very active in partnering theatre work involving older people. For example, they commissioned Glass Shot (Wales) to produce a community theatre project in 2008 as part of their Gwanwyn Festival, which dramatized the plight of older people, including dementia sufferers, in care situations; a follow-up project called 'Giving the Elderly a Voice' was also commissioned by Age Concern, devised around issues identified by older people (Cutler 2009: 48). Age Concern has also worked in partnership with The National Theatre to run a pilot year of a 'Discover for Life' programme for older people, and The Library Theatre, Manchester, is helping them to deliver a series of chair-based dance and fitness sessions in sheltered accommodation. The Library Theatre Company has prioritized work with older people for several years, and has offered workshops, residencies, play-reading sessions and in-depth activity days. Of the regional repertory theatres, however, West Yorkshire Playhouse, can claim one of the longest traditions of working with older people. Its 'Heydays' group for the over-fifty-fives has been meeting weekly for the last twenty-two years. Its total membership is over four hundred, and

> [s]everal members of the existing drama group have created their own 'Feeling Good Theatre Company'. This has created work on issues of ageing and has been commissioned to produce shows by the West Yorkshire Police and the National Osteoporosis Society. Both shows have toured including in residential settings. New work by the Company is showcased at the Playhouse. The Heydays group also gets special offers to performances at the Playhouse which therefore helps build its audience.
>
> (Cutler 2009: 50)

Intervention and healing

In the previous chapter we talked about theatrical representations of dementia. But theatre is beginning to explore the possibilities not only of representing dementia but also of offering interventions which might benefit dementia patients. The work of Helga and Tony Noice has (rightly) attracted attention among those interested in the potential of theatre for healing. Working with groups of community-dwelling older adults, the Noices have introduced theatre activities (acting classes in effect) into the curriculum of the care home and monitored the results. In a recent study, for example, they worked with participants of an average 81.7 years, not particularly well-educated, and half of whom needed mobility aids (walkers, canes, wheelchairs or motorized chairs). They organized regular sessions in which participants engaged in

> increasingly demanding exercises designed to have participants experience the essence of acting (i.e., to become engrossed in communicating the meaning of the dialogue so that obvious situation-specific cognitive/affective/physiological alterations occurred in their demeanor).
>
> (Noice and Noice 2009: 62)

There was a strict emphasis on active involvement in the course sessions, which were structured, like HE-level theatre arts instruction, so that passivity was never an option (Noice and Noice 2009: 72).

It might be thought that the one thing that acting classes would help with would be memory training. In fact, memorization was one of the things which the Noices' theatre-training programme deliberately left out. There were two reasons for this: firstly because the Noices differentiated their acting intervention programme from short-term training programmes targeted at improving the test measures themselves (such as mnemonic techniques designed to help participants learn lists). The problem with test-oriented training is that it tends to have only limited broader effects beyond the tests at which they were targeted. The programme was aimed at exploring the possibility of all-round cognitive gains which would be applicable in other areas of life. Secondly, while acknowledging the importance of memory as a form of 'deep processing' in the actor's task, the Noices expressly wanted the participants (many of whom perceived themselves, or were perceived, as having memory problems) to be able to focus on what the Noices regarded as the 'core process' of acting: that is to say the unitary process of understanding and communicating meaning through multiple modes of human action and interaction. This notion of the multimodal is an important one in the thinking of the Noices; and their training programme paid particular attention to the cognitive, emotional and physiological modes – that is to say, the actor's/character's thoughts; the emotions that these generate; and the body language, facial expressions and gestures that arise from them. In order to achieve this, participants were not required to memorize lines: dialogue was kept short and easy to assimilate, and all the scenes and exercises were performed script-in-hand.

Much social psychology involves proving through controlled experiment what was suspected at the level of common sense in the first place. Common sense might well suspect that for elderly participants, engagement with novel activities could produce cognitive gains – and there have been other studies which have suggested that this might be true. But not to the extent of this: in Noice and Noice's study the cognitive improvements of the acting participants in nearly all respects were significantly higher than expected, and higher, too, than those of participants in control groups (Noice and Noice 2009: 75).

Results were measured in relation to two sets of control groups – a no-treatment group and an other-treatment (singing) group – using standard psychological scales such as the Immediate East Boston Memory Test and the Ryff Personal Growth Scale. Noice and Noice report that 'the intervention produced significant cognitive and affective gains in the acting group. Of the eight cognitive measures, only the digit-span tests failed to demonstrate improvement' (Noice and Noice 2009: 70). Gratifyingly, the attributes where increase was measured were those whose absence or decline was most strongly associated with the likelihood of Alzheimer's.

The acting course also had a measurable knock-on effect in other aspects of participants' lives. For example, watching TV became a very active process, rather than a passive one, for participants, as they began to 'attend closely to the background events, analyze the actors' styles, or try to anticipate the next incident … basing their judgments on their newly acquired knowledge of Acting' (Noice and Noice 2009: 71–72). This increased evidence of active engagement elsewhere is itself beneficial to well-being.

The work of the Noices gives good experimental and empirical reason to think what many have long suspected: that acting is good for you. To engage in theatrical acting – even at a most basic aesthetic level – involves immersing oneself in a wide variety of simultaneous cognitive, emotional and physiological processes: the goals of a character, the characteristics of a character, the relationships (material, spiritual, emotional) between that character and others in her story, when to move and speak, how to hold the balance between immersion in the fictive world and awareness of the non-fictive reality of the rehearsal room or studio, the experience of that heightened and often disjunctive awareness of self that performance – especially in front of one's peers – generates. Furthermore, as the Noices argue,

> almost all dramatic situations involve some sort of problem to be solved. That is, one character wants something and the other character stands in the way. Therefore, in every dramatic transaction, the actor is trying to overcome an obstacle to achieving his or her objective, requiring the actor to stay alert to all input from the other characters that could affect achieving that objective. Once again, this effort requires a high degree of mental–emotional–physiological involvement. Also, this involvement must occur in any acting performance, whether in the short exercises and scenes we employ to avoid the need for memorization, or in full-length plays performed from memory by professional actors.
>
> (Noice and Noice 2009: 73)

Acting is a demanding multimodal activity and one which appears to lead to an 'increase of cerebral activation which, in turn, would contribute to improved cognitive performance' (Noice and Noice 2009: 74). But because acting is also such a holistic activity, it is not easy to isolate one aspect from the rest in order to say definitively that *this rather than that* is what accounts for the participants' increased cognitive benefits. Indeed, it may be that it is this very holism – 'the multiple and highly varied sources of stimulation involved in the acting process' (Noice and Noice 2009: 72) and the number of simultaneous levels on which the actor has to work, which is the key determinant of healthy cognitive development.

In a study which looked, not just at acting classes such as the Noices' but at the effect of stimulating activities in general on the ageing brain and the development of dementia, R. S. Wilson and D. A. Bennett suggested that such activities exert their influence by 'affecting the development or maintenance of the interconnected neural systems that underlie different forms of cognitive processing' (Wilson and Bennett 2003: 89). It has long been known that successful ageing can often be traced to habits built up in early years and mid-life, and that an enriched cognitive environment early in life can protect against cognitive decline; the Noices' claim, however, is more radical. It is that an intervention which provides a rich multimodal experience, even over a short period, *late* in life can also provide such protection. The proposition that actor training may be able to alter the physical structure of the brain in ways that make it harder for a dementia to take hold is an exciting one.

PART IV

The Value(s) of Old Age

Chapter 9

On Longevity

M uch of this book focuses on the way drama, theatre and performance engage either with old age as a socio-cultural category, or with old age as a lived experience, or with old age as a combination of the two. In this chapter, however, I will focus on something slightly different: on old age as an *idea*. In particular I want to explore some of our own culture's ideas about the notions of extreme old age, and to do so through a particular interplay between literature and performance on the one hand, and science, mythology and philosophy on the other. That may sound as if we are in the domain of science fiction, and that is not far from the truth. More strictly, though, we are in the realm of the 'theatre of ideas'.

'Theatre of ideas', it must be admitted, is a term which has rather fallen out of use in both literary and performance criticism: relationships between ideas, ideologies and performances are generally regarded as being too complex for such a neat formulation to be of much use. When the term *was* more critically current, however, it was generally used to refer to that 'intellectual movement which began to dominate [western theatre] towards the end of the [nineteenth] century' (Fallon 1944: 424) and to the successors of that movement. One writer who is usually held up as typifying the British theatre of ideas, with all its merits and all its faults, is George Bernard Shaw. It is with him that we begin.

'Our election cry is "Back to Methuselah!"': The politics of longevity

Shaw's *Back to Methuselah (A Metabiological Pentateuch)* is, perhaps, one of his works in which the 'theatre' most obviously takes a back seat to the 'ideas'. It is, as its title indicates, a cycle of plays, rather than a single drama, and it comprises five plays altogether: *In the Beginning: B.C. 4004 (In the Garden of Eden), The Gospel of the Brothers Barnabas: Present Day, The Thing Happens: A.D. 2170, Tragedy of an Elderly Gentleman: A.D. 3000* and *As Far as Thought Can Reach: A.D. 31,920*. All of these are contextualized by a lengthy philosophical *Preface*. The range of settings, from the Garden of Eden to thirty thousand years in the future, enables Shaw to deploy a variety of cultural as well as intellectual frames, from the mythical to the futuristic, by way of his own more familiar contemporary English settings; all five plays, however, are written in Shaw's unmistakable, provocatively ironic, dramatic voice.

The cycle was written in the years 1918–20, immediately after the Great War, and was Shaw's personal response and reaction to the War and its appalling carnage. And while many European cultural figures and movements responded to the questions raised by the War by an immersion in the irrational (Dadaism, Surrealism, etc.), Shaw typically reacted with his own peculiar and provocative form of rationalism, elaborating an argument he had made in an earlier anti-militaristic pamphlet in which he had advocated 'a general raising of human character through the deliberate cultivation and endowment of democratic virtue' (Shaw 1914: n.p.). In *Back to Methuselah* he sketches out a way in which this democratic virtue might actually be cultivated. Starting from the premise that the problems facing the industrialized societies of the early twentieth century are so complex that it has become impossible to govern them properly, he proposes the solution, which depends on a combination of 'Creative Evolution' and 'Voluntary Longevity'. These are ideas which he introduces in the *Preface* in the context of a rather general philosophical discussion of the possibilities of the improvement of humanity. Within the five plays, however, he takes these theoretical concepts to their imaginative conclusions.

In *The Gospel of the Brothers Barnabas* (set in the 'present day'), the eponymous brothers, Franklyn and Conrad, offer crisis-ridden post-war British politicians a new electoral policy:

FRANKLYN: Our program is only that the term of human life shall be extended to three hundred years.
LUBIN: (*Softly*) Eh?
BURGE: (*Explosively*) What!
SAVVY: Our election cry is 'Back to Methuselah!'

(Shaw 1965a: 882)

The world needs such a programme, according to the Brothers Barnabas, because it is the only way to avoid another world war. It is not that politicians are inept, they explain; rather that the skills and wisdom needed to govern a twentieth-century society simply cannot be attained within the traditional four-score and ten years of the human lifespan.

FRANKLYN: The war went England's way; but the peace went its own way, and not England's way nor any of the ways you had so glibly appointed for it. Your peace treaty was a scrap of paper before the ink dried on it. The statesmen of Europe were incapable of governing Europe. What they needed was a couple of hundred years training and experience: what they had actually had was a few years at the bar or in a counting-house or on the grouse moors and golf courses. And now we are waiting, with monster cannons trained on every city and seaport, and huge aeroplanes ready to spring into the air and drop bombs every one of which will obliterate a whole street, and poison gases that will strike

	multitudes dead with a breath, until one of you gentlemen rises in his helplessness to tell us, who are as helpless as himself, that we are at war again …
CONRAD:	We're not blaming you: you hadn't lived long enough. No more had we. Can't you see that three-score-and-ten, though it may be long enough for a very crude sort of village life, isn't long enough for a complicated civilization like ours? Flinders Petrie has counted nine attempts at civilization made by people exactly like us; and every one of them failed just as ours is failing … We shall go to smash within the lifetime of men now living unless we recognize that we must live longer.

(Shaw 1965a: 884)

This is the imaginative leap that sustains the entire cycle: what if the human lifespan could be extended sufficiently to enable political leaders to accrue the wisdom to govern well? Not that it would only be the élite that benefited from extended lifespans.

FRANKLYN:	When we get matured statesmen and citizens –
LUBIN:	(*Stopping short*) Citizens! Oh! Are the citizens to live three hundred years as well as the statesmen?
CONRAD:	Of course.
LUBIN:	I confess that had not occurred to me (*He sits down abruptly, evidently very unfavourably affected by this new light*).

(Shaw 1965a: 888–89)

Shaw's provocatively simple notion is part of a broadly utopian tendency in his writing that keeps surfacing through his satire. For all his apparent cynicism Shaw articulates a belief, if not in human perfectibility, then at least in the desirability of striving towards it. As one critic has put it, Shaw's 'perspective is evolutionary, and he thinks in terms of progress toward goals rather than their actual attainment' (Wisenthal 1974: 9). And since this progress is irrevocably time-based, the attainment of old age – Voluntary Longevity – becomes Shaw's not-entirely-frivolous answer to the failures of civilization.

The rest of the cycle then plays out the imaginative consequences of this basic idea. In *The Thing Happens: A.D. 2170*, longevity has not become an official policy, but it has been adopted by some enlightened souls, and this sets events in motion. In *Tragedy of an Elderly Gentleman: A.D. 3000*, the bleakest of the five plays, a race of long-livers has evolved, but it has been found to be incompatible with the rest of the world, which has remained more or less unchanged. These new humans have solved nearly all social and economic problems and have set up an isolated rational society on the islands of Ireland and England (the outer fringes of civilization), which a select few short-lived humans are occasionally allowed to visit: now a party of statesmen and military strategists have arrived to consult an 'oracle' about their own political problems. What they do not know is that the main political debate among the long-livers is, effectively, about whether to allow the short-livers to continue to exist at all. One of them explains to the Elderly Gentleman,

> We have two great parties: the Conservative party and the Colonization party. The Colonizers are of opinion that we should increase our numbers and colonize. The Conservatives hold that we should stay as we are, confined to these islands, a race apart, wrapped up in the majesty of our wisdom on a soil held as holy ground for us by an adoring world, with our sacred frontier traced beyond dispute by the sea … Five minutes ago that was my political faith. Now I do not think there should be any shortlived people at all.
>
> (Shaw 1965a: 924)

The very presence of the Elderly Gentleman manages to arouse in his guide some of the feelings of hate which the long-livers seemed to have transcended. She goes on to conclude

> that we who live three hundred years can be of no use to you who live less than a hundred, and that our true destiny is not to advise and govern you, but to supplant and supersede you. In that faith I now declare myself a Colonizer and an Exterminator.
>
> (Shaw 1965a: 925)

The play stops short of announcing the extermination of humanity as we know it as a general policy decision, but in the course of the action it becomes clear, not only to the long-livers but also to the Elderly Gentleman himself, that the superiority of the long-livers is such that '[w]e are worms before these fearful people: mere worms' (Shaw 1965a: 931). Like Gulliver, confronted, at the end of his travels, with the rational Houyhnhnms, the Elderly Gentleman loses his faith in what he thought to be human nature. Unable to return to normal 'civilization', he dies on the island, mercifully killed by the touch of the Oracle.

In *Back to Methuselah*, then, old age becomes the natural and necessary condition of an evolved – and improved – humanity. But this is old age only in a very specific sense: age measured in chronological years and moral enrichment, rather than in bodily change. There *is* bodily change as people age – at least in the society envisaged in *Tragedy of an Elderly Gentleman* – but it has been dramatically slowed down to enable the moral development to continue. But by the final play of the cycle, Shaw is attempting to imagine ways in which the body might be transcended completely. *As Far As Thought Can Reach: A.D. 31,920* is set in a 'far-distant future when humankind has evolved into god-like Ancients who live for centuries in their serene, intensely intellectual utopia' (Sparks 1997: 166). Into this world an inventor (named Pygmalion!) introduces a pair of beautiful, laboratory-made human figures: '*a man and woman of noble appearance, beautifully modelled and splendidly attired*' (Shaw 1965a: 951). Within minutes of their introduction, however, these androids/automata/

avatars of the New Adam and New Eve have shown enough of the old human spirit to turn vicious and kill their inventor. The Ancients destroy them painlessly, but their existence is used as a moral lesson. Tracing a line from the child's doll to Pygmalion's automaton with its 'perfection of resemblance to life' (Shaw 1965a: 956) they go on to describe the human body – even the long-lived body of the ancients – as a doll which needs eventually to be discarded.

THE HE-ANCIENT: Look at us. Look at me. This is my body, my blood, my brain; but it is not me. I am the eternal life, the perpetual resurrection; but (*Striking his body*) this structure, this organism, this makeshift, can be made by a boy in a laboratory, and is held back from dissolution only by my use of it. Worse still, it can be broken by a slip of the foot, drowned by a cramp in the stomach, destroyed by a flash from the clouds. Sooner or later, its destruction is certain.

THE SHE-ANCIENT: Yes: this body is the last doll to be discarded.

(Shaw 1965a: 957)

The play ends with an even more messianic note of transcendence. As a coda to the whole cycle, some of the characters from the first play reappear as (disembodied) spirits. We hear from Adam and Eve, but also from Lilith: Lilith, who came before Adam and Eve, who was present in the first play only by report, and who gave life to both Adam and Eve by dividing herself into their two bodies. Now, in the final moments of the play she visualizes the possibility of the total transcendence of these bodies, which were her bequest to humanity. She rejoices that

the impulse I gave them in that day when I sundered myself in twain and launched Man and Woman on the earth still urges them: after passing a million goals they press on to the goal of redemption from the flesh, to the vortex freed from matter, to the whirlpool in pure intelligence that, when the world began, was a whirlpool in pure force. And though all that they have done seems but the first hour of the infinite work of creation, yet I will not supersede them until they have forded this last stream that lies between flesh and spirit, and disentangled their life from the matter that has always mocked it.

(Shaw 1965a: 962)

The freeing of the consciousness (what Shaw calls 'pure intelligence') from matter is, in the tradition of much effective science-fiction writing, both very traditional and very forward-looking. It looks simultaneously back to medieval theology and forward to cyborg manifestoes and late twentieth-century debates about the conceptual challenges posed by the emergence of the virtual- or cyber-self in 'computer-mediated environments, [where] the representation is all there is … and the difference between on-line representation of self and "actual" self is utterly nonexistent' (Waskull and Douglas 1997: 389). It prefigures, too, some of the more dramatic reframing of concepts of consciousness, such as Donna Haraway's famous take on the Genesis myth: 'The cyborg would not recognize the Garden of Eden; it is not made of mud and cannot dream of returning to dust' (Haraway 1991: 32). Haraway's cyborg is not one of the children of Eve, but it may be a rather distant descendant of Lilith.

Bernard Shaw described *Back to Methuselah* as his *magnum opus* (Gahan 1997: 215). Critics and scholars since then have described it, depending on their viewpoint, either as 'an unwatchable dramatic dead end or an important modernist experiment that merits comparison with the work of Bertolt Brecht and James Joyce' (Moran 2010: 149). It is probably both of these, but for those who find it 'unwatchable' it may be that this is an ironic result of the relationship between its form and its content. At the heart of the play's ideology is a divorce between body and mind which enables the body to 'host' the maturing mind for longer. And this mirrors, in a strange way, another kind of divorce between mind and body, one that lies at the heart of the play's dramaturgy. Shaw has often been accused of being an over-cerebral playwright, one whose dramaturgy turns the theatre into a debating chamber, and who frequently offers a treatise on, rather than an embodiment of, the ideas with which his plays deal. The charge was made first, and most famously, by his contemporary Richard Aldington, who asserted that

> Bernard Shaw is a great literary journalist, which is just as rare as any other kind of great writer. He is a most fluent and effective pamphleteer, expounding his convictions with splendid clarity and vigour, buffeting his opponents, and animating his words with verve and wit. Moreover, he has an innate gift of theatre which he has disciplined to a high state of efficiency ... This excellent stage-craft has enabled him to give vigour, interest and even a semblance of life to ideas on the stage which, in the hands of a less splendid virtuoso, would have been flaccid and dull. But I cannot see him as a great creative artist, because he is almost wholly cerebral. There is no deep physical life in his writings, and his feelings are abstract and without passion – I don't mean sexual passion, though that is true as well. His writing is not of things, people, situations and relations, feelings, passions, but of ideas about them.
>
> (Aldington [1931] 1998: 98)

The accusation is not always justified, but in *Back to Methuselah* it is hard to contradict. Nor is this just the benefit of hindsight: the play was a cultural event without ever being a theatrical hit, admired for its 'sustained intellectual quality' but evoking only a lukewarm response in audiences and critics (see Evans 1976: 17).

The divorce between body and mind which is both a constant theme and an unintended structural feature of *Back to Methuselah* is itself a problematic issue in terms of contemporary ageing studies. Here the mind/body relationship is a complex affair, not one to be simply shrugged off by positing a body whose rate of deterioration has been slowed down. On one level, indeed, Shaw's imaginative solution to mankind's problems seems so unrealistic as to be simply naïve. His concept of Voluntary Longevity is deeply rooted in another of his scientific – or pseudo-scientific – views. In his Preface to the play, he offers a

> history of the conflict between the view of Evolution taken by the Darwinians (though not altogether by Darwin himself) and called Natural Selection, and that which is emerging, under the title of Creative Evolution, as the genuinely scientific religion for which all wise men are now anxiously looking.
>
> (Shaw 1965b: 507)

In this conflict Shaw places himself firmly on the side of 'Creative Evolution'. Describing himself as a 'neo-Lamarckian', he allies himself with that other major nineteenth-century theorist of evolution, and champions Lamarckian evolutionary theory in the following terms:

> Let us fix the Lamarckian evolutionary process well in our minds. You are alive; and you want to be more alive. You want an extension of consciousness and of power. You want, consequently, additional organs, or additional uses of your existing organs: that is, additional habits. You get them because you want them badly enough to keep trying for them until they come. Nobody knows how: nobody knows why: all we know is that the thing actually takes place.
>
> (Shaw 1965b: 510)

The force behind evolution, in Shaw's version of neo-Lamarckian theory, becomes not natural selection – or, as Shaw insists on calling it, 'Circumstantial Selection' – but sheer force of will: specifically, *human* will. Citing the work of German biologist August Weismann, Shaw asserts confidently that '[a]mong other matters apparently changeable at will is the duration of individual life' (Shaw 1965b: 506).

A few decades earlier, Weismann had published the first detailed formal theory of why ageing happens. His reflections on 'The Duration of Life' led him to the conclusion that 'the origin of death [lay], not in the waste of single cells, but in the limitation of their powers of reproduction. Death takes place because the worn-out tissue cannot forever renew itself, and because a capacity for increase by means of cell-division is not everlasting, but finite' (Weismann 1889: 21). Shaw argues that the logical implication of Weismann's position is 'that death is not an eternal condition of life, but an expedient introduced to provide for continual renewal without overcrowding' and that therefore ageing can be reprogrammed by sheer force of human will (Shaw 1965b: 506). Moreover, Shaw insists, three score and ten is insufficient; 'men do not live long enough … for all the purposes of high civilization', but '[p]resumably, however, the same power that made this mistake can remedy it. If on opportunist grounds Man now fixes the term of his life at three score and ten years, he can equally fix it at three hundred, or three thousand' (Shaw 1965b: 506).

Few plays can ever have been written with such an explicit intention of persuading an audience to take a particular view in a scientific debate: the energy that drives the imaginative narrative is completely grounded in the detailed scientific and philosophical argument with Darwin and Darwinianism which Shaw expounds in the Preface. Nor does Shaw's interest end with the theory of science: what really energizes him is the relationship between scientific theory and its social and political consequences. While it would be doing Shaw an injustice to say that the interlinked dramas 'merely illustrate' the ideas which he adumbrates there, the programmatic nature of the enterprise is clear.

Nearly a century on, it has become clear that Shaw was on the wrong side of the argument about evolution.

> Shaw's promotion of Creative Evolution was always wrong, always shallow, and often rather cheap ... [I]t is impossible to take Shaw's claim to being a ... deep biological thinker at all seriously, and this is not simply the result of hindsight strengthened by seventy years of genetics, 'chromosomes and hormones,' and the discovery of DNA. Even his contemporaries found Shaw easy to dismiss on this level ... Peter J. Bowler remarks that 'Shaw seems to have felt that he was part of a new wave of support for Lamarckism, but in fact his claim that it represented the spiritual salvation of the evolution movement was no longer fashionable even outside science.'
>
> (Shippey 1997: 202)

It is, however, by no means clear that what Shaw has to say is totally irrelevant. Twenty-first-century debates about the nature of ageing no longer turn to Lamarck or Weismann for validation, but the hard question of just *why* ageing occurs remains unresolved, even within a Darwinian framework. Tom Kirkwood, Britain's first Professor of Biological Gerontology, has written vigorously and repeatedly about the 'unnecessary nature of ageing', in tones and language that are sometimes unnervingly reminiscent of Shavian polemic.

> Two of the commonest ideas about ageing ... are wrong. The first of these is that ageing is *inevitable* because we just have to wear out. The second is that ageing is *necessary* and we are programmed to die because otherwise the world would be impossibly crowded. But ageing is neither inevitable nor necessary, at least not in the way that many suppose. This is good news if we hope eventually to improve the condition and quality of life in old age.
>
> (Kirkwood 1999: 52)

Broadly speaking, the main scientific theories of ageing can be divided into two camps: theories of programmed ageing and theories of non-programmed ageing. Both of these broad divisions have their internal disagreements and their subdivisions; there are several versions of programmed ageing theories, and there are also multiple competing non-programmed theories. It should be stressed, however, that these are scientific debates – debates within a mainstream community of biologists whose basic framework includes the mechanisms of Darwinian evolution through natural selection. They have nothing to do with pseudo-scientific or religiously motivated concepts such as 'Intelligent Design'. Among the advocates of both programmed and non-programmed ageing, there are differences of detail and emphasis. The central question, however, on which there is no consensus is: do organisms age by design or by mistake?

This is a controversy which has existed in one form or another for over 150 years, ever since the publication of Darwin's *On the Origin of Species by Means of Natural Selection, or the Preservation of Favoured Races in the Struggle for Life* (1859). While Darwin did not specifically address the question of ageing in any detail, the implications of his work were soon picked up by those with an interest in the ageing process. Weismann's theory, far from offering the potentially infinite longevity that Shaw wished to see in it, was actually one of the earliest contributions to what is now generally known as programmed ageing theory. This holds that 'life expectancy is predetermined and timed for individual species, with cells programmed to divide a certain number of times. Functional changes in the cells cause ageing of the cells and thus the organism' (*Mosby's Medical Dictionary*, eighth edition, 2009 online). Non-programmed ageing theories, on the other hand, hold that 'Ageing is not programmed but results from accumulation of somatic damage' (Kirkwood 2008: 117) either as a passive result of an organism's deterioration over time or as an unfortunate side effect of some function (such as reproduction) that is actually beneficial to the organism in its early life, but which exacts a price of molecular deterioration in later life.

The question of why ageing occurs remains a moot one, and majority opinion has leaned in different directions at different times. In the late 1970s, according to Kirkwood, 'most gerontologists inclined to the view that ageing was programmed, like development, and only a few supported the view that ageing was "stochastic" – that is, driven by the chance accumulation of mistakes' (Kirkwood 1999: 67). Today the balance has changed, and the majority of gerontologists and other medical researchers, including Kirkwood himself, are adherents of a version of non-programmed ageing theory. The debate, though, is far from over: the pendulum swings back and forth (see, for example, Goldsmith 2011), and any more detailed account of the contemporary scientific debates about programmed ageing lies outside the scope of this book. It is, however, valuable to see how deeply embedded these current debates are in the cultural history of the twentieth century, and the social and political meanings which became attached to them.

Now, in the early twenty-first century, we are experiencing at first hand some of the actual social, political and economic implications which have accompanied an increase in the longevity of average western lives that is (compared to Shaw's vision, at least) comparatively slight. Consequently, as Kirkwood argues, it has become increasingly important to explore the ways in which our understanding of the mechanisms of ageing may contribute to improvements in the condition and quality of life in old age. Shaw's own perspective on the problem was – in its own utopian way – a somewhat utilitarian one: how, he asked, might increased longevity (for some or all) benefit civilization as a whole? His characters debate the idea passionately, but in *Back to Methuselah*, it remains at the level of political fantasy. When the theme of longevity was taken up by another early twentieth-century, political playwright, however, the focus shifted from the societal and the utilitarian effects of longevity, to its personal and emotional effects.

'The end of immortality!': Karel Čapek's *The Makropulos Secret* (1922)

Karel Čapek's play *The Makropulos Secret* (also known as *The Makropulos Case*) is an important text in a consideration of old age in performance, not only in its own right, but also because of its operatic adaptation by Čapek's fellow-Czech, Leos Janáček, which will be discussed later in this section. Janáček's opera, in turn, became the inspiration for and the subject of a famous and much-quoted essay by Bernard Williams, whose discussion of *The Makropulos Secret*, and its implications for our understanding of death, old age and mortality, is one of the classic essays of twentieth-century British philosophy. Williams' position, broadly speaking, is that death gives meaning to life, and that immortality, or even extreme longevity, becomes intolerable because of the meaninglessness that it necessarily entails. But behind this rigorously argued philosophical proposition lies a complex history of ideas and performances. To follow the details of this history, we need to begin with the ill-defined relationship between George Bernard Shaw and Karel Čapek.

Čapek's play came out in 1922, just a year after the publication of *Back to Methuselah* and the relationship between the two texts has been much debated. In his own lifetime Čapek was seen as a 'Shavian' writer, and there are certainly details of plot and characterization which suggest that Čapek knew Shaw's play well. Čapek himself, however, always denied that he had read *Back to Methuselah* before writing *The Makropulos Secret*, insisting that he had heard of it only in summary. His actual inspiration, he said, came from the work on human longevity of the Russian biologist and pioneer of immunology, Elie Metchnikov. Metchnikov, like Shaw, was critical of Darwin, and in particular of those Malthusian aspects of Darwinian theory that insisted that 'overpopulation, intraspecific competition and natural selection were "the only basis of all phenomena"' (Todes 1989: 88). But there the similarity ends. While Shaw saw old age as the answer to mankind's problems, Metchnikov saw it as the problem itself: his Nobel Prize-winning work was based on the theory that physical ageing results from the 'self-poisoning' of the human organism (Kussi in Čapek 1990: 110). Čapek took Metchnikov's metaphor and both literalized and extended it: if ageing is poison, he reasons, might there not also be an antidote? *The Makropulos Secret* explores the emotional and ethical implications of such a possibility.

A quick synopsis of Čapek's play might be useful at this point. In fact, a very brief one has been provided by Bernard Williams. *The Makropulos Secret*, he explains,

tells of a woman called Elina Makropulos, *alias* Emilia Marty, *alias* Ellian MacGregor, *alias* a number of other women with the initials EM, on whom her father, the court physician to a sixteenth-century emperor, tried out an elixir of life. At the time of the action she is 342. Her unending life has come to a state of boredom, indifference, and coldness. Everything is joyless: 'in the end it is the same,' she says, 'singing and silence.' She refuses to take the elixir again; she dies, and the formula is deliberately destroyed by a young woman among the protests of some older men.

(Williams 1973: 82)

In fact, Williams's synopsis is rather *too* skeletal for present purposes – although its omissions are themselves interesting, in the light of his own interpretation of the Makropulos story. What Williams misses out, though, is the flavour of the drama itself. It opens in a lawyer's office, where a firm of solicitors is working on a complex inheritance case, one which (like Dickens' Jarndyce and Jarndyce) has been going on for over a hundred years. Unlike Jarndyce and Jarndyce, however, a judgement is imminent, and as the play starts it looks very much as if the firm and Gregor, their client, are going to lose. At this point, a mysterious woman arrives; she turns out to be a celebrity opera singer, but strangely, she knows about details of the case from a hundred years ago – including, crucially, the whereabouts of some essential papers. The woman is beautiful and fascinating, and during the play's first act an increasing number of clues is introduced to suggest that she is also very unusual. The situation is set up skilfully: the audience, on the whole, is rather ahead of the onstage characters in this deduction, but there are occasional dramatic twists – an early moment of horror, for example, when Gregor looks into her face and recoils, seeing something unexplained that the audience doesn't see.

GREGOR: Good God, what are you doing? What are you doing to your face? (*He steps back*) Emilia, don't do that anymore, you make yourself look old. You look horrible!

(Čapek 1990:126)

The event remains unexplained and the moment passes; but later developments make it clear that Čapek's reputation as one of the godfathers of twentieth-century science fiction has some bearing on the narrative of *The Makropulos Secret*.

The middle of the play, however, rather sags: we see Emilia's effect on various people, and gradually, the audience is allowed to put the picture together: although 'Emilia Marty' (i.e. Elina Makropulos) *looks* young, she is actually very very old. It turns out that she is now searching for the recipe for the elixir, the antidote to the poison of ageing, which has been the secret of her unnatural youthfulness, which she now needs to take again to sustain her longevity, and which she knows to be hidden among the papers in the inheritance case.

The notion that there might be a literal potion that would delay, halt or reverse the ageing process is both age-old and also utterly modern – a cultural myth that resurfaces with extraordinary frequency. A recent example is to be found in the 'science pages' of the *Daily*

Telegraph for 30 June 2011 under the headline 'Elixir of life discovered on Easter Island'. The article goes on to announce that

> A drug has been discovered which scientists believe can reverse the effects of premature ageing and could extend human life by more than a decade. Rapamycin, which has been nicknamed the 'forever young' drug, was created from a chemical found in the soil on Easter Island, one of the most remote places on Earth and 2,000 miles off the coast of Chile.
>
> (Anon. 2011c: n.p.)

Looking beyond the headlines, however, we discover that the story, which derives from a rather less sensationally presented report in the peer-reviewed journal *Science Translational Medicine*, is not quite what it seems. The clinical efficacy of this 'forever young drug' as an anti-ageing agent was actually related to a series of experiments which alleviated the symptoms of a group of children suffering from Hutchinson-Gilford Progeria Syndrome (HGPS), 'a rare genetic condition in which ageing is hyper-accelerated and sufferers die of "old age" at around 12 years'. Any suggestion that Rapamycin might be used more widely in reversing the effects of the normal ageing process is (at present) entirely speculative. My point, however, is that the fantasy of the elixir of life continues to haunt popular imagination, and continues to help sell newspapers.

It is only in the third act, after Emilia has been confronted with an accusation of fraud – with the audience now well ahead of the characters in their understanding of what is going on – that the philosophical debate to which the whole play has been leading takes place. An impromptu trial takes place, in which the truth comes out: Emilia admits her age, and establishes the truth of her claims. There follows a series of ethical and philosophical arguments in a fairly Shavian vein, about what should now be done.

Vitek, the political radical, takes a position very much like Shaw's own: 'My God', he exclaims,

> [W]hat can a man do in a mere sixty years of life? How much can he enjoy? How much can he learn? He can't even harvest the fruit from the tree he plants. He never learns what his ancestors knew. He dies before he begins to live! God in heaven, we live so briefly … A man needs more time to live. Sixty years! That is serfdom … Let's give everybody 300 years of life. This will be the greatest event since the creation. It will be a liberation and a new beginning. God, what can be done with a man in 300 years! … Oh, how valuable would a human life be if it lasted 300 years! There would be no wars, no more of that dreadful hunt for bread, no fear, no selfishness. Everyone would have dignity and wisdom.
>
> (Čapek 1990: 168–69)

Vitek sounds so very much like Shaw – even down to the detail of the three hundred years, the figure to which the Brothers Barnabas intended to extend the term of human life – that it is hard to take at face value Čapek's claim that he was not influenced by *Back to Methuselah*.

186

The final act of *Makropulos*, indeed, reads very much like a direct response to Shaw's play – although as we have seen, Čapek repeatedly claimed that the coincidence between his own work and Shaw's was 'entirely accidental, and, as it would seem from the resume, purely superficial, for Bernard Shaw comes to quite the opposite conclusions' (Čapek, cited in Sparks 1997: 174).

In the dramaturgy of the play, Vitek is a character who is quite close to the audience: the play opens with his soliloquy, in which the audience is invited to sympathize with his dreams of a fairer society. But in the argument at the end of the play about the moral implications of the elixir of life, his Shavian position is quickly dismissed by the legalistic Kolenaty:

> You had better realize, Vitek, that all you have said is legally and economically ridiculous. Our social system is founded upon a brief life span: contracts, pensions, insurance policies, salaries, inheritance laws, and I don't know what all. And marriage! Ha! Nobody would get married for 300 years! Nobody would make any kind of commitment for 300 years! You! You are an anarchist! You want to topple all our social systems!
>
> (Čapek 1990: 169)

Kolenaty's voice of pragmatic conservatism is soon supplanted by that of Prus, who disagrees even more vehemently with Vitek's vision of using the elixir for the benefit of all humanity. Prus, who is another claimant for the original inheritance, speaks with a voice that became increasingly chilling in the first half of the twentieth century:

VITEK: ... We must prolong life for all humanity!

PRUS: No, only for the strong. The life of the most capable ... We can begin an aristocracy of the everlasting ... Only the best are important. Only the leaders, only productive, efficient, men. I don't even talk about women.

(Čapek 1990: 170–71)

Eugenics in the first part of the twentieth century did not have the terrible reputation which became attached to it after the Nazi era in Germany. It was seen by many as the logical corollary of certain aspects of the theory of natural selection, and promoted by both individuals and governments as a social philosophy for the improvement of the human condition: Leonard Darwin, Charles's son, was the President of the first International Congress of Eugenics in 1912. Even so, it was surrounded, very early on, by political and ethical, as well as scientific controversies.

PRUS: ... [T]here are in this world about ten or twenty thousand men who are irreplaceable. We can preserve them. In these men we can

	develop superhuman brains and supernormal powers. We can breed ten or twenty thousand supermen, leaders and creators.
VITEK:	A race of supermen!
PRUS:	Exactly. Choice men who have the right to unlimited life.
DR. KOLENATY:	And tell me, if you will, who is going to choose the chosen?

(Čapek 1990: 171)

In the end, however, the voice that has the most influence is that of Emilia herself, and she speaks not from a socio-political perspective but from an experiential one. She talks about – and expresses – the great sense of *ennui* which her 'ageless' life has given her. It is much more than boredom, she explains.

EMILIA:	It is … It is … oh, you people you have no name for it. No language on earth has a name for it … It is horrible … One should not, should not, should not live so long!
VITEK:	But why not?
EMILIA:	One cannot stand it. For 100, 130 years one can go on. But then … then … one finds out … that … and then one's soul dies.
VITEK:	One finds out what?
EMILIA:	God, there are no words for it. One finds out that one cannot believe in anything. Anything! And from that comes this cold emptiness … Oh God if you knew how easy it is for you to live!
DR. KOLENATY:	Why?
EMILIA:	You are so near to everything! For you everything has meaning. For you everything has value because for the few years that you are here, you don't have time to live enough. God, if I could only once more …

(Čapek 1990: 173–74)

The horror of longevity lies in the mental, emotional and spiritual meaninglessness that accompanies it. It is death, the limitation of the lifespan, and the fact of age and change itself that give *meaning* to life. Emilia decides not to go on taking and retaking the elixir, but to submit to the ageing process and to eventual death. For the other characters, the decision is taken out of their hands. Krista, Vitek's daughter, takes the parchment on which the formula is written and burns it. In the final lines of the play the various characters react to this.

| | |
| GREGOR: | It's burning out. After all, it was a wild idea, to live forever. God, I feel lonely, but a bit lighter, knowing it isn't possible anymore … |

DR. KOLENATY:	We're no longer young, any of us. Only youth could burn such a thing so fearlessly. You did well, child.
HAUK-SENDORF:	Excuse me, but there is such a strange smell in here ... a smell like ...
VITEK:	(*Opening a window*) Like burning.
EMILIA:	(*Laughs*) The end of immortality.

(Čapek 1990: 176–77)

Čapek himself described *The Makropulos Secret* as a 'comedy'. If it *is* a comedy, then it is so in the Shavian sense of that word: a modern comedy of manners and ideas, which satirizes certain kinds of social types and certain kinds of notions about society. The tone of the play's ending, however, has caused some readers to question whether 'comedy' is the appropriate term for it at all. Yvetta Synek Graff and Robert T. Jones, the play's most recent translators, clearly found the term problematic, and felt obliged to add an addendum to their translation:

> Most readers will feel that the play ends tragically, with Emilia's final laugh a harsh, even bitter, welcome to death ... The stage directions in the following interpretation are purely the invention of the translators: it seems to us suitable to the comedic tone of much of the play.
>
> (Čapek 1990: 177)

They then add a detailed set of stage directions to accompany the last few lines of the play, so as to set it back on the right comedic road. In the Graff–Jones version, all the characters come together in joyful laughter to celebrate the end of immortality 'with genuine exuberance', while 'the bright midday sun shines in' (Čapek 1990: 177). It is a legitimate way of playing the final moments of *The Makropulos Secret*, but a somewhat ham-fisted one, and one which rather blunts the play's ending. By equating 'comedy' so straightforwardly with 'happy ending', and by insisting so strongly on the positive side of Emilia and Krista's decision, Graff and Jones destroy the careful ambiguity which Čapek had created. In Čapek's original we see once more a play which treats ageing and its associated issues with ambivalence. The Graff–Jones version offers something much more one-dimensional.

An equally one-dimensional, though rather different, reading of the play was offered by Leos Janáček when he came to produce his operatic version of *The Makropulos Secret* in 1926, for which he wrote both the libretto and the score. That the central character was an opera singer clearly offered opportunities to the composer; another reason for his interest may have been the fact that he himself was in his seventies at the time, and that – like the characters in the play – he, too, had been in love for many years with an unattainable Emilia-figure – in his case a married younger woman. Janáček's opera is generally agreed to be among his best works and is regularly revived as part of the modern operatic repertoire.

It does not make for easy listening, however: the music, with its expanded tonality and unorthodox chord spacings, is restless, difficult and continually unsettling. The ending, too, is handled very differently from Čapek's original: the potion wears off and Janáček's Emilia succumbs to old age before our very eyes, ageing with great rapidity and then expiring on stage (reciting, as she does so, the Lord's Prayer in Greek). This *grand-guignol* sequence, later to become a staple of science fiction and horror fiction and movies, owes, perhaps, more to Oscar Wilde than it does to Shaw; it bears traces of another famous version of the immortality myth, Wilde's Victorian Gothic *Picture of Dorian Gray*, which ends with a similar trope of rapid ageing:

> When they entered, they found hanging upon the wall a splendid portrait of their master as they had last seen him, in all the wonder of his exquisite youth and beauty. Lying on the floor was a dead man, in evening dress, with a knife in his heart. He was withered, wrinkled, and loathsome of visage. It was not till they had examined the rings that they recognized who it was.
>
> (Wilde [1891] 1988: 281)

But Janáček's harsh modernism is very different from Wilde's delicately balanced aesthetic – and different, too, from the ambivalent quality of Čapek's ending.

Perhaps because of this, Čapek's play has fared less well with posterity than Janáček's opera: it has not become part of the European dramatic canon, and, indeed, it is not particularly well-known in its own right today. Like Emilia, however, *The Makropulos Secret* turned up unexpectedly after an absence of many years, and in doing so, as I have already suggested, it made an indirect but important contribution to the philosophy of ageing. Bernard Williams' essay 'The Makropulos Case: Reflections on the tedium of immortality' became the most famous of his discourses on the *Problems of the Self* (1973) and is now regarded as a classic of modern moral philosophy. He uses Emilia's story as the focus for his consideration of the proposition (stated by Lucretius in *De Rerum Natura, Book III*) that death is never an evil. Putting this idea into dialectical opposition with the conclusions of Janáček's opera, Williams' essay develops the apparent paradox 'that immortality would be, where conceivable at all, intolerable, and that (other things being equal) death is reasonably regarded as an evil' (Williams 1973: 82ff.).

It was Janáček's version of the story which was best known to Bernard Williams, who was a great opera lover, a board member of English National Opera, and the author of a successful collection of essays, *On Opera*. Nonetheless, whether consciously or unconsciously, it is to the tone of Čapek's original, rather than of Janáček's adaptation, that Williams' essay owes greater allegiance. More so than Janáček, Williams sees a comic ambiguity and ambivalence in his exploration of the questions of immortality and the ageing process. Like Čapek's Emilia, Williams sees death as providing meaning to life, and he concludes that while death in itself may be regarded as an evil, 'as things are, it is possible to be … lucky in having the chance to die' (Williams 1973: 82). The ambiguity with which Čapek imbues the ending is important, and the voluntary renunciation of the possibility of immortality is bittersweet.

Myths of Tithonus: Old age and immortality

This early twentieth-century theatrical debate, between Shaw on the one hand and Čapek and his successors on the other, about the attractions or terrors of extreme longevity, can be seen in two contexts: the perennial and the immediate. Firstly, it seems that the notion of extreme old age holds a fascination for humankind which appears to be (ironically) timeless. We have already seen, from the Easter Island 'elixir of life' story, how potent the meme remains in contemporary culture. Myths and legends of superhuman longevity are etched too deep into the history and prehistory of human cultures, from China's eight-hundred-year-old Peng Zu to the Persian Shāh Jamshid, who, we are told, ruled the world for seven hundred years. In the Mesopotamian *Epic of Gilgamesh* (eighteenth-century to thirteenth-century BCE) Gilgamesh, on his fruitless quest to discover the secret of life and death, meets and seeks answers from Upnapishtim, the one mortal who (together with his wife) has been granted everlasting life by the gods. The Judaeo-Christian tradition – in which the notion of everlasting life later took on a rather different meaning – is no exception: the Bible contains a wide variety of characters who live well into a natural or supernatural old age. In particular those mythical patriarchs of the Hebrew Bible who lived before the Flood were generally credited with mind-bogglingly long lifetimes.

> And Enoch lived sixty and five years, and begat Methuselah: (22) And Enoch walked with God after he begat Methuselah three hundred years, and Enoch begat sons and daughters: (23) And all the days of Enoch were three hundred sixty and five years: (24) And Enoch walked with God: and he [was] not; for God took him. (25) And Methuselah lived an hundred eighty and seven years, and begat Lamech: (26) And Methuselah lived after he begat Lamech seven hundred eighty and two years, and begat sons and daughters: (27) And all the days of Methuselah were nine hundred sixty and nine years: and he died.
>
> (Genesis 5:21–27)

Adam and Eve, according to the genealogies of Genesis (4, 5 and 11) lived well into their ninth centuries, and Noah himself (who bears interesting similarities to Upnapishtim from *The Epic of Gilgamesh*) was six hundred years old at the time of the Great Flood. The stories of extreme longevity are part of a more general tendency within the Judaeo-Christian tradition to look back nostalgically to a utopian time before a rupture in man's relations with God caused a change for the worse in man's condition. The archetype of this is the Fall itself, and Adam and Eve's expulsion from Eden before which mankind lived in prelapsarian bliss;

and if the Fall brought with it the curse of work and eventual mortality, the disobedience of mankind which led to the Flood marked an acceleration of mortality, an acceleration which has speeded up at various key mythical moments (such as the time of the Flood) until the 'modern' span of three score and ten became a generally accepted touchstone for expected lifespan.

In these Old Testament examples, we can see traces of the ways in which earlier cultures use the attribution of the idea of great longevity as a form of honour, even of blessedness. The eighteenth-century Anglican minister Jonathan Swift took a rather different view, when he imagined the reverse side of this particular coin: long life as a curse from which there is no escape. The Struldbrugs that Lemuel Gulliver meets on his travels are a nightmarish vision of the prison of relentless senility. On first being told of a race of people who are effectively immortal, Gulliver first waxes lyrical, and is 'enlarged upon many other topics, which the natural desire of endless life, and sublunary happiness, could easily furnish me with'. He soon discovers, however, that 'through the common imbecility of human nature' he has misunderstood the case because he had 'supposed a perpetuity of youth, health, and vigour, which no man could be so foolish to hope, however extravagant he may be in his wishes'. The question which the Struldbrugs pose to Gulliver (and by extension to Swift's rational man) was 'how he would pass a perpetual life under all the usual disadvantages which old age brings along with it'. In fact, the plight of the deathless Struldbrugs is even worse than this, since their condition is one of continual deterioration so that '[a]t ninety, they lose their teeth and hair; they have at that age no distinction of taste, but eat and drink whatever they can get, without relish or appetite. The diseases they were subject to still continue, without increasing or diminishing.' When Gulliver eventually comes across some examples in the flesh, he concludes,

> They were the most mortifying Sight I ever beheld; and the Women more horrible than the Men. Besides the usual Deformities in extreme old Age, they acquired an additional Ghastliness, in Proportion to their Number of Years, which is not to be described; and among half a Dozen, I soon distinguished which was the eldest, although there was not above a Century or two between them.
>
> The Reader will easily believe, that from what I had heard and seen, my keen Appetite for Perpetuity of Life was much abated. I grew heartily ashamed of the pleasing Visions I had formed; and thought no Tyrant could invent a Death into which I would not run with Pleasure, from such a Life.
>
> (Swift [1726] 2005: 199)

The prototype of the Struldbrugs is to be found, not in Old Testament stories, but in the Greek myth of Tithonus. Recorded in the Homeric 'Hymn to Aphrodite', this tells the story of how Eos, the titan of the Dawn, fell in love with a mortal youth. She begged Zeus to make her lover immortal:

Zeus bowed his head to her prayer and fulfilled her desire. Too simple was queenly Eos: she thought not in her heart to ask youth for him and to strip him of the slough of deadly age. So while he enjoyed the sweet flower of life he lived rapturously with golden-throned Eos, the early-born, by the streams of Ocean, at the ends of the earth; but when the first grey hairs began to ripple from his comely head and noble chin, queenly Eos kept away from his bed, though she cherished him in her house and nourished him with food and ambrosia and gave him rich clothing. But when loathsome old age pressed full upon him, and he could not move nor lift his limbs, this seemed to her in her heart the best counsel: she laid him in a room and put to the shining doors. There he babbles endlessly, and no more has strength at all, such as once he had in his supple limbs.

(Evelyn-White [1914] 2012: V, lines 223–36)

A later version of the Tithonus story turns it into a 'metamorphosis' myth, of the kind later collected and retold by the Roman poet Ovid. Metamorphosis myths explain the origins of the natural world, often in terms of conflicts between mortals and immortals. In this instance, Tithonus is eventually offered a provisional freedom from his plight by being changed into a cicada – which was, in the ancient world, itself a symbol of longevity.

Tithonus and the Struldbrugs offer a grotesque and extreme image of the 'narrative of decline' taken to its logical conclusion. In their grim humour these stories present, of course, an ironic challenge to the naïve assumptions of Gulliver (and indeed of Eos) that eternal life should equal eternal youth; but their stark pessimism also challenges us to consider the limitations of our own hopes about positive ageing. The Tithonus motif, too, is a persistent one in both high and popular culture. Tennyson harnessed it when seeking a symbol for his own sense of the meaninglessness of existence.

The woods decay, the woods decay and fall,
The vapours weep their burthen to the ground,
Man comes and tills the field and lies beneath,
And after many a summer dies the swan.
Me only cruel immortality
Consumes; I wither slowly in thine arms,
Here at the quiet limit of the world,
A white-hair'd shadow roaming like a dream
The ever-silent spaces of the East,
Far-folded mists, and gleaming halls of morn.
Alas! for this gray shadow, once a man—
So glorious in his beauty and thy choice,
Who madest him thy chosen, that he seem'd
To his great heart none other than a God!

I ask'd thee, 'Give me immortality.'
Then didst thou grant mine asking with a smile.

(Tennyson 1987: II, 607)

The fantasy of extreme old age, then, has always had two faces. On the one hand there is the positive face: the wise and authoritative face of the prelapsarian patriarchs. This aspect flatly contradicts any narrative of decline; it resurfaces regularly in the benevolent elder figures of folklore and popular culture (Merlin, Tolkien's Gandalf, Lucas' Obi-Wan Kenobi and Yoda): Proppian helpers and guardians whose extreme old age gives them wisdom and experience to guide the hero or protagonist towards his or her destiny. This is the face that Shaw, at his most optimistic, imagines in *Back to Methuselah*. On the other hand there is the negative aspect: that which takes the notion of decline to its grotesque logical conclusion. This is the face of Tithonus, for whom longevity simply means a continual and drawn-out process of deterioration, either physical or mental/spiritual. In Emilia's case, this becomes the existential nightmare of the death of the soul and 'this cold emptiness' (Čapek 1990: 174).

If the prospect of extreme longevity has posed cultural questions down the ages, different historical periods have responded to these questions in their culture-specific ways. In late nineteenth-century England, for example, there was, according to Tom Kirkwood,

> an extraordinary surge of public interest in the question of extreme human longevity … Reports of centenarianism appeared frequently in the national and local newspapers, and a lively correspondence on the subject was carried on in the letters pages and in the 'Notes and Queries' column of the London *Times*.

(Kirkwood 1999: 42–43)

This is what I referred to earlier as the 'immediate' context of the debate. In particular it is the local historical context for Shaw's 'Metabiological Pentateuch': his Lamarckian dialectics are the direct outcome of this wider Victorian fascination with longevity. And this fascination, in turn, should be understood in connection with nineteenth- and early twentieth-century European preoccupations with notions of 'progress', a concept which informed the period's ideas about society, as well as (in the wake of Darwin's *Origin of Species* (1859)) its understanding of the natural world. The intertwined themes of progress, evolution and scientific rationalism informed theories about geological, social, economic, scientific, technological and intellectual change with equal influence, posing a formidable challenge to traditional theologies of the 'steady-state' universe created by God. It may well have been, then, as Kirkwood suggests, that 'the Victorians, triumphing so marvelously in their feats of engineering and exploration, imagined that even the secrets of ageing were in their grasp' (Kirkwood 1999: 42). Yet the Victorian age had its sceptics on the subject of human longevity, as well as its enthusiasts: William Thoms' *Human Longevity: Its Facts and Fictions* (1873), for example, provided a sober counterpoint to some of the more excited claims, debunking many of the dearly-held myths about cases of extreme longevity.

It is, then, the idea of extreme old age, rather than its actuality, that lies at the heart of both *Back to Methuselah* and the influential *The Makropulos Secret*. From the two cultural backgrounds, of an 'age-old' fascination with extreme longevity, and the more immediate concerns of nineteenth-century science, emerged this strange early twentieth-century debate, articulated through the medium of drama, between Shaw and Čapek. The debate and both writers were very much 'of their time'; however, as we shall see, the theme itself has continued to speak to later generations as well.

Chapter 10

On Institutions

In modern stage and screen drama, there are certain environments that have become so frequently used as to amount to 'stock' settings. The prison and the hospital, for example, offer the playwright or screenwriter dramatic opportunities resulting from the claustrophobically controlled environment; the heterocosm with its own rules and realities, within which personal interactions become more intense; and, frequently, the ready-made oppressive structure against which the individual can react. In the same vein, the care home, too, has become a frequently used dramatic setting: even a sub-genre in its own right, with its own conventions, repeatable stock characters and recyclable tropes and plotlines. It is a setting which has taken on a particular meaning in recent years, as crises within health care have their impact on homes for the elderly.

In this chapter, and part of the next, I shall explore the image of the nursing home in modern culture, and analyse the ways it has been used as a dramatic setting. I will pay particular attention to three rather different plays (one from the mid-twentieth century and two from the last few years) all of which use the care home as a dramatic setting. John Arden's *The Happy Haven* dates from the early years of the National Health Service and the post-war welfare state; *Juliet and Her Romeo* is a recent adaptation of Shakespeare's play which sets the action not in sixteenth-century Verona but in 'The Verona Nursing Home for the Elderly'. Erik Gedeon's *Forever Young* spans two of this book's themes, and is dealt with in the following chapter: it too, however, sets its action in a care home – in this case, a theatre which has been transformed into a care home for ageing actors.

'A Doctor Faustus of the present generation': *The Happy Haven* (1960)

The achievements of the British National Health Service during its first decade or so were many, not only in terms of equal health-care provision for rich and poor, but also in terms of erasing the stigma of charity, or the sheer fear of being unable to afford treatment, which many lower-paid workers had previously felt. The elderly, especially the frail elderly who were unable to look after themselves, had benefited particularly dramatically. As Geoffrey Rivett, historian of the National Health Service, explains:

> One of the early achievements in the NHS was the development of active geriatrics, when a start was made on dealing with the problem of the 'back wards', seldom visited by doctors, where people ended their days.
>
> (Rivett 2011: n.p.)

The NHS was not without its contradictions, however, and its birth had been made possible only after a large number of concessions had been made – largely to the medical establishment itself. Aneurin Bevan, Minister of Health in the 1945 Labour Government, had produced a plan for a fully nationalized health service based on the recommendations of the 1942 Beveridge Report, but a sizeable majority of doctors and consultants expressed concerns about loss of incomes, and about being demoted to the status of mere state functionaries. The British Medical Association campaigned vigorously against the introduction of a public health-care system in which treatment would be universally 'free at the point of delivery', and Bevan was forced into a series of compromises enabling consultants, senior doctors and GPs with richer practices to continue to earn large sums of money through a variety of private contracts while still being paid by the NHS. There was a manifest tension between the ideal (the provision of free universal health care) and the actuality (the continuing pursuit of self-interest among some echelons of the medical profession).

Some of these initial tensions were still visible in 1960, when *The Happy Haven* was first produced. The play's central character, the ambitious young doctor who is the Superintendent of the Happy Haven Nursing Home, articulates some of these continuing contradictions and tensions. He explains that the home is

> as yet only a small institution and our grant from the revenues of the National Health Service is alas not as generous as it might be – but, well, I dare say you'll know the old proverb – Time mends all. I'd like you to meet some of the old people who are in our care. As the phrase is, the evening of their lives – well, I've more to say about that later – but at present sufficient to indicate that this hospital for the amelioration of the lot of the aged is situated in pleasant rural surroundings, almost self-supporting – own produce, eggs, butter, and so on – within easy reach of London, and, I am happy to say, the most up-to-date facilities for both medical treatment and – most important of all from my point of view – research. I'm the Superintendent, my name's Copperthwaite.
>
> (Arden 1964: 195)

The contradiction between Copperthwaite's duty of care to his patients, and his own personal and self-aggrandizing agenda as a researcher forms the basic conflict of the play.

The style of *The Happy Haven* is a key element of its meaning. Before it transferred to the Royal Court Theatre for its professional premiere, the play's first production took place, in April 1960, in the Bristol University Drama Department 'on an open stage, following roughly the Elizabethan model' (Arden 1964: 193) – a fairly radical form of staging at the time, when the generation of open-stage repertories that characterized theatre design in the later 1960s and early 1970s had not yet been built. This staging was the one which Arden himself greatly preferred. It proved to his own satisfaction that the leanings I have long had towards the open stage and its disciplines were justifiable in practice as well as in theory. I would urge anyone who wishes to produce this play to do so, if at all possible on an open stage.

(Arden 1964: 193–94)

The advantage of this kind of staging was that it offered a greater directness of address between the stage and the audience, which suited the traditions of popular theatre on which the play draws. In particular, the play makes use of masks in various ways: there are anonymizing surgical masks for the nurses and orderlies who act as extras, and Arden also specifies that 'The Five Old People wear character masks of the *commedia dell'arte* type, covering the upper part of their faces only' (Arden 1964: 193). Placing them so clearly within the *commedia* tradition establishes them, of course, as stereotypes of old age rather than as individuals, although both within the dialogue and in the stage directions and speech tags they are referred to by their names: Mrs Phineus, Mrs Letouzel, Mr Golightly and so on.

Arden's stage directions do not go so far as to link each character to any specific figure from the *commedia* tradition; and indeed the analogy breaks down quite quickly, since these are characters in a state of dependence, and as such are much more closely aligned to the younger servant characters of the *commedia* – Arlecchino, Brighella and so on – rather than the older master figures such as Dottore and Pantalone. Even so, several of the episodes in the play are effectively Arden's own versions of the *commedia* performers' *lazzi* or set-piece routines. For example, an extended routine based around a drugged coffee cup takes up much of the final scene, while a recurring *lazzi* involving a dog, which the audience cannot see but which the onstage characters can, is a source of several comic moments throughout the play. *The Happy Haven* inhabits a larger-than-life aesthetic in which a broadly Brechtian epic style is combined with the kind of *commedia* tradition of popular theatre that Brecht himself enjoyed.

This larger-than-life style enables Arden to make some larger-than-life statements about the politics of old age. Copperthwaite is, as he indicates in his opening speech, primarily interested in the research that will make his reputation rather than the care of his patients. The play's opening monologue establishes his attitude towards the residents, as the language which Copperthwaite uses to describe them slips from one register to another:

On Mrs Phineus's right we have Mr Golightly, seventy-five years old, bachelor, very good state of preservation. Fitted six years ago with improved Walschaerts valve-gear replacing original Stephenson's link motion and injectors also recently renewed. Latent procreative impulses require damping down on the firebox, but less so than formerly. Next one, number three, on Mrs Phineus's left, you will observe the only other female member, Mrs Letouzel. Aged seventy, all moving parts in good condition, cross-head pins perhaps slightly deteriorated, and occasional trouble from over-heated bearings when financial gain is in question. General report, extremely favourable. Now next to her we have

Mr Hardrader, number four, our best running specimen. Very firm original design in smokebox and blast pipe has resulted in continual first-class steaming conditions. Age eighty-eight on the thirteenth of next month.

(Arden 1964: 196–97)

As the language of the motor mechanic replaces that of the care worker, Copperthwaite's monologue effectively satirizes an overly objective, and indeed *mechanical* medical model of patient care. Copperthwaite himself is a caricature of the uncaring manager who exploits those whom he should be protecting. As the plot unfolds we discover (perhaps without too much surprise) that the subjects, and indeed the eventual guinea pigs of Copperthwaite's research are to be his aged patients themselves.

The play strikes a note of paranoia that was to become increasingly common in the popular culture of the 1960s: the fear that behind the apparent benevolence of state (and sometimes private) care lay a more sinister purpose – in this case, one involving scientific experiments on human beings. It is hard to be definitive about the reason for this recurring fear: perhaps it had something to do with very real and all-too-recent memories of the atrocities of some of the Nazis' experiments in eugenics in their 'hospitals' and perhaps, too, with an increasing awareness of the animal experimentation on which both the beauty industry and the pharmaceutical industry relied. Perhaps, too, it was an ironic consequence of the very success of the NHS. The centralization and nationalization of health care had had enormous benefits, but it had also created a large bureaucratic machine which already threatened to depersonalize health care and create a sense of alienation among its clients.

In all likelihood, a combination of these factors contributed to a paranoid political fantasy which has a particular force in the context of a care home for the elderly. A sense that other people are controlling your environment, disempowering you, doing things to you which you do not fully understand and which frighten you: such fears and anxieties are frequently associated with the experience of dementia. They are also, of course, literal truths about being subject to any kind of institutional care at any age.

The inhabitants of Arden's Happy Haven range from the fully cognisant, such as the cunning Crape, to the apparently confused (the easily deceived Mrs Phineus – who, in fact, shows her own kind of cunning as the play unfolds). For the most part they live in contented ignorance of just how the experimental strand of Copperthwaite's work impinges upon them. But for the audience the sense of the Happy Haven as a kind of prison camp rather than a place for 'the amelioration of the lot of the aged' is enhanced by our realization that – like any efficient prison governor – Copperthwaite has an informer. Crape (played in the Royal Court production by Gordon Gostelow) spies on the other residents, and betrays to the authorities their small secrets: Mrs Letouzel's pilfering, Mr Hardrader's secret ownership of the dog. And – like any efficient informer – Crape is sufficiently curious about what is going on around him to begin to uncover some of Copperthwaite's own secrets.

In fact Dr Copperthwaite's experiments – while unethical, dangerous and driven by his own egotistical desire for professional glory – are not quite what the audience may first suspect. Staged as a pantomime parody of laboratory practice, complete with retorts full of multicoloured liquids and nonsensical jargon ('the solution … reading nine-by-three by four-and-a-half scantlings, ledged braced battened and primed … To it I am about to add nought point three-double-six degrees of *this*' (Arden 1964: 199)), the demonstration has more about it of alchemy than of twentieth-century scientific method. And, indeed, the aim of Copperthwaite's experiments draws on age-old alchemical fantasies.

> My research. My project … To quote, somewhat tentatively, a literary example as being perhaps most appropriate for this audience, you can call me if you like, a Doctor Faustus of the present generation. It's not an exact parallel – Faustus sold his soul to the Devil, I believe. I'm selling mine to nobody. But what I have here or what I shall have here, ladies and gentlemen, is nothing less, or will be nothing less, than the Elixir of life – of Life, and of Youth.
>
> (Arden 1964: 198)

The Happy Haven, it turns out, is playing another variation on the theme of extreme longevity. The tone here, however, is very different from either Shaw or Čapek. Copperthwaite's self-conscious Faustus reference brings with it all the connotations of that medieval legend: the Faustus of folk tradition and of Marlowe's play was an hubristic 'over-reacher', whose arrogant faith in his own rational but limited view of the world led to his downfall and damnation. And if this modern Faustus is not, as he claims, selling his soul, the audience may suspect it is only because he does not have much of a soul to sell in the first place.

He, however, sees himself as a benefactor to mankind – and indeed to the patients under his care.

> Those five old people you saw go to bed last night are to be the raw material upon which I shall work. They don't know it yet, but they are. If I am successful and the Elixir is found – Copperthwaite's Elixir – or might I call it the Happy Haven Elixir – the institution is greater than the man – *if* I am successful; then those five old people will be not at the end of their established term of years but at the beginning! They will be able, they will be able, to be completely reborn! To any age we may see fit to lead them. Think of that. Think of that!
>
> (Arden 1964: 199)

Copperthwaite's speech winds up the spring of the play; its unwinding is concerned with the questions of (a) whether he will successfully complete his quest to perfect the elixir; and (b) if so, what will happen when/if he administers it to the patients. The middle of the play is baggy and lacking in focus, but after some predictable mishaps and interruptions to the experiments, and some slightly less predictable shenanigans among the residents, the elixir is finally produced. After a final test on the invisible dog, the doctor arranges for a public trialling of the drug, to be carried out on the enthusiastic residents in the presence of local dignitaries and civil servants.

The early part of the play is largely a satire on institutionalized health care for the elderly; as it develops it becomes more concerned with philosophical debates about longevity, immortality and the life-course – the kind of territory already traversed by Čapek and, to some extent, Shaw. Like Čapek, Arden concludes that it would be a bad thing for life (and perhaps even of youth, health and beauty) to be extended indefinitely – or even just beyond the traditional allotted span. He complicates the argument, however, by making the 'spokesperson' for this point of view the malcontent and disaffected Crape.

Crape, it turns out, has been excluded from the trials because of a bronchial indisposition. Feeling betrayed, he turns on the other residents, confronting them with negative images of what it would be like to be given back their youth. To Mrs Phineus, for example, he says.

CRAPE:	Now answer me this one. Supposing you … were born again. Young strong. Not beautiful. You never were beautiful until you were old – I've seen your wedding photograph so I know what you were like … Suppose you were born again –
PHINEUS:	I don't know –
CRAPE:	I do. You wouldn't dare to face it. Oh Lord, it would be far too much like hard work … Truth or lie? Truth or lie?
PHINEUS:	Truth, truth.

(Arden 1964: 251)

His arguments are born of resentment and envy, but one by one Crape convinces the residents that they do not want the doctor's gift of renewed youth. His argument is a bleakly pessimistic one: youth, he insists, would be a curse rather than a blessing because their memories of past happiness are actually all illusory. And it is at this point that the significance of the character's name becomes apparent: 'Crape' is John Arden's version of Beckett's 'Krapp' (in fact, *Krapp's Last Tape* had played at the same London theatre, the Royal Court, a couple of years earlier). Caricatured now, and with none of the poignancy or nuance that characterized Beckett's original creation, the message that Crape repeats to one after another of the residents is a bald restatement of Krapp's own contempt for his own lost youth. The final line of Beckett's play – 'No, I wouldn't want them back' – is the refrain of Crape's whole argument, as he successfully manipulates the residents to the point where they 'don't want to die, but none of [them] dare state that [they] want any more life' (Arden 1964: 254).

The play itself, however, does not endorse either Crape's bleak vision or the nuanced philosophical resignation of Čapek's *The Makropulos Secret*. Instead, the ending of *The Happy Haven* reverts to comic mode. When the residents finally rebel against Copperthwaite in the final scene, they do so in order to regain control of their own destinies. Overwhelming the doctor – after a few comic mishaps – they inject him with a dose of his own medicine, sending him back to infancy: '*He is now*', say the stage directions, *wearing a little boy's suit, with short pants, and wears a mask that entirely covers his own face. It resembles the actor's own features closely, but is round, chubby and childish.* MRS LETOUZEL *puts a lollipop into his hand and he sucks at it in a formal fashion.*

(Arden 1964: 271)

In this way he becomes the infant which Mrs Phineus had wanted, and which for her would have been the only real advantage of rejuvenation. The doctor's Brechtian 'transformation' ties up loose ends and becomes the punchline of what is, after all, a fairly short joke.

The Happy Haven, then, is an oddly complicated play. Arden's satire on institutionalized elderly care in the early years of the NHS sits rather uncomfortably with a disquisition on the elixir of life and the folly of human dreams of immortality, and an intertextual *riposte* to his fellow Royal Court playwright, Samuel Beckett. Nonetheless, the various strands of the play are brought together in an ending which sees the elderly residents re-empower themselves, and eventually regain control of their own destinies. The play's last moments contain a serious choric address, spoken by the old people.

Everybody, listen! Take warning from us. Be cheerful in your old age. Find some useful hobby. Fretwork. Rugmaking. Basketry. Make yourselves *needed*. Remember: a busy pair of hands are worth ten thousand times the Crown of a Queen. Go home and remember: your lives, too, will have their termination.

(Arden 1964: 272)

On the page, the content may seem overly didactic, even trite. Yet as the play's 'chorus of elders' usurps both Copperthwaite and Crape in their function of directly addressing the audience, their group voice also takes on a kind of authority, delivering a message which has something of the *memento mori* about it, but which also contains pragmatic advice for positive ageing.

'A workhouse that has been converted into a hospital': The care home as a total institution

The ending of *The Happy Haven* is a response, not just to Beckett's pessimism, but to one of the common fears about ageing: the fear that in the process, we may somehow become less ourselves, less human. As western society has learned to rely less on the extended family for late-life care and more on the professional services of trained care workers in controlled environments, the parallel fear of the dehumanized institutionalized environment raises its head.

I have already suggested how Erving Goffman's notions of everyday performance might be applied to the elderly, and how one of the central aspects of Goffman's explanation of social dramaturgy is his insistence that effective 'impression management' depends on the performer being able to keep a clear distinction between the 'front' and 'back' regions. In *Asylums*, his work on mental hospitals, Goffman explored the way in which under certain circumstances, stigmatized individuals are exiled to special places where such separation does not exist. The first sentence of his book explains with admirable clarity what he intends to study:

> A total institution may be defined as a place of residence and work where a large number of like-situated individuals, cut off from the wider society for an appreciable period of time, together lead an enclosed, formally administered round of life.
>
> (Goffman [1961] 1991: 6)

Goffman's *Asylums* both pre-dates and to some extent prefigures the work of Michel Foucault and his analysis – both in *The Birth of the Clinic* ([1963] 1988) and *Discipline and Punish* ([1975] 1977) – of the workings of institutionalized power. Like Foucault, Goffman focuses on some of the more extreme examples of total institutions; and like Foucault, his findings have implications elsewhere. Just as Bentham's Panopticon, which haunts the pages of *Discipline and Punish*, controls prison inmates of the prison through a (potentially) constant denial of privacy, so Goffman's analysis of total institutions, like the asylum, shows the effect of a regime in which there is no 'backstage', no place in which to develop the performance whose quality is so essential to a sense of self. Goffman's examples of total institutions include the prison, the mid-twentieth-century mental institution and – that archetypal image of dehumanization, whose ghost still haunted the western imagination throughout the 1950s and 1960s – the concentration camp. He goes into some detail about the processes of 'mortification of the self' which becoming an inmate (or 'recruit') in such an institution involves: processes such as subjection to degrading and humiliating treatments which are designed to mark a clear separation between the inmates' former selves and their institutional selves.

> The recruit comes into the establishment with a conception of himself made possible by certain stable social arrangements in his home world. Upon entrance he is immediately stripped of the support provided by these arrangements. In the accurate language of some of our oldest total institutions, he begins a series of abasements, degradations, humiliations, and profanations of self. His self is systematically, if often unintentionally, mortified. He begins some radical shifts in his *moral career*, a career composed of the progressive changes that occur in the beliefs that he has concerning himself and significant others ... The processes by which a person's self is mortified are fairly standard in total institutions.
>
> (Goffman [1961] 1991: 24)

Like Foucault, Goffman emphasizes not the individual humanity or brutality, the thoughtfulness or the callousness of the orderlies, nurses, warders or guards, so much as the structural and institutional constraints which are involved in setting up 'a place of residence and work where a large number of like-situated individuals, cut off from the wider society for an appreciable period of time, together lead an enclosed, formally administered round of life.' The point is not that care homes for the elderly in the UK or elsewhere in Europe are like prisons or concentration camps. It is that there exists a popular nightmare – a *meme*, if you like – which dwells upon the possibility that they might become so. This is the nightmare that plays such as *The Happy Haven* articulate, and it is grounded in the reality that care homes *do* share some of the structural characteristics of the total institution, and some of the same interactional dynamics.

The point is made (wittily and rather gracefully) in a stage direction in a play by Alan Bennett, a writer whose plays have repeatedly maintained a strong and sympathetically comic focus on ageing and the aged. His television play *Rolling Home* is set in a nursing home for the elderly. He describes it as 'a nineteenth-century building – a workhouse, probably, that has been converted into a hospital' (Bennett 2003: 2). This apparently throwaway description speaks volumes, and in his introduction to the play Bennett makes it clear that the visual specifics are as important as the dialogue.

> In my experience – and this applies to stage as well as television – authors are seldom given much credit for visual sense, the setting one carries in one's head when writing not being thought to be of much relevance when it comes to the design. To my mind, though, it's as pertinent as the words themselves.
>
> (Bennett 2003: xi)

The setting that Bennett carries in his head for *Rolling Home* makes explicit the link between the workhouse and the care home. And although the two have had rather different connotations, the care home is to an extent a direct descendant of the Victorian workhouse. Largely because of the influence of fictional accounts such as Charles Dickens' *Oliver Twist* and *Our Mutual Friend*, the workhouse has come to symbolize some of the worst abuses of a welfare system. While various kinds of workhouses (or poorhouses) had existed since Elizabethan times, it is the Victorian version which is so infamous for the dread in which it was held by the working class of its day. It was a product of the 1834 Poor Law Amendment Act, an Act which led to the building of more than six hundred of these grim edifices, so similar to the prisons to which contemporary writers frequently compared them (see Bruce 1961: 92). The Act's inspiration can be traced (like the Panopticon mentioned previously) to the philosopher Jeremy Bentham, whose pilot plan for a workhouse-based poor-relief system was published as *Pauper Management Improved* in 1798. If the central ideological platform of the Act was its attempt to establish a clear distinction between the 'deserving' and the 'undeserving' poor, its actual effect was a welfare structure which at worst was characterized by 'systematic, institutional cruelty informed by abstract economic principles' (Stokes 2001: 711), and which even at its best risked dehumanizing 'the poor' by treating them as a group that must be institutionally managed and controlled, rather than as individuals. Bentham's monolithic vision was of a system which he estimated would involve a million or more poor people; not all of these would be elderly, of course, but in an economic system with no old age pension (which was introduced in 1928) and with little other provision for those too old to earn a living wage, the elderly made up a large percentage of the residents of workhouses. Bentham's stipulation that relief would be dependent upon admittance to and residence in a workhouse was formalized by the 1834 Act as its key mechanism for poverty management, and a single central authority was established to regulate and supervise all poor relief.

While institutional cruelty was certainly evident in the nineteenth-century workhouse, Dickens' critique tells only part of the story. The Victorian workhouse was a genuine attempt to deal with the increasing number of particularly urban poor and elderly in a context where some of the traditional rural care structures of both family and parish had broken down along with the large-scale migration into the cities. Certainly Bentham himself, in his project 'to organize every aspect of the lives of the poor, and thereby make charity an institution, not just an arbitrary, unhelpful interference with the labor market' saw his institution as being – in a rather Foucauldian way – simultaneously nurturing *and* controlling (Stokes 2001: 713).

The workhouse, too, functioned as an infirmary and hospital for the poor and the elderly – inefficiently at first (again, Dickens wrote passionately to newspapers about the poor quality of medical care in workhouses) but increasingly well as the century progressed. The following anonymous report on nursing in workhouse infirmaries, from the *British Medical Journal* of 1896 explains that

> The Workhouse Infirmary Nursing Association was founded in 1879 in order to supply Boards of Guardians with competent and duly trained nurses. Before the Association was started workhouse nursing was of a very casual character; in many places it was carried out by paupers, and much of the nursing was in the hands of unskilled and untrained people. The humane treatment of the poor was a matter of much importance, and the Association set to work to improve it.
>
> (Anon. 1896: 1004)

Even so, that account was written in the context of a call to the authorities for further regulation to ensure that only staff with medical or nursing qualifications were employed in that capacity in workhouses. Institutional and state-sponsored care for the elderly was clearly felt to be a case for concern at the end of the nineteenth century – not so much on account of deliberate cruelty, but because of widespread inefficiency, ignorance and inadequate staffing.

'Inefficient units': The elderly care home in the contemporary media

The BBC situation comedy series *Waiting for God*, written by Michael Aitkens, ran for forty-seven episodes over five series in 1990–94, and featured Stephanie Cole and Graham Crowden as two elderly people dumped in a care home by unloving relatives. Cole's Diana Trent, a highly intelligent and very angry woman joins forces in an unlikely partnership with Graham Crowden's kindly and mildly demented Tom Ballard in order to undermine the smoothly oppressive regime of Bayview Retirement Home. The comedy arises partly from a subversion of expectations regarding how old people in care homes 'ought' to behave, and partly from the clash both of personalities and world-views which underlies the anarchic partnership of Diana and Tom: Diana's rational atheism coming into conflict with Tom's benign Christianity. The target of much of the series' satire (and of Tom and Diana's stratagems) is the greedy and arrogant manager, Harvey Bains – a man who sees his residents purely in economic terms and whose great regret is that these 'oldies' are 'inefficient units'. Not one of the BBC's most groundbreaking sitcoms, *Waiting for God* is nonetheless significant on a couple of levels. Firstly, appearing as it did, in the last year of Margaret Thatcher's premiership, it offered the care home as a metaphor for the wider erosion of social values which had been such a significant outcome of the politics and policies of the 1980s. Secondly, for our purposes, its setting establishes the theme of the care home as a site of oppression and resistance – a theme we will see developed elsewhere in this chapter.

In the news media, this theme took a little longer to establish itself. When *Waiting for God* was first produced, the unfamiliarity of the idea that care homes might be run by unfeeling entrepreneurs motivated only by money contributed to the satirical 'bite' of the series. In more recent years, however, the idea has become virtually commonplace. The care home – or in some cases, the caricature of the care home as produced by the media and particularly the tabloid press – has increasingly been characterized as a place of institutional oppression. Headlines such as '5,000 complaints a month over care home abuse fears' (*Daily Mail*, 5 May 2008) and 'Caught on camera: Care home workers arrested for hitting and taunting naked dementia patient, 78' (*Daily Mail*, 8 April 2011) and even 'Couple who ran care home are arrested "for murder of five elderly residents"' (*Daily Mail*, 10 December 2007) have fanned the flames of a natural concern about institutionalization in old age into something like the dread felt by the Victorian working classes for their workhouses. A 2011 Care Quality Commission report on dignity and nutrition in elder hospital care, which received a very high level of media attention, found that over half of hospitals inspected were falling short to some degree in the basic care they provided to elderly people. Media headlines in the national press tended to be along the lines of *The Guardian's* 'Hospitals lambasted for "alarming" treatment of older people', and Michelle Mitchell, director of Age UK, commented, 'This shows shocking complacency on the part of those hospitals towards an essential part of good healthcare and there are no excuses' (*The Guardian*, 13 October 2011). The care of the elderly in their homes has received similarly bad press. Only a month later, a review of home care for the elderly carried out by the Equality and Human Rights Commission found that basic care for the elderly in their own homes in England is so bad that it regularly breaches human rights. Highlighting cases of physical abuse, theft, neglect and disregard for privacy and dignity, the report concluded:

Many of these incidents amount to human rights breaches. The cumulative impact on older people can be profoundly depressing and stressful: tears, frustration, expressions of a desire to die and feelings of being stripped of self-worth and dignity.

(Anon. 2011b: 5)

Care homes of all kinds had increasingly come under the spotlight during 2010–11, starting with the dramatic collapse of Southern Cross. In the summer of 2011 Southern Cross – which at the time was Britain's largest private provider of care homes for older people, looking after more than thirty-one thousand residents in seven-hundred-and-fifty homes – went into financial administration. This was a company whose success in the market place had seemed to promise a golden future for private involvement in health care. In the years after its foundation in 1996, running care homes for the elderly had 'seemed an easy way to make money in a country where the population was greying at a faster rate than anyone could remember' (*The Guardian*, 16 July 2011). However, following a series of complex financial deals (including – disastrously – a policy of buying up care-home properties then selling them again, while keeping a long-term lease) Southern Cross hit a financial wall in 2008, when it found itself unable to meet a £43 million repayment deadline. The signs were unmistakeable and in a single day its share price crashed from over £3 to just £1.30. Its attempt over the next two years to ride out the storm was unsuccessful. Cuts to the public sector meant that its main clients, the local authorities, had been forced to cut their own spending on social care by 10 per cent or more: they were able to send fewer clients to Southern Cross and were pressing for a reduction in fees for those they did send. At the same time, standards of care were deteriorating: by 2009, 30 per cent of Southern Cross homes had been served with improvement orders by Care Quality Commission inspectors, and the group's reputation as a care provider was on the slide. By June 2011 the company's half year results showed a loss of £311 million, and Southern Cross found itself unable to pay rent demands to the landlords who now owned its properties.

The catastrophic prospect that thousands of elderly and vulnerable residents might find themselves with nowhere to live led to calls for the coalition government to bail out Southern Cross in a way similar to that in which the banks had been rescued following the financial crash, but ministers refused to intervene. This response was driven in part by the government's ideological opposition to state intervention in what they insisted were local difficulties between private sector providers and their local authority customers. However, the situation was complicated by cabinet fears that the government's longer-term programme to involve more private sector firms in health care might be damaged if Southern Cross were to fail completely. At the same time, local authorities also seemed helpless to intervene in what was recognized to be the largest single collapse of social care provision that the UK had ever experienced. But many authorities had already sold off their portfolio of care homes to private sector concerns – in many cases to Southern Cross itself – and now lacked both the capacity and the expertise to take over the running of homes, or to provide care and accommodation for any but the poorest of residents. The Southern Cross crisis brought into sharp focus debates that were already under way: debates about whether private-sector operators can be trusted to provide social care, and about how we can continue to provide and pay for the increasing numbers of elderly people who desperately need such care.

The image of care homes got worse during that summer for other reasons, too. In June 2011 a BBC *Panorama* programme was broadcast; using an undercover cameraman, it documented systematic abuse of residents at Winterbourne View, a facility for adults with learning disabilities in Bristol run by Castlebeck Care Group. Experts on the programme described the abuse as amounting to torture: staff members were shown pinning residents to the floor, slapping and taunting them, verbally abusing them; in one particularly disturbing sequence a resident was forced into a shower fully dressed, then taken outside and left there until she shook from cold. As a direct result of the broadcast, four staff members were arrested; CQC (who had been severely criticized for ignoring earlier warning signs) carried out an in-depth review of all Castlebeck Care's facilities, finding approximately half of them to be non-compliant with one or more essential care standards; and the Commons health committee launched a wide-ranging inquiry into the state commissioning of social care facilities for the elderly and vulnerable adults.

Significantly, although Winterbourne View was not specifically an elderly persons unit, it had the effect of directing press and public attention once more towards conditions in care homes for the elderly. There are several reasons for this. The story picked up general themes and concerns about elderly care which were already in the air and which had been intensified by the ongoing Southern Cross story. Then again Winterbourne View was simply one type of institutional care facility, and the type of institutional facility with which the majority of the public are most likely to have some personal familiarity is the care home for the elderly. It is impossible, of course, to know for how many people this concern might have been intensified by the thought that at some point they themselves might be a resident of such a facility. Nonetheless, such considerations probably increased the tendency to transfer concerns from one type of facility to another. Thirdly, the Winterbourne View story was only the most vivid story of its kind: the kind of abuse which was so dramatically documented on national television had also featured in several less high-profile court cases relating to abuses in elderly care around the country. Many of these were reported only in local newspapers, while others made the national press. And so Winterbourne View began to stand, iconically, for care homes in general.

Stories in the press are predictably dramatic and predictably focus on *hiatus* – in this case on reports of breakdowns and failures of care, rather than on the undeniable good practice to be found elsewhere. The overwhelmingly bad press that elderly care – in hospitals, care homes and private homes – has received, has attracted an understandable response from some quarters. Writing in the *British Medical Journal*, Graham Mulley, Emeritus Professor of Elderly Care at Leeds University, attempted to redress the balance and focus on 'what the media forget to tell us' about social care homes. His narrative starts with a request from the BBC for him to participate in another Winterbourne-style exposé programme.

The programme producer told me that a care home employee had reported that a culture of poor quality care was going unchecked. The plan was for a journalist to apply for work experience and surreptitiously film examples of inadequate care. Would I consider being a consultant adviser, providing guidance on what constituted good practice?

I had just returned from doing a teaching round in an excellent care home, where nurses and care assistants provided first rate care – despite low wages and at times inadequate staffing levels. I knew how the staff were buffeted by relentless negative media stories, and how another undercover report might demoralise diligent workers. I declined to help, and disingenuously asked why they did not consider making a truly original programme, one which celebrated all the excellent work that is taking place in many care homes. There was a long silence.

(Mulley 2011: 5391)

It is hard not to sympathize with Mulley's position. Citing a further CQC report, Mulley stresses the excellent quality of care that exists in so many facilities, and all the good work that is being done in nursing homes to provide residents with a better quality of life. Media stories may sometimes actually create the very phenomenon that they appear merely to describe, and Mulley warns (realistically) that 'gloomy' reporting is likely to have negative effects both on care-home staff morale and on the state of mind of relatives of elderly residents, increasing their sense of guilt at having left their loved ones to the mercies of such a place. 'Perhaps', he concludes, 'all of us who witness excellence in care homes – relatives, professionals, and other visitors – should write or tweet positive messages to balance the prevailing nihilism' (Mulley 2011: 5391).

And perhaps we should. It is quite true that very frequently the reports themselves, by bodies such as CQC and EHRC, paint a rather more balanced picture than newspaper headlines would imply, citing instances of good practice as well as bad, and of successful units as well as of failing ones (Anon. 2011b: 4). Even so, these reports *are* predominantly critical, and there *is* a widespread concern that the human rights of many old people are being neglected or abused by the very structures which are intended to protect and enhance them. The over-riding feeling about elderly care is negative, and it amounts to a crisis of confidence. It is against this background of a crisis of confidence that the setting of the care home in contemporary theatre now operates.

Juliet and Her Romeo (2010)

One of the most unexpected recent uses of the care home as dramatic setting was to be found in the Bristol Old Vic's 2010 production of *Juliet and Her Romeo*. Subtitled on the rehearsal script as *A geriatric Romeo & Juliet. Adapted by Sean O'Connor & Tom Morris (with apologies to Shakespeare)*, the play is actually a fairly faithful version of Shakespeare's play – with the major twist that Romeo and Juliet (along with Tybalt, Mercutio and a few others) are imagined as two octogenarians into whose lives, in the Verona Nursing Home, love crashes unexpectedly and destructively. In this re-visioning of the classic story, the site of conflict is relocated from the streets and villas of a thriving Italian city state to the wards and corridors of a British care home.

As far as their textual adaptation was concerned, O'Connor and Morris did not need to apologize too much to Shakespeare: audience members who know the original play well would spot the occasional cuts, rewordings and narrative restructurings that they made, but these amount to no more than is the common practice of a lot of modern productions – especially those mounted by small-scale touring companies, where necessary economies sometimes have to be negotiated (as they were in Shakespeare's day) through textual adjustments.

The action takes place in the Verona Nursing Home for the elderly, a decaying Victorian building with unsympathetic modern additions. These do little to erase the vestiges of the home's original function as a civic hospital.

(O'Connor and Morris 2010: 3)

Morris, the artistic director of the Old Vic, argues that what is radical about the production is the notion of taking the 'emotional situation of the characters seriously' – something almost unheard of in a youth-obsessed culture. '[W]hy shouldn't people who are 80 have the same life-transforming experience when they fall in love as a 14-year-old?' he argues (cited in Costa 2010: n.p.). And indeed the idea of a late-life *Romeo and Juliet* seems to be one that *is* being taken seriously in contemporary theatrical culture, and *Juliet and Her Romeo* is not the only rewriting of the play for older actors that has been seen recently. Ben Power's *A Tender Thing* had been commissioned and performed by the Royal Shakespeare Company the previous year and at the time of writing is due for a Stratford revival. This was a much more radical reworking of the play which cut the characters down to just the two lovers, and cut the text up, re-presenting it as a collage which tells the story of an older 'married couple who discover that their lifetime together is drawing to a close [and] realize that they cannot contemplate being apart' (Power 2009: 47). O'Connor and Morris' adaptation, however, interests me more for three reasons: it makes much fewer changes to the text that most people know; it foregrounds the care home as an institutional setting; and it maintains Shakespeare's theme of interfamilial conflict, while giving it a contemporary twist. In *Juliet and Her Romeo*, the values of age and youth are reversed: family opposition to the love of Juliet and Romeo comes, plausibly enough, from their children's generation. The younger generation of Capulets, in particular, are portrayed as post-Thatcherite opportunists looking to cement the family finances through a late-life liaison for a mother who seems to have ceded power of attorney to them: as such they are as rigid, as oppressive and as self-centredly destructive as Shakespeare's older generation of feuding families.

The casting of the production was both age-appropriate and age-inappropriate. On the one hand veteran actors were playing fictional characters who were meant to be more or less their own age: Siân Phillips (Juliet), Michael Byrne (Romeo), Dudley Sutton (Mercutio):

all of them in their seventies and eighties. As a result they did not need to 'act old'. On the other hand, of course, the lines were written for – and we are used to hear them spoken by – young actors playing young characters. This basic disparity, between the familiar star-crossed adolescents – barely out of their childhoods, as Juliet's Nurse reminds us – and their new manifestations as the senescent care home residents, was the play's main producer of meaning.

The transposition of the action from youth to age has several consequences. The first – and one of the most positive – is the wonderful surprise of hearing actors like Siân Phillips speak the verse. It is a frequent complaint of theatre critics (and of directors and playwrights) that young actors today do not have the technique to speak Shakespeare's verse, that voice training is not what it used to be, and that the emphasis which young actors have to place on televisual naturalism and acting for the camera in order to make anything like a living wage have impoverished the classical stage, to the extent that the younger generation of actors find it increasingly difficult to physicalize the poetry of the text. That there is some truth in all this can be seen when an actor of Siân Phillips' calibre takes ownership of the verse, making lines such as these sing and resonate:

> Gallop apace, you fiery-footed steeds,
> Towards Phoebus' lodging: such a wagoner
> As Phaethon would whip you to the west,
> And bring in cloudy night immediately.
> Spread thy close curtain, love-performing night,
> That runaway's eyes may wink and Romeo
> Leap to these arms, untalk'd of and unseen.

(Shakespeare 1974: 1077)

Phillips' presence on stage in Abi Morgan's *Lovesong* has already been discussed, and if I return to another of her performances here, it is not, perhaps entirely coincidental. She may not have entirely cornered the market in beautiful old women, but her performances have enriched the vocabulary of the older woman in contemporary British theatre. Her delivery of this speech made it something unique. On one level there was her sheer technical ability, which enabled her to find those connections between sounds, meaning, her own voice and body, as well as her capacity to represent emotional range and her capacity to connect with an audience. And just as a good young Juliet will bring to this speech many of the stereotypical characteristics of youth in love (including excitement, naivety and thoughtlessness) so a good old Juliet brought to it many of the stereotypical characteristics of old age in love (including excitement, naivety and thoughtlessness). The young actress playing Juliet brings to all this the context of an implied personal history which an audience is encouraged to fill in, helped by hints from Juliet herself, her Nurse and her parents. This context might include a privileged but sheltered upbringing; fond but controlling parents who believe they have her best interests at heart when they have their own; a thirteen-year (or more) childhood of dutiful obedience and occasional mischief which is now turning into an adolescence which puts her into unprecedented conflict with those parents. Various individuals will bring various details to this, but there will be much that is shared. The older actress brings a different implied history – one which in Phillips' case spoke of a lifetime of disappointment and emotional deprivation. And so, on another level, the moment offers the human poignancy of this extraordinary and passionate discovery of love in older age. In the stage directions of the rehearsal script, this speech is introduced by the phrase 'So this is what it is like to be in love!' With or without the Shakespeare play in the background, the moment is a moving one.

However, there were also some other, less positive consequences of the play's transposition of the story of Romeo and Juliet from youth to old age. This was, in part, the result of the play's trying to do too much. For example, the play attempted to develop a class politics which seemed to have something to do with the feud between the families. The Verona Nursing Home was divided into two very separate wards: the Capulet Ward, 'for Private clients' only; and the Montague Ward, for 'Patients on benefits' – Juliet's Nurse became an NHS nurse and so on. It was a brave attempt to infuse the classic love story with a contemporary satire on the dismantling of the health service, but not an entirely successful one.

Since another underlying theme was that of the oppression of the elderly in institutional care, neither Capulet Ward *nor* Montague Ward were presented as particularly attractive places; and in the original conception of the production, the Montague/Capulet feud seemed to have roots in a dystopian vision of the future:

We are imagining a Soylent Green-type near future whereby the elderly, living longer are in 'protective care' and are sometimes forced into alliances by their families in order to protect cash and inheritances. All of the residents are old enough to remember the civil war. Some of them fought in it, the Capulets on the victorious monarchist side, the Montagues on the losing republican side.

(O'Connor and Morris 2010: 3)

This 'alternative history' (which may have been of greater importance in early rehearsals than it ever was in performance) was hardly developed, and an audience would have had a hard time picking it up, or understanding quite what the origin of the enmity between the two families actually was. That, of course, is equally true of Shakespeare's original play – but the impression we were left with was that the play was somehow 'about' current crises in the NHS, and in these terms the play did not entirely hold together. The class politics of the contemporary crisis in welfare are very different from the class politics of the two equally powerful Veronese families that Shakespeare envisaged; and the attempt to overlay the one onto the other raised more problems than it solved.

The production divided the critics, garnering both very positive and very negative reviews, and the different critical responses are good indicators both of the successes and the failures of the production. Critics were unanimous in praising Siân Phillips' performance. Paul

Taylor, writing in *The Independent*, described her Juliet as 'a physically frail but spiritually intrepid lady, almost like the ghost of herself in her white nightdress and lace shawl and yet at the same time still situated within a body that she refuses to consign to some socially dictated scrap heap' (Taylor 2010: n.p.). However, Taylor went on to say,

> I wish that I could be as complimentary about the rest of the proceedings. Watching this well-meant but incoherent – and I'm afraid sophomoric-seeming – farrago, I kept thinking two things. Why not just do the play straight but with elderly actors in the lead parts? That would raise all the 'issues' laboriously invoked here with a tacit eloquence ... Nearly every detail grates and fails to convince.
>
> (Taylor 2010: n.p.)

He is unconvinced by the deadly feud between the private patients and the second-class NHS Montagues, by the duel between Tybalt and Mercutio with Zimmer frames and walking sticks and – in particular by the idea – in the balcony scene, that Michael Byrne's Romeo has scaled walls to get there, a line which, on the night he was there, was greeted with indulgent laughter for the audience.

The Guardian critic Susannah Clapp, in contrast, read the audience's laughter in a more positive way; the laughs which greeted, for example, Benvolio's 'Let's retire', she suggests, were evidence that the audience was in sympathy with the aims of the production. 'This translation of the lovers from youth to old age will look like travesty rather than tragedy only if you think the centre of *Romeo and Juliet* is youthful rather than forbidden love', she argues, adding, 'Tom Morris's inventive production shows that isn't so' (Clapp 2010: n.p.).

And both responses are, in their way, right, since the issue, in the end, is one of *tone*. My own experience of watching *Juliet and Her Romeo* was a complex one, since the tone of the production seemed continually uncertain – an uneasy balance between one thing and another. The play works through quotation and opposition, and its meaning is produced through the constant tension between the 'geriatric' narrative, and the phantom presence of that 'other' narrative which we know we are also seeing: western culture's iconic tragedy of young love's struggle to try to assert itself in the face of ancient enmity. This kind of juxtaposition can, at its best, offer startling new insights of the kind that Siân Phillips gave us by her inflection of lines we thought we knew; or of the kind that Susannah Clapp saw in Michael Byrne's portrayal of a Romeo who 'begins ... as a man who is tottering towards decrepitude, but grows ... into a man for whom love means Lazarus-like regeneration' (Clapp 2010: n.p.). And yet, however good its heart is, this kind of juxtaposition does also run the continual risk of collapsing into the wrong kind of comedy – especially in those moments of physical violence and physical intimacy which are at the heart of Shakespeare's play.

Juliet and Her Romeo did have gaps in its logic, and it did fall over itself when it tried too hard to follow in detail the logic of its own future dystopian nursing-home setting. But on a general level, the institutional tensions, cruelties and petty bureaucracies of the Verona Nursing Home *did* offer a plausible context for this tragedy of circumstance, and there was a genuine poignancy in the narrative of the lovers who, trapped in this environment, are too old, rather than too young, to deal with the 'adult' world of their families. Moreover, in its juxtapositions, and in its respect both for the language of youthful characters and for the presence of the elderly actors, it also occasionally transcended the dichotomy between youth and age and allowed Juliet and her Romeo the space to meet each other with a passion, a tenderness, and an intimacy which did not call attention to itself but which simply *was*.

Chapter 11

On Song and Dance

'A really rather serious piece of work': *Forever Young* (2010–12)

On one level, Erik Gedeon's *Forever Young* (2010–12) has a good deal in common with texts and performances analysed in the previous chapter. Like them, it deals with the theme of the institutional oppression of the elderly, and – like *The Happy Haven* in particular – it stages and celebrates the residents' solidarity in resistance to that oppression. The overall effect, however, is very different, for *Forever Young* is a play in which form and content are seriously at odds with each other. On the one hand, the play and its creators claim to have something serious, positive and socially progressive to say about the condition of the elderly in our society; yet the play gains much of its theatrical effect by exploiting negative stereotypes of old age, stereotypes which are intensified by the popular music which constitutes the play's primary dramatic language. It is this contradiction, and some of its wider implications, that I want to explore in this chapter.

The first thing to say about *Forever Young*, however, is that it was a resounding local hit – a theatrical triumph within a specific community: that of Nottingham and the East Midlands. It played on the main stage of the Nottingham Playhouse in the spring of 2010 as an apparent piece of ephemera, and did so so triumphantly that it was revived the following year, and then the year after that for two more immensely popular runs. Repeat runs are comparatively rare in present-day regional theatres, and to achieve not one but two repeats is quite a sizeable success. It remains to be seen, at the time of writing, whether there will be a 2013 revival as well. The story, as such, is simple, and the play's director Giles Croft, who is also the artistic director of Nottingham Playhouse, describes it as follows. The action takes place at a time when

> Nottingham Playhouse is closed, it's forty years in the future and it's been turned into an old people's home, and some of the residents are actors who used to work in the theatre, and once a week they're allowed onto the stage – to reminisce, if you like, to replay scenes. But on the night that we meet them something very different happens.
>
> (Croft 2011: n.p.)

The 'something very different' that happens is that the elderly actor/residents, who are continually being bullied, patronized and generally oppressed by the care home staff in the person of 'Sister Sara' eventually rebel and attack her. As we have seen, medical care as a site of oppression is a frequent trope in popular culture, and the resistance of the inmates can become a metaphor for resistance to other sorts of political repression. *Forever Young's* nightmarish care home bears some similarity to that of Bayview Retirement Home in *Waiting for God*, while the domineering and destructive Nurse Ratched in Ken Kesey's *One Flew Over the Cuckoo's Nest* is perhaps the prototype for the figure of Sister Sara in *Forever Young*, the nurse/warden/controller of the Nottingham Playhouse Nursing Home, who masks the malevolent pleasure she takes in her power over the elderly residents with a veneer of efficient caregiving. At the climax of the play, when the residents finally overpower her, the audience is encouraged to cheer.

Insofar as *Forever Young* contains a serious dimension – and Croft maintains that it does – its message is a socio-political one:

> It superficially seems to be an entertainment but actually once you begin to investigate it it's a really rather serious piece of work about the condition that old people are put into – not the condition that they are in but the condition they are put into and how it may be better for all of us to rebel to some degree, to claim back part of our lives, which can be taken away from us when we grow old.
>
> (Croft 2011: n.p.)

Croft is an excellent artistic director and an intelligent director of plays, and while what he is saying here is in the context of an interview on the Nottingham playhouse website, whose main job – by definition – was to sell the show, he is clearly sincere when he says that he takes the show seriously. I, too, feel that it is a play that needs to be taken seriously – not least because the theatrical style of the piece depends entirely on exploiting stereotypes of old age in ways which are startlingly unreconstructed. *Forever Young* is problematic on a number of levels; all of these levels, however, are illuminating about theatre, ageing and popular culture.

The Nottingham Playhouse production was adapted and translated from an original German text by the Swiss playwright Erik Gedeon. *Ewig Jung* premiered in Dresden in 2007 and has had great success at regional theatres throughout Europe. The title page of the Playhouse rehearsal script, in fact, describes it as 'A *Songdrama* by Erik Gedeon. Translated by Ian Black with contributions from Gareth Morgan. Version by Giles Croft with a few additional gags by Andy Barrett' – which suggests something about the nature of the piece: not exactly collaborative, but involving many 'authors' including both Gedeon himself and Croft the director even before it reaches the stage. The composite German neologism *Songdrama* which appears on the title page denotes the particular genre of the piece: it is a genre – or perhaps more correctly, a technique of construction – which Gedeon himself is popularly credited with inventing, following his

> collaboration with the dramaturg Christiane Baumgartner. Out of this developed the new dramatic art form of the *Songdrama*. In this form – an advancement of the *Liederabend*

[song recital] – spoken text is almost entirely omitted. Action and dialogue take place exclusively through songs.

(Anon. 2007: n.p.; my translation)

There is, in fact, some minimal dialogue to help the plot along, but very little. And what distinguishes *Songdrama* from opera is the fact that the songs are predominantly not original, but are a collage of existing pop songs. One local Nottingham reviewer described the overall effect as 'a JiveBunny-style medley of tunes ... a bit like the film *Moulin Rouge*' (Douglas 2011: n.p.). There is nothing new, of course, in adopting popular songs for dramatic purposes. John Gay started the trend in England in 1728 with *The Beggar's Opera* – but when he did it he also wrote new words for the songs, whereas the technique of *Songdrama* involves leaving the original lyrics intact. In one sense, then, Gedeon's *Songdrama* exemplifies some of the key tenets of postmodernist construction: it is a collage of found texts, knitted together into a whole which is necessarily and consciously intertextual, in which meaning is created through continual quotation and there is nothing outside the text.

After a protracted opening sequence in which the caricature oppressor-nurse enters and sets the scene, much of the action of the play consists of a series of *lazzi* – comic sequences, each with their own logic, strung together to make a longer routine. These include a few local jokes (such as references to Nottingham sporting heroes Torvill and Dean, and a portrait on the wall of the director, Croft, which Sister Sara ritualistically worships), but on the whole there are basically three interlinked themes to these *lazzi*: the first theme is that of the actors growing old, remembering past performances and trying to relive past glories. The second is that of bodily malfunctions: fart jokes, jokes about false hair and false legs falling off, jokes about old people taking a long time to get out of their chairs, or up off the floor when they fall down, or back onto the stage when they fall off it. The third is that of rebellion: a series of *lazzi* built around small acts of defiance involving drink, drugs (some weed is smoked, some sherry sipped!), rude words ('twat!') and, above all, rock and roll. Rock music becomes the residents' mode of rebellion, in contrast to the anodyne songs and hymns favoured by Sister Sara: the anthem 'I love rock 'n' roll' provides the evening's first show-stopper. As the *lazzi* build, a party develops – only to be called to a halt, Malvolio-like, by Sister Sara, who tries to reduce the residents to their former subservient status. This is the point at which the rebellion finally happens: one of the residents shoots Sara (twice to make sure). Elated, the residents prepare to 'torch the cathedral, storm the BBC' – at which point the apparently dead nurse inexplicably revives and sings a song ('Thanks for the laughs') before treating the residents once more as children and sending them all off to bed. It is an extraordinary ending, and one in which it is quite unclear what stage logic is at work. Did they miss? Was she only wounded? Was it all a dream? Was the 'dead' nurse playing a trick on them? Was it all a shared ritual which they played out together? All these answers were theatrically possible but the play committed to none of them and refused to resolve the ambiguities. What seemed certain was that any potential for liberation which seemed to have been offered in their rebellion had either failed or was illusory in the first place. Despite which, the evening's finale and curtain call was a rousing chorus of 'We shall overcome', together with words dropped from the flies in music-hall/panto singalong style so that the audience could join in. This was followed by a *carpe diem* exhortation to the audience: 'Don't let the bastards grind you down' because 'we will all grow old'. Like *The Happy Haven*, then, the play ends both with a revolution, and with a positive exhortation to the audience. But whereas the revolt of the residents at the end of *The Happy Haven* amounts to a reclamation of personal power which emerges from the dialectic of the play, there is no such logic to the ending of *Forever Young*, where the death (and the subsequent resurrection) of the monster-nurse seems oddly random, and the final message of defiance consequently lacking in conviction.

Forever Young draws heavily on popular culture – not only in the shape of the pop songs from which its fabric is woven, but in terms of its whole method. For, when translated to a British context, it can be seen that Gedeon's *Songdrama* is actually a close relation to the modern British pantomime – another theatrical form which typically makes great use of the technique of quoting the pop songs of the day. Giles Croft speaks openly of the way in which the Nottingham version of the show makes use of panto – and indeed pantomime is central to the whole conception of the piece. The real-life actors – who then turn into the elderly fictional characters of *Forever Young* – are all from the actual Nottingham panto cast, and much of the marketing of the play was aimed at getting an audience who had enjoyed the actors' panto performances to come back to the theatre in order to share the joke about the theatre becoming an old people's home in 2050. Indeed, regional pantomime being what it is, the panto audience will probably have seen most of them time and again over the last few years, playing repeated stereotypes of Dames, princes, wicked uncles and the like. Throughout the play, the relationship with the audience is predicated on the assumption that the majority of the spectators will be regular Playhouse patrons, and as such familiar with these actors as local celebrities because of their pantomime background.

Familiarity is also the touchstone of the musical aesthetic of Gedeon's *Songdrama*. There is very little that is new: rather the audience is expected to (and does) recognize the melodies and lyrics which make up most of the evening's entertainment. The only character for whom this is not the case is Sister Sara. The songs *she* sings – with titles such as 'Silver Hair, Trembling Hands' and 'Dying', are not popular favourites, but are specially written by Gedeon for the show; they veer in tone between the patronizing and the ominous, between lullaby and threat. Cowed in her presence, the residents become themselves only when she is offstage, and the *lack* of familiarity in the songs she sings enhances this sense of her difference from the inmates.

Because the original lyrics of the rest of the songs remain more or less untouched, however, they retain an importance in terms of narrative and characterization: the choice is all. The songs tended to fall into various groups. Many of them emphasized youth or eroticism or both: songs such as Nirvana's 'Smells Like Teen Spirit', The Who's 'My Generation', Tom Jones' 'Sex Bomb' and 'You Can Leave Your Hat On', and Aqua's 'Barbie Girl'. These songs for the most part pointed up the disparity between their original articulation as part of rock 'n' roll/

youth culture and their performance now by the care home residents. They also contributed to the play's favourite trope and the source of a great number of its gags: the incongruity of octogenarian sexual desire. A few were popular love songs which, when sung by older characters, transcended this kind of sniggering humour: songs such as The Eurythmics' 'Sweet Dreams' and the Mamas and Papas' 'I Got You Babe' manifested something very much like tenderness. Others were classic pop anthems, which worked in a very different way: Gloria Gaynor's 'I Will Survive', and a rousing – if incongruous – final singalong chorus of 'We Shall Overcome' were all being repeated in a context other than their original uses as anthems for civil liberties, anti-racism and sexual equality – but survival, respect and overcoming are terms that can translate easily enough to a politics of positive ageing. Some of the songs were simply rather puzzling, such as the eponymous 'Forever Young' – not the sentimental bittersweet Bob Dylan ballad, but the 1984 hit by the German synth-pop band Alphaville, the lyrics of which include the immortal couplet 'It's so hard to get old without a cause/I don't want to perish like a fading horse'.

I quote that, not to dismiss it, but to make a point about structure, technique, and about the aesthetics and the ethics of theatre and ageing. Collage technique can be a very powerful mode of artistic creation but it has certain consequences. Dramatic character is created largely out of the words that that character has to say (or indeed sing) and if those words are going to be derived entirely or predominantly from existing texts, all of which are embedded in their own pre-existent contexts, structures and logic, then the actor has to find ways of negotiating any resulting inconsistencies, contradictions and fuzzy edges. (You do not have to be a card-carrying Stanislavskian to start to ask, 'But *why* am I saying this line? What do I actually mean by it?') The form of the *Songdrama*, with its more or less unbroken sequence of pop songs, demands that the choices of those songs be good ones, and the order in which they are presented be carefully and precisely orchestrated. If juxtaposition is going to be the primary dramaturgical principle of a performance, that juxtaposition needs to be particularly well thought through: better, I would argue, than it is in *Forever Young*.

There are two further juxtapositions which lie at the heart of the play. The first involves the disparity between the ages of the characters and the actors. The result of projecting the action of the play into the dystopian future of 2050 is, of course, that the 'characters' are forty years older than the actors who play them; thus, with the exception of the nurse, there is a cast of actors who are predominantly in their thirties and forties, playing characters in their seventies and eighties. They do so in terms of predictable stereotypes: stiff joints, problems standing and sitting, digestive disorders: all the stereotypes of young-playing-old are mobilized. (These, incongruously, included a costume design built around items such as flowery frocks, smoking jackets, fox furs and black lacy dresses – clothes which were plausible enough signifiers of old age in 1980, but which would be historical curiosities by 2050!)

I have suggested, in an earlier section which looked at the work of Frank Randle, that such stereotypes can, when handled well, be turned against themselves, and that the elder-as-trickster can have a subversive, even a liberating effect. This, clearly, was the intention in *Forever Young* with its narrative of resistance and rebellion. Two things, however, prevented it from working in these subversive terms. Firstly there was the fact that, unlike Randle's act, the play was not rooted in the politics of regional identity in a way that could make *use* of the stereotypes of old age. Secondly, and more importantly, the tone of the play was set by the way in which its second key juxtaposition was handled: the juxtaposition of – and the implied incongruity between – pop music and old age.

A prime example of the way this was handled was the sequence which involved 'Respect' – the iconic rock number written by Otis Redding, and which, in Aretha Franklin's version, became a feminist anthem. Franklin's explosive performance, and the lyrics in which a strong confident black woman demands respect from her partner, had lasting resonance in terms of liberation movements and the struggle for equal rights. In a production which aspired to be 'a really rather serious piece of work about the condition that old people are put into' (Croft 2011: n.p.), this was a song which seemed to have great potential in terms of encouraging the sort of respect for the elderly that might have some impact on the way that they are treated by society. In the event, the song was performed, by Douglas Jardine, in a way that brought the house down, but which cancelled out the meaning of the lyrics. His elderly actor postured and strutted in a grotesque geriatric caricature of the gestures of youth, quoting an 'attitude' to which he could no longer lay claim, or trying to channel the sexual energy of past rock 'n' roll heroes. The audience loved it: old age parodying the gestures of youth was a joke of which they did not get tired. And the entire routine negated any sense that old age should be treated with respect – or indeed, anything other than derision.

When the play co-opts popular music in the service of dramatic form, it sets in motion a particular set of ideas, beliefs and prejudices. The age dynamics of popular music are complex, and will be explored in more detail later this chapter; but in *Forever Young* the disparity between youth-culture songs and 'doddering' performances nearly always worked in such a way as to mock the elderly and to reinforce stereotypes of senility. It was this, more than anything, which prevented the play from being a serious piece of work 'about the condition that old people are put into' (Croft 2011: n.p.) and it was this which worked *against* any of the positive messages about the value of rebellion in ageing which the story might have delivered. This is what I meant when I talked about the relationship between form and content in *Forever Young*. Collage and juxtaposition can be powerful dramaturgical tools. In many postmodern texts they both highlight and mimic the way in which consciousness is constructed from the fragments around us (and held together, one might add, by the glue of ideology), in ways that can be both aesthetically effective and culturally valuable. But although, as I have suggested earlier, the play gestures towards some of the techniques of postmodernist performance, this is not really the game that is being played in *Forever Young*. And the result of the various juxtapositions in Gedeon's play was confusion rather than complexity; in the end, for all its goodwill concerning the situation of the elderly, it offered a theatrical experience which simply reasserted the master narrative of decline.

Too old to rock 'n' roll?: Young@Heart (2002)

Perhaps one of the reasons I was so disappointed by *Forever Young* was that a few years earlier I had been present at a performance by 'Young@Heart', an ensemble of senior citizens from Massachusetts, with an average age of around eighty, who specialize in covers of classic and contemporary pop numbers. The performance was at the 'Giving Voice Festival 2002: The Voice Politic' in Aberystwyth, organized by Joan Mills in association with the Centre for Performance Research, and the concert they gave really did combine joyous musical celebration with an implicit political statement about the value of older people. There has since been a documentary film made about the group, directed by the British film-maker Stephen Walker and simply called *Young@Heart* (2008). This follows the group through preparations for a particular performance, and is interesting in its own right, but what follows refers essentially to the Aberystwyth performance.

The concert took place for the most part on a bare stage, but occasionally a song would be contextualized by a surreally minimalist set or costumes (hospital beds, cowboy hats) which gave a faint narrative to the proceedings. In general, however, the performance was as simple as possible. Some old – and in one or two cases *extremely* old – people sang numbers from James Brown to Jimi Hendrix, from the Ramones to Coldplay. In some cases, these were the same songs that were used in *Forever Young*: it is probably hard to resist including, for example, Gloria Gaynor's 'I Will Survive' in such a context. As with *Forever Young*, some of the songs made explicit reference to old age – or at least, had lyrics which had particular meanings in relation to old age – but many others were simply love songs. The company were all good singers and some were exceptional, although it was also clear that for many of them the breath was not as strong as it had once been, the control a little less certain. The Giving Voice festival audience, which was highly knowledgeable in all things vocal, were there both for the music itself and because of the special status which 'Young@Heart' had as an elder choir, and they were well-equipped to read the various levels on which the performance operated.

Occasionally, the frame of old age gave new interpretative possibilities to songs we thought we knew well. The Police's 'Every Breath You Take', for example, is a song about a stalker, a sinister character – perhaps a jealous ex-lover – who is watching a woman obsessively:

Every breath you take
Every move you make
Every bond you break
Every step you take
I'll be watching you

(Sumner 1983: n.p.)

Restaged as the words of an old husband watching over his aged wife, whose every move was both frail and painful, it became a love song of extraordinary tenderness, redolent with the possibility of imminent loss. In such simple ways, the concert took well-known songs and created new meanings from them.

Both 'Young@Heart' and *Forever Young* share a single aesthetic principle – the juxtaposition of old bodies and a musical genre that is more usually identified with youth. It is such an important juxtaposition – not only in regard to these performances but also in relation to broader cultural experience – that it demands unpicking.

Pop music, its meanings and its values are, after all, intensely bound up with ideas about age and 'generation' (a term about whose exact definition demographers still argue). This is particularly true of that branch of popular music which comes under the broad, but vague heading of 'rock'. The paradox which that generates was handled in a 2010 BBC documentary – also, coincidentally titled *Forever Young* but with the subtitle *How Rock 'n' Roll Grew Up*. It opened with the following statement:

> From the first moment it fell upon alarmed old ears, it was clear that rock and roll was a young person's game. Music made by young people for young people, that never intended to grow up, or grow old. And yet it did. So what happened as the music refused to die, and its performers refused to leave the stage. What happens when rock's youthful rebelliousness is delivered wrapped in wrinkles?
>
> (Lunghi 2010: n.p.)

There is no single point at which pop music began, but for the sake of the current argument, let us take – as cultural historians frequently do – the release of Bill Haley's 'Rock Around the Clock' (1954) as providing a convenient marker, both in terms of the meaning of pop music and youth culture. The song started out as a B-side to another Haley number that sank without trace, but achieved cult status as part of the soundtrack of the film *The Blackboard Jungle* (1955) and it is generally agreed to mark the point at which rock 'n' roll entered mainstream culture. Thus a boy who was eighteen when Haley's record was achieving its first success in the pop charts would have been born in 1937, so is now (at the time of writing, 2012) seventy-five. The fifteen-year-old girl who screamed hysterically while the Beatles sang 'She Loves You' and 'Please Please Me' in 1963 is now herself sixty-four – that Methuselan age at which Lennon and McCartney imagined themselves scrimping and saving to rent their cottage on the Isle of Wight if its not too dear, and dandling on their knees their grandchildren: Vera, Chuck and Dave. There is nothing remarkable about this, of course. Generations grow up; children grow old and eventually die. There are countless songs about it, from Shakespeare onwards: 'Golden lads and lasses must, Like chimney sweepers come to dust.'

So there should be nothing unusual about contemplating Bill Haley's audience, or that of John, Paul, Ringo and George, growing old after all, and having to confront what it's like when they're sixty-four. Except that this is the generation that invented rock 'n' roll – or for whom rock 'n' roll was invented by the entertainment industry. And by the same token, the generation that invented teenagers, the generation that (according to Philip Larkin's wry poem) invented, just a little too late for him, sex. It is taking it too far to suggest that it invented youth itself. It is not even quite true to say that 'the teenager' was invented in the 1950s. The word itself had been in use for a decade or so by then, and while many social historians have assigned the invention of the teenager and the formation of teen culture to the period immediately after World War II, others (e.g. Schrum 2004) have pushed the periodization back into the 1920s. But it was during the 1950s that manufacturers, marketers and promoters began to take seriously the idea that 'teenagers could be counted on to spend their parents' money' (Palladino 1997: xiii), and nowhere more enthusiastically than in the music industry:

> As rock 'n' roll, teenage rhythm and blues became a marketing category in its own right, a category based on age, not race, a demographic shift that would change the very nature of pop music. All of a sudden, it was the beat, not the melody, that drove record sales: Teenagers accounted for 80 percent of the market by 1955, according to one industry spokesman, and if the beat they wanted was rhythm and blues, there's no reason not to give it to them.
>
> (Palladino 1997: 124)

And during the decade or so between 'Rock Around the Clock' and 'Sgt. Pepper's Lonely Hearts Club Band', both youth and old age were constructed and reconstructed in new ways and took on new meanings. Teen culture became increasingly distinct from adult culture, and popular music lay at the very heart of that reconstruction of generational identity. Youth culture constituted itself through a defining generational referent, one which gave it a sense of distinctiveness and vision. Or as Stuart Hall and Paddy Whannel put it at the time,

> For many young people, Britain in the fifties and sixties has been a society in transition, a society throwing out a number of confusing signals. Teenage culture is, in part, an authentic response to this situation, an area of common symbols and meanings, shared in part or in whole by a generation, in which they can work out or work through not only the natural tensions of adolescence, but the special tensions of being an adolescent in our kind of society.
>
> (Hall and Whannel [1964] 2006: 46)

As never before, youth itself became a cohesive force for the baby boomers, and the popular music of the period was one of its most potent symbolic expressions.

There was a particularly sharp edge to this youth culture's perception of age. 'Hope I Die Before I Get Old' sang Pete Townshend and Roger Daltrey in 1965 – a single, sharp, cruel and utterly memorable phrase, one of the defining rock lyrics, a line which cuts through the cliché, the age-old paradox that we may flinch at the prospect of old age, yet no one really wants to die young either. The Who had no qualms about it in 1965, no prevarication: old age is so distasteful, so disgusting that an early death is preferable, and they proclaimed the fact in a song whose very title claimed to speak for youth itself: 'My Generation'. That reaction is of course an extreme one – the strutting and posturing of a careless Peter Pan energy which has had neither the need nor the imagination to take seriously the universal human condition of ageing.

> People try to put us d-down (Talkin' 'bout my generation)
> Just because we g-g-get around (Talkin' 'bout my generation)
>
> (Townshend 1965: n.p.)

And in fact, of course, Pete Townshend and Roger Daltrey themselves, did not die before they got old, and at the age of sixty-six and sixty-seven, respectively, they seem, at the time of writing, to be enjoying a reasonably happy old age, continuing, among many other activities, to record and perform sets that include 'My Generation'. Bob Dylan turned seventy as I was drafting this chapter, Sir Mick Jagger and Keith Richards headlined at Glastonbury 2013 at the age of sixty-nine, to varying responses from journalists and satirists. Sir Paul McCartney is now sixty-nine. Such professional and artistic longevity is not without its ironies: as a result of years on the road standing in front of The Who's massive amplification equipment, Pete Townshend suffers from that caricature infirmity of old age, deafness. And the sight of the former cultural icons of a youth generation themselves becoming old is always easy meat both for the cynical and the nostalgic.

It is important to remember, though, that, like the 'invention of the teenager', youth culture and youth identity of the period were always, in part at least, the product of the market. In the words of Iggy Pop,

> 'Youth movement', 'youth culture', 'youthfulization' of pop and all that has always been mostly complete shit and its just been about seizure and marketing of a folk movement by the same old commercial and industrial forces that take anything.
>
> (*Forever Young*, BBC4)

What with one thing and another, then, we might be entitled to take that line – 'Hope I Die Before I Get Old' – with more than a pinch of salt. Entitled, perhaps, to respond to Townshend's childish outburst with a ringing affirmation of the positive ageing agenda, to spread the good news that even in the 1960s old people were already living longer, healthier and more capable lives than ever before, and that that upward trend is continued apace; to insist that the narrative of decline is not the only narrative available; to point out that the overall percentage of old age per head of population which is now spent in a state of sickness or disability is greatly decreasing (at least in advanced capitalist economies); and that by paying attention to the social, economic, medical and spiritual needs of the elderly, societies can – and often do – make it possible for many individuals to reach old age in a state of optimum health, and to enjoy a good quality of life with a high degree of independence.

And yet …

And yet the starkness of the line continues to resonate. It resonates in part because – despite all these qualifications – it did (and does?) claim so defiantly to speak for 'My Generation', and in doing so it emphasizes the importance of the notion of generation itself as an essential element of the identity narrative, and reminds us of the urgency with which those rising post-war generations defined themselves in terms of their youth. In an unidentified television programme from the BBC archives circa 1965, which was included in *Forever Young: How Rock 'n' Roll Grew Up*, we see Townshend being posed questions by his young audience. A well-spoken young woman asks him, 'In "My Generation" you write "I hope I die before I get old." Do you in fact mean it?' Townshend replies immediately and bluntly: 'Yes.' The young woman looks anxiously at her companions. That was not the answer she really wanted to hear.

The cultural binary, then, which places pop music and old people in opposition is deeply rooted in the politics and the ideology of pop. But although it is a powerful idea, it is not an invincible one, and what the 'Young@Heart' concert achieved, with its simplicity and openness of staging, was to resist the implicit assumption that the joyful energy of pop music and the concerns of old age are mutually exclusive. Whereas *Forever Young* used the juxtaposition of pop and old age to point out the incongruities, and thus wring some laughs out of the evening, 'Young@Heart' used the same juxtaposition to stress continuity – to reclaim the genre for a generation who were young when youth culture was in its own infancy. Like all such victories, it was temporary: assaults on ideological 'givens' need to be remounted time after time, and generational identity has become so central to the culture industry that the environment is a particularly hostile one. But the achievement of 'Young@Heart' was to demonstrate convincingly the possibilities of positive ageing by means of performance.

'Those little walls that people construct between themselves': *Kontakthof* (2010)

If pop music involves one kind of inbuilt ageism, dance involves another. In *Forever Young*, once more, dance was repeatedly used, like pop music, to make fun of the elderly characters: whenever the inmates of the care home tried to dance they did so badly, stiffly and, invariably, to humorous effect. And the joke is based in the undeniable physical realities not only of the ageing process but of dance itself. Dance is above all an athletic art form, and one which both embraces and celebrates an aesthetic of physical difficulty that is as demanding as any field or track event. Its practitioners need to achieve and display a level of technical and physical ability which, for the most part, is attainable only by the young. Classical ballet, in particular, sets its own standards of physical perfection and will callously reject those who fail to live up to it, through being too tall, too short, too fat, too disproportioned – or, eventually, too old! But in all forms of dance, a premium is set on youth. Injury cuts short many careers, but even without injury, few dancers' careers survive beyond their mid-thirties. After that there is a general expectation that dancers will move into teaching or choreography or arts management or directing (see Edward and Newall 2011). Dance as performance is generally a young person's game.

Generally, but not always. In the spring of 2010, the Barbican Theatre, London, mounted a short season of Pina Bausch's *Kontakthof* in honour of Bausch, who had died the previous year. The show was staged in two versions: a performance with a cast of 'Ladies and Gentlemen over 65' alternated with one with a cast of 'Teenagers over 14'. *Kontakthof* had originally been created by Bausch for her company Tanztheater Wuppertal in a 1978 production. A contemporary review described the piece as being set in

a large dingy rectangular room – some sub-prefecture transformed into a dance hall – containing a piano in a far corner and rows of identical wooden chairs along the walls. A group of 22 men and women, no longer in the bloom of youth, walk, dance, parade, touch each other, take flight, struggle, grimace. The men are stiffly dressed in double-breasted suits and ties; the women wear tight-fitting tacky satin dresses and bargain-basement high heels. Corpselike in pallor, these unglamorous, deprived figures fascinate for over three hours.

Whether dancing the tango, moving their hips disjointedly to *The Third Man* theme, or parading in a circle, grimacing or smiling coyly at the audience, the group creates a social universe of cold automatism in which conventionality betrays the frantic search for intimacy, desire, and inexpressible longing. Couples form and immediately separate, looking for yet another partner; a woman comes up to a man, leans over as if to kiss him, viciously bites his ear and glacially walks off; a man approaches a prospective partner, takes her hand, bends her fingers back painfully, and withdraws, totally indifferent. Yet another yanks out a hair from his partner's head, but instead of reprisals, they go off arm in arm, while others listlessly applaud. Sometimes, but oh so rarely, tenderness sneaks through.

(Wehle 1981: 529–30)

Kontakthof came from a period of Bausch's work which was marked by productions known for their bleakness and melancholia, and the German title is ambiguous; it means, roughly, a place of meeting (a 'contact-yard'), but the promise of human interaction is offset by harsher connotations: 'a place of difficult encounters, a prison courtyard, for example, or a brothel "salon" where clients and prostitutes carry out their furtive deals' (Wehle 1981: 529). And intimate human contact is certainly rare and fleeting in the world of Bausch's *Kontakthof*: in this place of difficult encounters Bausch constructs a narrative about men and women seeking tenderness and closeness, but continually being unable to find it, or losing it after only a brief moment. 'It is as if in reality they could not stand the dream about closeness after all, and as if they would be afraid of the big feelings, the big stories, the uncontrollable and impossible ones' (Hoghe and Tree 1980: 67).

The 1978 production, then, was not specifically 'about' age or ageing. Although the cast was 'no longer in the bloom of youth' they were not noticeably elderly by ordinary standards: photographs show images of men and women who seem to be in their twenties and thirties. But of course, in the world of dance age has a different meaning from its meaning in everyday life, and a dancer is 'old' in his/her thirties. Thus, while Bausch's slight deviation from the norm of youthfulness in her casting made a statement about ageing, it was a comparatively quiet one. Its focus was rather on 'those little walls that people construct between themselves' (Bausch, quoted in Wehle 1981: 530).

When she went back to the piece and reworked it, however, Bausch used the piece to focus more explicitly on issues of age – in terms of both youth and seniority. In 2000 she had produced a revival of *Kontakthof* which featured a cast of seniors, dancers over sixty-five; in 2008 it was staged once again with a cast of teenagers, the youngest only fourteen years old. The Barbican tribute season juxtaposed these two versions of the production, and in so doing created a new work, seen in two parts, and whose primary meaning was now derived from the relationship, and in particular from the contrast, between the two age-specific casts. The *Evening Standard*'s Sarah Frater, for example, found this relationship 'almost unbearably poignant', although she did find some problems with the level of technique shown by the older cast.

> The senior cast seem to preordain the young, who could be their former selves or their children, or remembered mistakes. In this respect, the elders dominate the two shows, although they were less good performers and not as able to imbue their gestures with meaning.
>
> (Frater 2010: n.p.)

Reviewer Judith Mackrell, however, disagreed with the judgement that the elder performers were inferior. Writing in *The Guardian*, she reports having found that

> the teens' performance fell far short of the seniors', which was rich in surreal comedy and human interest. *Kontakthof* is about the games people play in order to communicate; the older cast were able to bring a more knowing, cussed, tender, disruptive life to the material. Next to them, the teens appeared almost generic.
>
> (Mackrell 2010b: 21)

In a separate article, which focuses solely on the seniors' cast, Mackrell elaborates this sense that the older dancers were able to bring more to their performance than the younger ones:

> The fact that we don't expect to see older people engaged in such a public search for intimacy makes some of the material doubly shocking ... When the women, in unison, adjust their bra straps, suck in their stomachs, pull at their dresses, their

vanity and uncertainty seem extra vulnerable. But age brings power, too. One routine is choreographed entirely from small acts of spite – a flick of the ear, a slap of the cheek – and the dancers trade these punishments like old married couples. Another dance has the two sexes alternately barking orders at each other – again with a lifetime's expertise.

(Mackrell 2010a: n.p.)

The Barbican's programming drew attention to what we know instinctively – that *presence* counts for a great deal, and age is not value-free on stage. The 'embodied' performance relies for much of its meaning on the bodies that are doing that embodying, and on the meanings that we read from – or bring to – those bodies, and the 'same' dance performed by the two separate casts has two different meanings.

In song and dance performance we may see some of the delineations of the narrative of decline in their clearest outlines. We see ways in which certain kinds of art form are popularly constructed so as to exclude, in the first instance at least, the ageing body, and perhaps the ageing mind, too. The undeniable physical demands of modern dance, the history of youthful rebellion which is so central to the myth of popular music: these continue to undertake the cultural work of validating youth at the expense of age. Yet again, it has to be insisted that even in such instances, gerontideology is not monolithic. The 'Young@Heart' singers were able to make new meanings by exploiting and critiquing the assumptions underlying the cultural binary between pop music and old age; *Kontakthof* was able to deconstruct the unspoken association between dance and youth in ways that made the older body of the dancer culturally visible. Cultural forms can be turned against themselves, and made to question their own implicit assumptions, and the identity politics to which they appear to subscribe. It can be hard to do this, it is true; but it is possible.

Epilogue

The Amazing One-Hundred-and-Sixty-One-Year-Old Woman

Recent models of cultural history (I am thinking here in particular of the Foucauldian tradition) have frequently concentrated on the task of demonstrating that many of those things which we assume are 'natural' are actually social inventions, discursive structures which arose at specific times in response to particular societal and ideological pressure. Such models stress cultural rupture rather than continuity. They illuminate the paradigm shifts that have taken place in the way we conceptualize ourselves and our society; and they chart how old ways of thinking about ourselves at even the most basic of levels – gender and body, sanity and madness, self and society - are replaced by new social constructions, as successive ages reconfigure these aspects in ways that relate to contemporary concerns. In this exploration of old age and theatre, one implicit question was the extent to which this was also true of old age.

I would suggest that the answer is: only partially. Old age is – as social gerontology insists – culturally constructed. And different generations, certainly, have put their own 'spin' on its construction. But in the social construction of old age, what is most noticeable is the element of continuity that characterizes different generations' attitudes to and experiences of ageing. Rather than the decisive breaks with the past which the 'paradigm shift' model suggests, we find repeated themes and tropes recurring through the centuries. We may find, indeed, that the great paradigm shift in relation to ageing is just about to take place, as the current generation begins to come to terms with the full implications of an ageing global population. This has not, however, happened yet; and looking back over the last couple of thousands of years, the thing we see most clearly is a pattern either of acquiescence, or of various strategies of resistance to the master narrative of decline.

Earlier in this book, I referred to the angry critique of the 'Face Aging' exhibit at the Boston Museum of Science with which Margaret Morgenroth Gullette opens her analysis of that master narrative. Her outrage is fuelled in part at least by the combination of apparent scientific authority and bad science which the exhibit represents.

Everything promised them scientific 'truth' – their location in a 'Museum of Science' and the prestigious array of complex and nonhuman technologies involved: the robot eye with no human behind it, the computer-driven graphics, the 'interactive' button that produced the same effect forward or backward, invariably. And children are deeply curious about their life course, that mystery where your particularity scrunches up against unknown laws … Invariability was implied in the title of the exhibit too: 'This is the way all faces age'.

When I interviewed the children exiting I asked 'What did you learn?' The answer, in short was, 'I don't want to get old'. They had nothing more to add.

(Gullette 2004: 4)

In fact, the 'Face Aging' exhibit, for all its scientific dressing, had more in common with another, particularly North American, kind of 'museum'. In American culture (to a greater extent than in European culture) there has long been an explicit, and uneasy, relationship between the museum and the carnival sideshow. As one very knowledgeable nineteenth-century commentator put it:

The show business [meaning the business of exhibitions] has all phases and grades of dignity, from the exhibition of a monkey to the exposition of that highest art in music or the drama which entrances empires and secures for the gifted artist a worldwide fame which princes well might envy.

(Benton 1891: n.p.)

The speaker is the most famous proprietor of these exhibitions, the entrepreneur whose contempt for the intelligence of his customers has become a byword for cynical commercial exploitation: P. T. Barnum. Long before he gave his name to Barnum and Bailey's Circus, he was the first proprietor of the American Museum, New York, part of a long career spent exhibiting 'scientific' curiosities to a clientele that seemed eager to prove him right in his belief that nobody ever lost a dollar by underestimating the taste of the American public. And P. T. Barnum's very first exhibit, which he first displayed in 1835, was an old lady.

Her name was Joice Heth, and she was a slave, owned by one R. W. Lindsay, who had already been exhibiting her at the Masonic Hall in Philadelphia, with the following billing:

Curiosity – The citizens of Philadelphia and its vicinity have an opportunity of witnessing at the Masonic Hall one of the greatest natural curiosities ever witnessed, viz.: Joice Heth, a negress, aged 161 years, who formerly belonged to the father of General Washington. She has been a member of the Baptist Church one hundred and sixteen years, and can rehearse many hymns, and sing them according to former custom. She was born near the old Potomac River in Virginia, and has for ninety or one hundred years lived in Paris, Kentucky, with the Bowling family.

All who have seen this extraordinary woman are satisfied of the truth of the account of her age. The evidence of the Bowling family, which is respectable, is strong, but the original bill of sale of Augustine Washington, in his own handwriting, and other evidences which the proprietor has in his possession, will satisfy even the most incredulous.

(Benton 1891: n.p.)

The young Barnum had travelled to Philadelphia specifically to see Joice Heth; when he did, he was so impressed that he sold his grocery business and bought her on the spot. The cost was $1000, the price to include various 'proofs' of her age and claims: a bill of sale, dated 5 February 1727, from Augustine Washington, county of Westmoreland, Virginia, to Elizabeth Atwood, a half-sister and neighbour of Mr Washington, conveying 'one negro women named Joice Heth, aged fifty-four years, for and in consideration of the sum of thirty-three pounds lawful money of Virginia'.

According to Barnum, Joice Heth

> was certainly a remarkable curiosity, and she looked as if she might have been far older than her age as advertised. She was apparently in good health and spirits, but from age or disease, or both, was unable to change her position; she could move one arm at will, but her lower limbs could not be straightened; her left arm lay across her breast and she could not remove it; the fingers of her left hand were drawn down so as nearly to close it, and were fixed; the nails on that hand were almost four inches long and extended above her wrist; the nails on her large toes had grown to the thickness of a quarter of an inch; her head was covered with a thick bush of grey hair; but she was toothless and totally blind, and her eyes had sunk so deeply in the sockets as to have disappeared altogether.
>
> Nevertheless she was pert and sociable, and would talk as long as people would converse with her.

(Barnum 1869: n.p.)

Throughout his career, Barnum intermittently claimed that he bought Joice in good faith, and that he 'honestly and with good reason believed [her] to be genuine' (Benton 1891: n.p.). If so, it would have been one of the few examples of Barnum having been taken for the kind of sucker that he exploited so successfully in the rest of his career. But it is unlikely that this is the case.

Barnum travelled with her to New York, and after a vigorous advertising campaign – which stressed not only her great age, but also her status as the nurse of George Washington, 'the Father of our Country' (Barnum's poster text), he put her on display, where she would sit and weep and tell stories of the young George Washington to anyone who would pay to hear. Thousands did, and Barnum reputedly earned approximately $1500 a week over the course of several months. When, inevitably, the novelty wore off in New York, he took her on the road and repeated the success. He also, as he tells in his autobiography,

> kept up a constant succession of novel advertisements and unique notices in the newspapers, which tended to keep old Joice fresh in the minds of the public, and served to sharpen the curiosity of the people.
>
> When the audiences began to decrease in numbers, a short communication appeared in one of the newspapers, signed 'A Visitor,' in which the writer claimed to have made an important discovery. He stated that Joice Heth, as at present exhibited, was a humbug, whereas if the simple truth was told in regard to the exhibition, it was really vastly curious and interesting. 'The fact is,' said the communication, 'Joice Heth is not a human

being. What purports to be a remarkably old woman is simply a curiously constructed automaton, made up of whalebone, India-rubber and numberless springs ingeniously put together, and made to move at the slightest touch, according to the will of the operator. The exhibitor is a ventriloquist, and all the conversations apparently held with the ancient lady are purely imaginary, so far as she is concerned, for the answers and incidents purporting to be given and related by her, are merely the ventriloquial voice of the exhibitor.'

(Barnum 1855: n.p.)

The writer of the letter was, of course, Barnum himself, and it had the desired effect. Intrigued by Barnum's own claims that he was a fraud, the public flocked back to check out the reality, or otherwise, of his exhibit.

Joice Heth did not survive long on the road. She died in 1836, after touring with Barnum for seven months. Once more, however, Barnum ingeniously exploited his own dubious reputation. Joice's body was examined in public, and the surgeons who carried out the autopsy concluded unanimously '[t]hat Joice Heth could not have been more than *seventy-five*, or, at the utmost, *eighty years of age!*' The report in *The New York Sun* goes on to accept Barnum's own protestations of good faith.

We believe, however, that the person[s] who exhibited her in this city are not inculpated in the deception, but that they took her, at a high price, upon the warranty of others. Still it is probable that $10,000 have been made by this, the most precious humbug of modern times.

(Anon. 1836: n.p.)

In this last estimate, the *Sun* was on the conservative side. Barnum had charged admission to the public autopsy, and fifteen hundred people had attended at 50 cents per head: Joice's autopsy alone netted Barnum $750.

Before the revelations of the autopsy, however, New York newspapers had been greatly impressed by Joice, or at least, so Barnum would have us believe. In his autobiography he quotes the *New York Daily Advertiser* as having enthused that

since the flood, a like circumstance has not been witnessed equal to one which is about to happen this week. Ancient or modern times furnish no parallel to the great age of this woman. Methuselah was 969 years old when he died, but nothing is said of the age of his wife. Adam attained nearly the age of his antiquated descendant. It is not unlikely that the sex in the olden time were like the daughters at the present day – unwilling to tell their age. Joice Heth is an exception; she comes out boldly, and says she is rising 160.

(Barnum 1855: n.p.)

The invocations of Methuselah, Noah and Adam are both predictable and appropriate. In the light of these accounts, Joice Heth's one-hundred-and-sixty-one years seem fairly modest.

But then, these are stories set in a sacred mythical past, stories with a particular explanatory function. Joice Heth's narrative is more closely akin to those local tales of long-lived individuals in which British and European folklore abounds. These stories – like urban myths – are usually located at a short but significant distance from the teller: they are tales of someone who lived and died at the age of (say) a hundred-and-twenty 'a few years ago' and 'in the next town but one'. Sometimes they find their way into print, sometimes they remain as part of an oral tradition; either way, they greatly complicate the task of any historical demographer who is trying to construct a reliable history of ageing. These folkloric tales of superhuman longevity are usually no more reliable than the claims of Barnum for Joice Heth; constant retelling, however, may give them authority and the apparent attestation of fact. The 'museum' exhibition of her living body simply added a level of visual 'proof' to what, in many folk cultures, might have been taken on trust.

Joice Heth's story has, rightly, been told as part of the narrative of race and slavery in the United States (see Reiss 1999, 2001). It is also, however, part of the narrative of attitudes towards ageing. The point of including this account of Joice Heth is not to sneer at the gullibility of the American public (Barnum himself did quite enough of that). Rather, it is to emphasize the way in which notions of old age have held a certain kind of horrified fascination for audiences – a fascination which exists somewhere between attraction and repulsion, and which Gullette identifies in the responses of the children to the Face Aging exhibit at the Boston Museum of Science. But one person's museum is another person's freakshow; and freakshows are of interest to performance scholars, because there is something very naked about what they suggest about the ethics of performance, spectatorship and 'the gaze': the freakshow comes from a modality of culture in which there is no attempt to soften the edges of this. Joice Heth offers a good example of the way in which the freakshow illuminates a relationship between old age and a certain mode of spectatorship. In the eyes of the punters who paid Barnum their dollars and cents to view Heth's extra-ordinary body, the fascination of the experience was supplemented, no doubt, by Heth's apparent status as a living historical 'document', one which claimed to offer spectators an intimate link to the childhood of the Founding Father. But, as Barnum's final successful attempts to wring something out of his exhibit demonstrate, Joice Heth seems to have raised more profound questions than this in the minds of her audience. The publicity stunt claiming that she was simply a doll made out of whalebone, India-rubber and springs, sounds, at first hearing, merely comic. It also suggests, however, that the spectacle of this hundred-and-sixty-one-year-old woman touched on something in the minds of spectators which was to do with the very limits of their sense of humanity.

Barnum's 'show' presents us with a particularly cynical and exploitative performance of old age. Why am I concluding this study of *Staging Ageing* with such a downbeat case study, rather than with, say, an upbeat and inspirational example such as that of the 'Young@Heart' singers?

The aim of this book, I said at the start, would be to juxtapose the procedures and the analysis of theatrical scripts and various kinds of performances with the concerns and insights of age studies in order to try to discover what light each might throw on the other. But the ethics of performance are far from simple, and if, as I suggested earlier, most gerontologists are studying 'something that is not quite ourselves', just how far does that place us from Barnum's gawping public? When, in Chapter 1, I laid out some of the broad principles of contemporary age studies, I omitted one of its most important tenets – a tenet that is ethical rather than methodological. This is the expectation that the discipline should make a positive difference to the elderly and how they are treated. Age studies can (and, it is argued, *should*) make a contribution towards more people being able to age successfully through discovering and promulgating greater knowledge about ageing processes, so as to enable people to make better choices and engage in more positive behaviours, and through encouraging and understanding the best of way of providing positive interventions. It can explain both the experience of ageing and the ways in which the elderly can interact with society in ways that promote, enable and facilitate positive ageing.

The broad aim is unexceptionable, but I would like to focus, for a moment, on nuance. For example, an almost messianic note is struck by Ian Stuart-Hamilton's rallying cry in the introductory chapter of his *Introduction to Gerontology*:

> Should we ... view old age as a heroic summation of all that has passed, or as an agonizing brooding on all that has been lost? It is the responsibility of gerontology to address this question and ensure that in the future there is only one possible answer.
>
> (Stuart-Hamilton 2011: 17)

While applauding Stuart-Hamilton's crusading zeal and his conviction that 'gerontology's role is both to explain ageing and improve the experiences and lives of older people' (Stuart-Hamilton 2011: 17), I have reservations about the way in which he articulates his programme. The binary opposition of 'heroic summation' versus 'agonized brooding' appears to me to be an unhelpfully reductive way of thinking about the emotional textures of old age. And even if it were not, the complete elimination of the one at the expense of the other seems (at the very least) an unfeasible objective.

In this book I have tried to look at a variety of performances, ranging from the very complex to the very simple, from the highly artificial to the quotidian, from the emotionally empathic to the coldly exploitative, from the scripted to the improvised, from the inspirational to the depressing. The function of art has traditionally been to engage with the whole range and complexity of human experience, both positive and negative. The difference that this book seeks to make is based on whatever contribution it may make to our fuller understanding of the range and complexity of human experiences of ageing, as seen through the optic of drama, theatre and performance. Even performances such as Barnum's show of the 'One-Hundred-and-Sixty-One-Year-Old Woman'.

References

Adams, Kathryn Betts, Leibbrandt, Sylvia and Moon, Heehyul (2011), 'A critical review of the literature on social and leisure activity and wellbeing in later life', *Ageing & Society*, 31:4, pp. 683–712.

Adorno, Theodor (1964), '*Spätsil Beethovens' in moments musicaux*, Frankfurt: Edition Suhrkamp, pp. 13–17.

Ahrensdorf, Peter J. (2008), 'Blind faith and political rationalism in Sophocles' *Oedipus at Colonus*', *The Review of Politics*, 70:2, pp. 165–89.

Alakas, Brandon (2006), 'Seniority and mastery: The politics of ageism in the Coventry Cycle', *Early Theatre*, 9:1, pp. 15–36.

Aldington, Richard ([1931] 1998), Review of Frank Harris, *Bernard Shaw*, in *The Sunday Review*, 6 December 1931, reprinted in *SHAW, The Annual of Bernard Shaw Studies*, 18, pp. 95–99.

Alvarez, Alfred (1974), *Beckett*, London: Woburn Press.

Amoss, Pamela T. and Harrell, Stevan (eds) (1981), *Other ways of growing old: Anthropological perspectives*, Stanford CA: Stanford University Press.

Anon. (1836), 'Dissection of Joice Heth – Precious Humbug Exposed', *The New York Sun*, 26 February, http://www.lostmuseum.cuny.edu/archives/sun2261836.htm. Accessed 12 October 2012.

——— (1896), 'Nursing in workhouse infirmaries', *British Medical Journal*, 1896:1004.

——— (2007), 'Erik Gedeon', entry in German-language version of *Wikipaedia*, http://de.wikipedia.org/wiki/Erik_Gedeon. Accessed 9 November 2012.

——— (2011a), 'India – Family life and family values', *Marriage and family encyclopaedia*, http://family.jrank.org/pages/859/India-Family-Life-Family-Values.html. Accessed 8 July 2012.

——— (2011b), *Close to home: An inquiry into older people and human rights in home care*, London: Equality and Human Rights Commission.

——— (2011c), 'Elixir of life found on Easter Island', *The Telegraph: Science News*, http://www.telegraph.co.uk/science/science-news/8607582/Elixir-of-life-discovered-on-Easter-Island.html. Accessed 15 July 2011.

Arber, Sara and Ginn, Jay (eds) (1995), *Connecting gender and ageing: A sociological approach*, Buckingham and Philadelphia: Oxford University Press.

Arden, John (1964), *Three plays: The waters of Babylon, Live like pigs, The happy haven*, Harmondsworth: Penguin.

Arts Council England (2007), *Paving the way. Mapping of young peoples' participatory theatre*, http://www.artscouncil.org.uk. Accessed 14 June 2011.

Auslander, Philip (1999), *Liveness: Performance in a mediatized culture*, New York and London: Routledge.

Bacon, Helen H. (1995), 'The Chorus in Greek life and drama', *Arion*, 3:1, pp. 6–24.

Baird, Joseph L. and Baird, Lorrayne Y. (1973), 'Fabliau form and the Hegge *Joseph's Return*', *Chaucer Review*, 8:2, pp. 159–69.

Barnum, Phineas Taylor (1855), *The life of P. T. Barnum, written by himself*, http://www. lostmuseum.cuny.edu/archives/lifeofptbheth.htm. Accessed 14 September 2012.

—— (1869), *Struggles and triumphs or, forty years' recollections*, http://www.lostmuseum.cuny. edu/archives/strugglesheth.htm. Accessed 14 September 2012.

Baron-Cohen, Simon (2011), *Zero degrees of empathy: A new theory of human cruelty*, London: Allen Lane.

Basting, Anne Davis (1995), 'The stages of age: The growth of Senior Theatre', *TDR*, 39:3, pp. 112–30.

—— (1998), *The stages of age: Performing age in contemporary American culture*, Ann Arbor: University of Michigan Press.

—— (2001), '"God is a talking horse": Dementia and the performance of self', *TDR*, 45:3, pp. 78–94.

—— (2006), 'Beyond the stigma of Alzheimer's', *Journal of Medical Humanities*, 27:2, pp. 125–26.

—— (2010), 'Visions of Aging', *Journal of Aging Humanities and the Arts*, 4:1, pp. 65–67.

—— (2011), *Forget Memory: Creating Better Lives for People with Dementia*, Baltimore: Johns Hopkins University Press.

Battye, Marguerite (1957), *Stage Movement*, London: Herbert Jenkins.

BBC (2006), 'The original BBC Radio Ballads – History', http://www.bbc.co.uk/radio2/radioballads/ original/orig_history.shtml. Accessed 19 July 2012.

—— (2011), *Service review, BBC Radio 3, BBC Radio 4 & BBC Radio 7*, http://www.bbc. co.uk/bbctrust/assets/files/pdf/regulatory_framework/service_licences/service_reviews/ radio_347/radio_347_final.txt. Accessed 3 September 2012.

BBC Radio 4 (2011), *Mr Jones goes driving*, Promotional website, http://www.bbc.co.uk/ programmes/b00z58bj. Accessed 4 April 2011.

Beauvoir, Simone de (1972), *Old age (La vieillesse)*, translated by Patrick O'Brian, London: Andre Deutsch and Weidenfeld and Nicholson.

—— (1949), *Le deuxieme sexe*, Paris: éditions Gallimard.

Beckett, Samuel (1986), *The complete dramatic works*, London: Faber and Faber.

Bennett, Alan (1991), *Forty years on, and other plays*, London: Faber and Faber.

—— (2000), *Telling tales*, London: BBC.

—— (2003), *Rolling home*, London: Faber and Faber.

—— (2007), *Talking heads*, London: BBC.

Benton, Joel (1891), *A unique story of a marvellous career: Life of Hon. Phineas T. Barnum*, Edgewood Publishing, http://www.gutenberg.org/cache/epub/1576/pg1576.html. Accessed 2 March 2012.

Beugnet, Martine (2006), 'Screening the old: Femininity as old age in contemporary French cinema', *Studies in the Literary Imagination*, 39:2, pp. 1–20.

Bevington, David (1975), *Medieval drama*, Boston: Houghton Mifflin.

Billington, Michael (2010), Review of *On ageing*, at the Young Vic, *The Guardian*, 30 September, http://www.guardian.co.uk/stage/2010/sep/30/on-ageing-michael-billington. Accessed 20 July 2012.

Birren, James E. and Cochran, Kathryn (2001), *Telling the stories of life through guided autobiography groups*, Baltimore: Johns Hopkins University Press.

Blackmore, Susan (2003), *Consciousness: An introduction*, London: Hodder and Stoughton.

Blaikie, Andrew (1999), *Ageing and popular culture*, Cambridge: Cambridge University Press.

Botelho, Lynn and Ottaway, Susannah R. (2008), *The history of old age in England, 1600–1800*, Eight volumes, London: Pickering and Chatto.

Botelho, Lynn and Thane, Pat (eds) (2001), *Women and ageing in British society since 1500*, Harlow: Longman.

Bruce, Maurice (1961), *The coming of the welfare state*, London: B. T. Batsford Ltd.

Brustein, Robert (1960), Review of *Krapp's Last Tape*, in *New Republic* magazine, 22 February, p. 21.

Burian, Peter (1974), 'Suppliant and saviour: *Oedipus at Colonus*', *Phoenix*, 28:4, pp. 408–29.

Butler, Robert. N. (1963), 'The life review: An interpretation of reminiscence in the aged', *Psychiatry*, 26, pp. 65–76.

—— (1969), 'Age-ism: Another form of bigotry', *The Gerontologist*, 9:4, pp. 243–46.

—— (1971), 'Age: The life review', *Psychology Today*, 7, pp. 49–51.

—— (1974), 'Successful aging and the role of the life review', *Journal of the American Geriatrics Society*, 22:12, pp. 529–35.

Butler, Robert N. and Lewis, Myrna I. (1982), *Aging and mental health*, St Louis, MO: Mosby.

Bytheway, Bill (1995), *Ageism*, Buckingham and Philadelphia: Open University Press.

Čapek, Karel (1990), *Toward the radical center: A Karel Čapek reader*, edited by Peter Kussi, North Haven, CT: Catbird Press.

Care Quality Commission (2011), 'CQC publish first of detailed reports into dignity and nutrition for older people', Press release, 26 May.

Carlson, Marvin (2003), *The haunted stage: The theatre as memory machine*, Ann Arbor: University of Michigan Press.

Chamberlain, Clair (2011), Interview with Abi Morgan for Chichester Festival Theatre, http://www.cft.org.uk/uploads/documents/doc_856.doc. Accessed 28 August 2012.

Charney, Maurice (2009), *Wrinkled deep in time: Aging in Shakespeare*, New York: Columbia University Press.

Chivers, Sally (2011), *The silvering screen: Old age and disability in cinema*, Toronto: University of Toronto Press.

Christie, Sheila K. (2008), 'A crisis of gerontocracy and the Coventry play', *Early Theatre*, 11:1, pp. 13–32.

Cibber, Colley (1756), *An apology for the life of Colley Cibber, comedian, and late patentee of the Theatre-Royal. With an historical view of the stage during his own time*, Fourth edition, London: R. and J. Dodsley.

Clapp, Susannah (2010), Review of *Juliet and Her Romeo* at Bristol Old Vic, *The Observer*, 21 March, http://www.guardian.co.uk/stage/2010/mar/21/juliet-her-romeo-and-juliet-review. Accessed 28 August 2012.

Classen, Albrecht (2007), *Old age in the middle ages and the renaissance: Interdisciplinary approaches to a neglected topic*, Berlin and New York: Walter de Gruyter.

Clegg, David (2007), *Ancient mysteries: Stories from the Trebus Project*, https://sites.google.com/site/trebusprojects/projects-2/ancient-mysteries. Accessed 29 November 2012.

Cohler, Bertram J. (1982), 'Personal narrative and the life course', in Paul Baltes and Orville Gilbert Brim (eds), *Life span development and behavior 4*, New York: Academic Press, pp. 205–41.

Cokayne, Karen (2003), *Experiencing old age in ancient Rome*, London and New York: Routledge.

Cole, Thomas R. and Sierpina, Micelle (2007), 'Humanistic gerontology and the meaning(s), of aging', in Janet M. Wilmoth and Kenneth F. Ferraro (eds), *Gerontology: Perspectives and issues*, Third edition, New York: Springer Publishing Company, pp. 245–264.

Coleman, Peter G. (1986), *Ageing and reminiscence processes*, New York: John Wiley and Son.

—— (1994), 'Reminiscence within the study of ageing', in Joanna Bornat (ed.), *Reminiscence reviewed*, Buckingham and Philadelphia: Open University Press, pp. 8–20.

Collective Encounters (2012), *Third Age acting company*, http://collective-encounters.org.uk/arts-health-well-being/third-age-acting-company/. Accessed 12 December 2012.

Congreve, William ([c. 1690–1700] 1982), *The comedies of William Congreve*, edited by Anthony G. Henderson, Cambridge: Cambridge University Press.

Cornell, Paul, Day, Martin and Topping, Keith (1996), *The Guinness Book of Classic British TV*, Enfield: Guinness.

Costa, Maddy (2010), '*Juliet and her Romeo*: Star-crossed senior citizens', *Guardian.co.uk*, 14 March, http://www.guardian.co.uk/stage/2010/mar/14/juliet-and-her-romeo-bristol-old-vic#history-link-box. Accessed 28 August 2012.

Coveney, Michael (2010), Review of *On Ageing*, *What's on Stage*, http://www.whatsonstage.com/reviews/theatre/london/E8831285796429/On+Ageing.html. Accessed 20 July 2012.

Craig, Hardin (ed.) (1902), *Two Coventry Corpus Christi plays. 1. The shearman and taylor's pageant, re-edited from the edition of Thomas Sharp, 1825; and 2. The weaver's pageant, re-edited from the manuscript of Robert Croo, 1534,* London: Early English Texts Society.

Croft, Giles (2011), Video interview: Nottingham Playhouse production of *Forever Young*, http://www.youtube.com/watch?v=3xT-dAvBCys. Accessed 14 April 2011.

Cuffe, Henry (1607), *The difference in the ages of man's life*, London: Martin Clearke.

Cutler, David (2009), *Ageing artfully: Older people and professional participatory arts in the UK*, London: Baring Foundation.

Daily Mail (2009), 'Gosh, Posh, is this you in 2020? How our favourite celebrities might look in ten years' time', http://www.dailymail.co.uk/tvshowbiz/article-1239309/Victoria-Beckham-2020-How-favourite-celebrities-look-10-years-time.html#ixzz1gzDJFZRP. Accessed 30 December 2009.

Daily Telegraph (2008), 'OAP celebrities: Photoshop masters imagine what the stars will look like in old age', http://www.telegraph.co.uk/news/picturegalleries/celebritynews/3533709/OAP-celebrities-photoshop-masters-imagine-what-the-stars-will-look-like-in-old-age.html. Accessed 28 November 2010.

Darwin, Charles R. (1859), *On the origin of species by means of natural selection, or the preservation of favoured races in the struggle for life*, London: John Murray.

Davis, Rowenna (2010), 'Dementia training puts care staff in residents' shoes', *Guardian Online*, 2 November, http://www.guardian.co.uk/society/2010/nov/02/dementia-training-care-staff-antipsychotics. Accessed 5 September 2012.

Demastes, William W. (2002), *Staging consciousness: Theater and the materialization of mind*, Ann Arbor: University of Michigan Press.

Dhuga, Umit Singh (2005), 'Choral identity in Sophocles' *Oedipus Coloneus*', *American Journal of Philology*, 126:3, pp. 333–62.

Douglas, Ian (2011), Review of *Forever Young, Left Lion*, 6 February, http://www.leftlion.co.uk/articles.cfm/title/forever-young/id/3437. Accessed 10 July 2012.

Downes, John ([1708] 1929), *Roscius Anglicanus*, edited by Montague Summers, London: Fortune Press.

Duckworth, George Eckel (1994), *The nature of Roman comedy: A study in popular entertainment*, Second edition, Norman, OK: University of Oklahoma Press.

Duncan, Theodore G. (1982), *Over 55. A handbook on health*, Philadelphia: Franklin Institute Press.

Eagleton, Terry (2007), *The meaning of life*, Oxford: Oxford University Press.

Eaton, Mick (1978), 'Television situation comedy', *Screen*, 19:4, pp. 61–90.

Edward, Mark and Newall, Helen (2011), *Temporality of the dancing body: Tears, fears and ageing dears*, eBook Publication, IDP Press, http://www.inter-disciplinary.net/wp-content/uploads/2011/04/edwardppaper.pdf. Accessed 13 January 2012.

Ellis, Antony (2009), *Old age, masculinity and early modern drama*, Farnham: Ashgate.

Erikson, Erik (1959), *Identity and the life cycle: Selected papers*, New York: International Universities Press.

—— ([1959] 1997), *The life cycle completed – Extended version with new chapters on the ninth stage of development by Joan M. Erikson*, New York and London: W.W. Norton.

Evans, T.F (ed) (1976), *Bernard Shaw: The critical heritage*, London & New York: Routledge.

Evelyn-White, Hugh G. (ed. and trans.) ([1914] 2012), *Hesiod, Homeric Hymns and Homerica*, Adelaide: eBooks@adelaide, http://ebooks.adelaide.edu.au/h/hesiod/white/complete.html. Accessed 30 November 2012.

Falkner, Thomas M. (1995), *The poetics of old age in Greek epic, lyric, and tragedy*, Norman: University of Oklahoma Press.

Fallon, Gabriel (1944), 'The theatre of ideas', *The Irish Monthly*, 72:856, pp. 424–29.

Fisher, John (1973), *Funny way to be a hero*, London: Frederick Muller Ltd.

Fiske, Susan T. and Taylor, Shelley E. (1991), *Social cognition*, Second edition, New York: McGraw-Hill Inc.

Flanagan, Owen (1992), *Consciousness reconsidered*, Cambridge, Mass. and London: MIT Press.

Fletcher, Beryl S. and Fletcher, John (1978), *A student's guide to the plays of Samuel Beckett*, London: Faber and Faber.

Foucault, Michel ([1963] 1988), *The birth of the clinic: An archaeology of medical perception*, translated by Alan M. Sheridan, London: Routledge.

—— ([1975] 1977), *Discipline and punish: The birth of the prison*, translated by Alan M. Sheridan, New York: Vintage.

Frank, Arthur W. (2009), 'Tricksters and truth tellers: Narrating illness in an age of authenticity and appropriation', *Literature and Medicine*, 28:2, pp. 185–99.

Frater, Sarah (2010), '*Kontakthof* breaks the age barrier', *This is London*, http://www.thisislondon.co.uk/theatre/review-23821595-kontakthof-breaks-the-age-barrier.do. Accessed 17 January 2011.

Frith, U., and Frith, C.D. (2003), 'Development and Neurophysiology of Mentalizing', *Philosophical Transactions of the Royal Society, Series B*, 358, pp. 459–73.

Furstenberg, Frank (2000), 'The sociology of adolescence and youth in the 1990s: A critical commentary', *Journal of Marriage and Family*, 62:4, pp. 896–910.

Gagnier, Regenia (1991), *Subjectivities. A history of self-representation in Britain, 1832–1920*, New York: Oxford University Press.

Gahan, Peter (1997), '*Back to Methuselah*: An exercise of imagination', *Shaw*, 17, pp. 215–38.

Galton, Ray and Simpson, Alan (1962) *The offer*, directed by Duncan Wood, BBC Comedy Playhouse, broadcast 5 January 1962.

——— (1972), *Steptoe and son*, 'Divided we stand', directed by David Croft, BBC 1, broadcast 27 March 1972.

Gardner, Lyn (2012), '*Autobiographer*' review, *Guardian Online*, http://www.guardian.co.uk/stage/2012/apr/29/autobiographer-review. Accessed 18 September 2012.

Gennep, Arnold van ([1908] 2004), *The rites of passage*, translated by Monika B. Vizedom and Gabrielle L. Caffee, London: Routledge.

Gibson, Andrew (2006), *Beckett and Badiou: The pathos of intermittency*, Oxford: Oxford University Press.

Goffman, Erving ([1959] 1990), *The presentation of self in everyday life*, London: Penguin.

——— ([1961] 1991), *Asylums: Essays on the social situation of mental patients and other inmates*, Harmondsworth: Penguin.

——— (1963), *Stigma: Notes on the management of spoiled identity*, New York: Simon & Schuster.

Goldsmith, Theodore C. (2011), *An introduction to biological aging theory*, Crownsville, MD: Azinet Press.

Graham, Scott and Hoggett, Steven (2011a), '*Lovesong*' rehearsal Interview 1, http://zomobo.net/play.php?id=Zb4Hd5k2WuE. Accessed 29 December 2011.

——— (2011b), '*Lovesong*' rehearsal Interview 2, http://zomobo.net/play.php?id=ubXLHpQmtmg. Accessed 29 December 2011.

Gullette, Margaret Morganroth (2004), *Aged by culture*, Chicago: University of Chicago Press.

——— (2011), *Agewise: Fighting the new ageism in America*, Chicago: University of Chicago Press.

Hall, Stuart and Whannel, Paddy ([1964] 2006), *The popular arts*, London: Hutchinson.

Haraway, Donna (1991), *Simians, cyborgs and women: The reinvention of nature*, New York: Routledge.

Hayman, Ronald (1968), *Samuel Beckett*, London: Heinemann.

HelpAge (2011), *Report on elder abuse and crime in India*, New Delhi: HelpAge India Publications.

Hoghe, Raimund and Tree, Stephen (1980), 'The theatre of Pina Bausch', *TDR*, 24:1, pp. 63–74.

Hougan, Glen (2011), 'Impact of image: Designers and ageism', *Academia.edu* website, http://nscad.academia.edu/GlenHougan/Papers/864864/Impact_of_Image_designers_and_ageism. Accessed 20 December 2011.

Howe, Elizabeth (1992), *The first English actresses*, Cambridge: Cambridge University Press.

Hume, David ([1739] 1978), *A treatise of human nature*, edited by P. H. Nidditch, Oxford: Oxford University Press.

Hyde, Lewis (2008), *Trickster makes this world: How disruptive imagination creates culture*, Edinburgh, London, New York and Melbourne: Canongate Press.

Janáček, Leoš (1926), *Die Sache Makropulos*, London: Universal Edition.

Jalley, Émile (1998), *Freud, Wallon, Lacan. L'enfant au miroir*, Paris: Éd. EPEL.

Johnson, Malcolm L. (ed.) (2005), *The Cambridge handbook of age and ageing*, Cambridge: Cambridge University Press.

Johnson, Paul and Thane, Pat (eds) (1998), *Old age from antiquity to post-modernity*, London and New York: Routledge.

Jung, Carl Gustav (1933), *Modern man in search of a soul*, London: Kegan Paul Trench Trubner.

Kaminsky, Marc (1984), *The uses of reminiscence: New ways of working with older adults*, New York: Haworth Press.

Kazan, Elia (1988), *A Life*, New York: Alfred A. Knopf.

Kemper, Susan (1994), 'Elderspeak: Speech accommodations to older adults', *Aging, Neuropsychology, and Cognition*, 1:1, pp. 17–28.

Kenyon, Gary, Clark, Phillip, and de Vries, Brian (eds) (2001), *Narrative gerontology: Theory, research and practice*, New York: Springer.

Kenyon, Gary and Randall, William (1997), *Restorying our lives: Personal growth through autobiographical reflection*, Westport, CT: Praeger.

Kermode, Frank (2006), 'Going against', *London Review of Books*, 28:19, pp. 7–8.

Kershaw, Baz (1993), 'Building an unstable pyramid: The fragmentation of alternative theatre', *New Theatre Quarterly*, 9:36, pp. 341–56.

Keysers, Christian and Fadiga, Luciano (2008), 'The mirror neuron system: New frontiers', *Social neuroscience*, 3:3–4, pp.193–98.

Langley, Gordon and Kershaw, Baz (eds) (1981–82), *Reminiscence Theatre*, Dartington: Dartington Theatre Papers.

Kirkwood, Tom (1999), *The time of our lives: The science of human aging*, Oxford: Oxford University Press.

———— (2001), *The end of age: Why everything about ageing is changing* (Reith Lectures 2001), London: Profile Books.

———— (2008), 'Understanding ageing from an evolutionary perspective', *Journal of Internal Medicine*, 263:2, pp. 117–27.

Kirkwood, Thomas B. L. and Melov, Simon (2011), 'On the programmed/non-programmed nature of ageing within the life history', *Current Biology*, 21:18, pp. 1–6.

Knowlson, James (1971), *Samuel Beckett: An exhibition*, London: Turrett Books.

———— (1972), *Light and darkness in the theatre of Samuel Beckett*, London: Turret Books.

———— (1992), *The theatrical notebooks of Samuel Beckett. Volume 3, Krapp's Last Tape*, London: Faber and Faber.

Lacan, Jacques (1992), *The ethics of psychoanalysis 1959–1960: The seminar of Jacques Lacan. Book 7*, translated with notes by Dennis Porter, New York and London: W.W. Norton and Routledge.

Lee, Chris P. (1996), 'The Lancashire shaman. Frank Randle and Mancunian Films', in Steve Wagg (ed.), *Because I tell a joke or two*, London: Routledge, pp. 32–49.

Lieberman, Morton A. and Tobin, Sheldon S. (1983), *The experience of old age: Stress, coping and survival*, New York: Basic Books.

Linforth, Ivan Mortimer (1951), *Religion and drama in 'Oedipus at Colonus'*, California: University of California Publications in Classical Philology.

Lipscomb, Valerie Barnes and Marshall, Leni (2010), *Staging age: The performance of age in theatre, dance, and film*, London and New York: Palgrave Macmillan.

Loftus, Elizabeth F. and Palmer, John C. (1974), 'Reconstruction of automobile destruction: An example of the interaction between language and memory', *Journal of Verbal Learning and Verbal Behavior*, 13:5, pp. 585–89.

Luders, Alexander, Tomlins, Thomas E., and Raithby, John ([1810–28] 1963), *The statutes of the realm*, London: Record Commission.

Lukowski, Andrzej (2012), 'Review: *Autobiographer*', *Time Out*, http://www.timeout.com/london/theatre/event/259954/autobiographer. Accessed 25 July 2012.

Lunghi, Cherie (narrator) (2010), *Forever young: How rock 'n' roll grew up*, directed by Chris Rodley, BBC4, 2 July 2010.

MacColl, Ewan (1964), *The travelling people*, Radio programme produced by Charles Parker, BBC Home Service, first broadcast 17 April 1964.

Mackrell, Judith (2010a), Review of *Kontakthof*, *The Guardian*, 3 April, http://www.guardian.co.uk/stage/2010/apr/02/kontakthof-review. Accessed 6 May 2011.

—— (2010b), 'Give me an over-65 dancer any day', *The Guardian G2*, 8 April, http://www.guardian.co.uk/culture/2010/apr/07/critics-notebook-judith-mackrell. Accessed 6 May 2011.

Mangan, Michael (2002), *Staging Masculinities: Gender, History, Performance*, Basingstoke: Palgrave.

Manns, Joseph R. and Eichenbaum, Howard (2012), 'Consciousness and memory', in Tim Bayne, Axel Cleeremans and Patrick Wilken (eds), *The Oxford companion to consciousness*, Oxford Reference Online, Oxford University Press, http://www.oxfordreference.com/views/ENTRY.html?subview=Main&entry=t313.e206. Accessed 18 July 2012.

Marowitz, Charles (1978), *The act of being*, London: Secker and Warburg.

Marshall, Norman (1947), *The other theatre*, London: John Lehmann.

Marx, Stephen (1985), '"Fortunate Senex": The pastoral of old age', *Studies in English Literature, 1500–1900*, 25:1, pp. 21–44.

Maus, Katharine Eisaman (1979), '"Playhouse flesh and blood": Sexual ideology and the restoration actress', *English Literary History*, 46:4, pp. 595–617.

McConachie, Bruce (2008), *Engaging audiences – A cognitive approach to spectating in the theatre*, New York and Basingstoke: Palgrave Macmillan.

McKenzie, Jon (2004), 'The liminal norm', in Henry Bial (ed.), *The performance studies reader*, New York and London: Routledge, Taylor and Francis, pp. 26–31.

Merrill, Deborah (2001), *Life review interview manual*, www.clarku.edu/faculty/dmerrill/soc180/manual.doc. Accessed 29 August 2012.

Mignon, Elisabeth (1947), *Crabbed age and youth: The old men and women in the Restoration comedy of manners*. Durham, NC: Duke University Press.

Milhous, Judith (1979), *Thomas Betterton and the management of Lincoln's Inn Fields, 1695–1708*, Carbondale: Southern Illinois University Press.

Minois, Georges (1989), *History of old age, from antiquity to the Renaissance*, Cambridge: Polity Press.

Moran, James (2010), 'Meditations in time of civil war: *Back to Methuselah* and *Saint Joan* in production, 1919–1924', *SHAW: The Annual of Bernard Shaw Studies*, 30, pp. 147–60.

Morgan, Abi (2011), *Lovesong*, London: Oberon Books.

Mulley, Graham (2011), 'Social care homes: What the media forget to tell us', *British Medical Journal*, 343, p. 5391.

Myerhoff, Barbara (1992), *Remembered lives: The work of ritual, storytelling and growing older*, Ann Arbor: University of Michigan Press.

Nagel, Thomas (1974), 'What is it like to be a bat?' *The Philosophical Review*, 83:4, pp. 435–50.

Nathan, David (1971), *The laughtermakers: A quest for comedy*, London: Peter Owen.

Neale, Steve and Krutnik, Frank (1990), *Popular film and television comedy*, London: Routledge.

Nicholson, Helen (2005), *Applied drama: The gift of theatre*, Basingstoke and New York: Palgrave.

Noice, Helga and Noice, Tony (2009), 'An arts intervention for older adults living in subsidized retirement homes', *Aging, Neuropsychology, and Cognition*, 16:1, pp. 56–79, http://www.tandfonline.com/doi/pdf/10.1080/13825580802233400. Accessed 15 August 2011.

Norton, David L. (1976), *Personal destinies: A philosophy of ethical individualism*, Princeton, NJ: Princeton University Press.

Nuttall, Jeff (1978), *King Twist: A portrait of Frank Randall*, London: Routledge and Kegan Paul.

O'Connor, Sean and Morris, Tom (2010), *Juliet and her Romeo: A geriatric Romeo & Juliet. Adapted by Sean O'Connor & Tom Morris (with apologies to Shakespeare)*, London: Oberon.

Oglesby, Tamsin (2010), *Really old, like forty-five*, London: Oberon Books.

Orr, Jake (2012), 'Review: *Autobiographer*' in *A younger theatre. Theatre through the eyes of the younger generations*, 20 April, http://www.ayoungertheatre.com/review-autobiography-melanie-wilson-toynbee/. Accessed 27 July 2012.

Otway, Thomas ([c. 1670–80] 1968), *The works of Thomas Otway*, edited by Jyotish Chandra Ghosh, Oxford: Clarendon Press.

Pacala, James T., Boult, Chad and Hepburn, Ken (2006), 'Ten years' experience conducting the Aging Game workshop: Was it worth it?' *Journal of the American Geriatrics Society*, 54:1, pp. 144–49.

Palladino, Grace (1997), *Teenagers: An American history*, New York: Basic Books.

Parkin, Tim G. (1998), 'Ageing in antiquity', in Paul Johnson and Pat Thane (eds), *Old age from antiquity to post-modernity*, London and New York: Routledge, pp. 19–42.

Pavis, Patrice (2011), 'Aging in the performing arts', *Studies in Theatre & Performance*, 31:1, pp. 47–59.

Pennell, Steve et al. (2010), *Gay and gray*, performed at *ATHE Conference 2010*, Chicago.

Perotta, Peter and Meacham, John A. (1981–82), 'Can a reminiscing intervention alter depression and self-esteem?', *International Journal of Aging and Human Development*, 14:1, pp. 23–29.

Phythian-Adams, Charles (2002), *Desolation of a city: Coventry and the urban crisis of the late middle ages*, Cambridge: Cambridge University Press.

Plato ([c. 380 BCE] 1970), *The dialogues of Plato, 4: The republic*, translated by Benjamin Jowett, London: Sphere Books.

Plautus ([c. 205–184 BCE] 1912), *The comedies of Plautus, Volume I*, translated and edited by Henry Thomas Riley, London: G. Bell and Sons.

———— ([c. 205–184 BCE] 1913), *The comedies of Plautus, Volume II*, translated and edited by Henry Thomas Riley, London: G. Bell and Sons.

Plutarch ([c. 100 CE] 1936), *Moralia*, translated by Frank C. Babbitt (Loeb Classical Library Edition Volume 10), London: Heinemann.

Population Division, UN Department of Economic and Social Affairs (2002), *World population ageing: 1950–2050*, New York: United Nations Publications.

Power, Ben (2009), *A tender thing*, London: Nick Hern Books.

Prinz, Jesse (2011), 'Against empathy', *The Southern Journal of Philosophy*, 49 (Spindel Supplement), pp. 214–33.

Pullen, Kirsten (2005), *Actresses and whores: On stage and in society*, Cambridge: Cambridge University Press.

Randle, Frank (1938a), 'The old hiker' (Recording), http://www.youtube.com/watch?v= Goiam 3NFnzY. Accessed 3 September 2012.

———— (1938b), 'The old hiker' (Sound recording), http://www.youtube.com/watch?v=5_2QZF6 eCkU&feature=BFa&list=ULiPBLzBPHMsE. Accessed 3 September 2012.

———— (1942a), 'Wanted, a housekeeper', from *Somewhere in camp*, directed by John E. Blakeley, Mancunian Films, http://www.youtube.com/watch?v=iPBLzBPHMsE&feature=BFa&list=U LiPBLzBPHMsE. Accessed 3 September 2012.

———— (1942b), 'Putting up the banns' from *Somewhere on leave*, directed by John E. Blakeley, Mancunian Films, http://www.youtube.com/watch?v=jX8xI3CQsas. Accessed 3 September 2012.

Rappaport, Steve (2002), *Worlds within worlds: Structures of life in sixteenth-century London*, Cambridge: Cambridge University Press.

Reinhardt, Karl (1979), *Sophocles*, translated by Hazel Harvey and David Harvey, Oxford: Basil Blackwell.

Reiss, Benjamin (1999), 'P. T. Barnum, Joice Heth and antebellum spectacles of race', *American Quarterly*, 51:1, pp. 78–107.

———— (2001), *The showman and the slave: Race, death, and memory in Barnum's America*, Cambridge, MA: Harvard University Press.

Reuter, Edward B. (1937), 'The sociology of adolescence', *American Journal of Sociology*, 43:3, pp. 414–27.

Revere, Virginia and Tobin, Sheldon (1980–81), 'Myth and reality: The older person's relationship to his past', *International Journal of Aging and Human Development*, 12:1, pp. 15–26.

Rifkin, Jeremy (2009), *The empathic civilization: The race to global consciousness in a world in crisis*, Cambridge: Polity Press.

Rivett, Geoffrey (2011), *National Health Service history: The start of the NHS*, http://www. nhshistory.net/shorthistory.htm. Accessed 20 March 2011.

Rolinson, David ([2002] 2012), '"You dirty old man!" Masculinity and class in *Steptoe and Son* (1962–74)', *British Television Drama* website, edited by David Rolinson, http://www. britishtelevisiondrama.org.uk/?p=2346. Accessed 2 December 2012.

Rosenthal, Laura J. (2008), '"All injury's forgot": Restoration sex comedy and national amnesia', *Comparative Drama*, 42:1, pp. 7–28.

Rudlin, John (1994), *Commedia dell'arte: An actor's handbook*, London and New York: Routledge.

Runnell, Marti R. (1989), *Lee Breuer and his cross-cultural American classicism* (unpublished Ph.D. thesis, Texas Tech University), http://etd.lib.ttu.edu/theses/available/etd-02262009-31295005654149/. Accessed 21 June 2011.

Said, Edward (2004), 'Thoughts on late style: A lecture', *London Review of Books*, 26:15, pp. 3–7.

—— (2006), *On late style: Music and literature against the grain*, London: Bloomsbury.

Scala, Flaminio ([1611] 1967), *Scenarios of the commedia dell'arte: Flaminio Scala's Il teatro delle favole rappresentative*, New York: New York University Press.

Schrum, Kelly (2004), *Some wore bobby sox: The emergence of teenage girls' culture, 1920–1945*, New York: Palgrave Macmillan.

Schweitzer, Pam (2007), *Reminiscence theatre: Making theatre from memories*, London and Philadephia: Jessica Kingsley.

Searle, John R. (1997), *The mystery of consciousness*, London: Granta Books.

—— (2002), *Consciousness and language*, Cambridge: Cambridge University Press.

Segal, Erich (1987), *Roman laughter: The comedy of Plautus*, Oxford: Oxford University Press.

Shahar, Shulamith (1997), *Growing old in the Middle Ages*, London and New York: Routledge.

—— (1998), 'Old age in the high and late Middle Ages: Image, expectation and status', in Paul Johnson and Pat Thane (eds), *Old age from antiquity to post-modernity*, London and New York: Routledge, pp. 43–63.

Shakespeare, William (1974), *The Riverside Shakespeare*, edited by Gwynne Blakemore Evans et al., Boston: Houghton Mifflin.

Shaw, George Bernard (1914), 'Common sense about the war', *New Statesman*, December, full text archived at http://www.archive.org/stream/newyorktimescurr13635gut/13635-8.txt. Accessed 12 May 2011.

—— (1965a), *The complete plays of Bernard Shaw*, London: Paul Hamlyn.

—— (1965b), *The complete prefaces of Bernard Shaw*, London: Paul Hamlyn.

Sherman, Edmund (1991), *Reminiscence and self in old age*, New York: Springer Publishing.

Shippey, Tom (1997), 'Skeptical speculation and *Back to Methuselah*', *Shaw*, 17, pp. 199–213.

Silk, Avril (2012), 'Quiet courage and unsung heroes: Review of *The Exeter Blitz Project*', 9 May, http://www.remotegoat.co.uk/review_view.php?uid=8494. Accessed 20 July 2012.

Small, Helen (2007), *The long life*, Oxford: Oxford University Press.

Somers, John (2009), 'Drama and well-being: Narrative theory and the use of interactive theatre in raising mental health awareness', in Sue Jennings (ed), *Dramatherapy and social theatre: Necessary dialogues*, London: Routledge, pp. 193–202.

Snow, Charles Percy (1959), *The two cultures and the scientific revolution. The Rede lecture 1959*, Cambridge: Cambridge University Press.

Sophocles ([406 BCE] 1928), *Oedipus the King, Oedipus at Colonus, Antigone*, with an English translation by Francis Storr, Loeb Classical Library, London: William Heinemann, New York: G. P. Putnam and Sons.

—— (1955), *Oedipus Colonus*, edited by Richard C. Jebb, Cambridge: Cambridge University Press.

Sparks, Julie A. (1997), 'Shaw for the utopians, Čapek for the anti-utopians', *Shaw*, 17, pp. 165–83.

Spector, Stephen, (ed.) (1991), *The N-Town play*, Early English Texts Society, Oxford: Oxford University Press.

Spencer, Charles (2010), '*Gospel at Colonus*, Edinburgh Playhouse, Review', *Telegraph*, http://www.telegraph.co.uk/culture/theatre/edinburgh-festival-reviews/7959799/Gospel-at-Colonus-Edinburgh-Playhouse-review.html. Accessed 15 November 2011.

Steele, Richard ([1711] 1891), *The Spectator*, edited by Henry Morley, London: Cassell.

Steiner, George (1978), *On difficulty and other essays*, Oxford: Oxford University Press.

Stokes, Peter M. (2001), 'Bentham, Dickens, and the uses of the workhouse', *Studies in English Literature*, 41:4, pp. 711–27.

Stuart-Hamilton, Ian (2011), *An introduction to gerontology*, Cambridge: Cambridge University Press.

Stueber, Karsten (2008), 'Empathy', in Edward N. Zalta (ed.) *The Stanford encyclopedia of philosophy* (Fall edition), http://plato.stanford.edu/archives/fall2008/entries/empathy/. Accessed 26 October 2012.

Sumner, Gordon (1983), 'Every breath you take', on *Synchronicity*, Los Angeles: A & M Records.

Swift, Jonathan ([1726] 2005), *Gulliver's Travels*, edited by Claude Rawson, Oxford: Oxford University Press.

Tattrie, Jon (2009), 'Empathy suit simulates ageing', *Metro*, http://metronews.ca/news/151960/empathy-suit-simulates-aging/. Accessed 1 December 2010.

Taylor, Paul (2010), Review of *Juliet and her Romeo*, Old Vic, Bristol, *Independent online*, 18 March, http://www.independent.co.uk/arts-entertainment/theatre-dance/reviews/juliet-and-her-romeo-old-vic-bristol-1922947.html. Accessed 24 March 2010.

Tennyson, Alfred (1987), *The poems of Tennyson in three volumes*, Second edition, edited by Christopher Ricks, Harlow: Longman.

Thane, Pat (2000), *Old age in English history: Past experiences, present issues*, Oxford and New York: Oxford University Press.

—— (ed.) (2005), *A history of old age*, London: Thames and Hudson.

Thompson, Evan (2001), 'Empathy and consciousness', *Journal of Consciousness Studies*, 8:5–7, pp. 1–32.

Thompson, Paul (1992), '"I don't feel old": Subjective ageing and the search for meaning in later life', *Ageing and Society*, 12:1, 23–47.

Thompson, Paul, Itzin, Catherine and Abendstern, Michele (1990), *I don't feel old: The experience of later life*, Oxford and New York: Oxford University Press.

Thoms, William (1873), *Human longevity: Its facts and fictions*, London: John Murray.

Todes, Daniel P. (1989), *Darwin without Malthus: The struggle for existence in Russian evolutionary thought*, New York: Oxford University Press.

Townshend, Pete (1965), *My generation*, London: Brunswick Record Label.

Trueman, Matt (2012), 'An attic full of life's flotsam. *Autobiographer*, Toynbee Studios, London', *Culture Wars*, http://www.culturewars.org.uk/index.php/article/an_attic_full_of_lifes_flotsam/. Accessed 25 July 2012.

Turner, Janice (2012), 'What advice would Janice Turner give her 80-year-old self?' *The Times Magazine*, 28 January, pp. 26–33.

Turner, Victor (1977), 'Variations on a theme of liminality', in Sally Falk Moore and Barbara G. Myerhoff (eds), *Secular ritual*, Assen and Amsterdam, Netherlands: Van Gorcum Press, pp. 36–52.

Uhry, Alfred ([1986] 2010), *Driving Miss Daisy*, New York: Theatre Communications Group.

United Nations Department of Economic and Social Affairs Population Division (2009), *World population ageing 2009*, New York: United Nations.

Varkey, Prathibha, Chutka, Darryl S., Lesnick, Timothy G. (2006), 'The Aging Game: improving medical students' attitudes toward caring for the elderly', *Journal of the American Medical Directors Association*, 7:4, pp. 224–29.

Wadsworth, Philip A. (1977), *Molière and the Italian theatrical tradition*, Columbia, SC: French Literature Publications Co.

Waskull, Dennis and Douglass, Mark (1997), 'Cyberself: The emergence of self in on-line chat', *The Information Society*, 13:4, pp. 375–97.

Webb, Eugene (1972), *The plays of Samuel Beckett*, London: Peter Owen.

Wehle, Philippa (1981), Review of *Kontakthof* by Pina Bausch, *Theatre Journal*, 33:4, pp. 529–31.

Weismann, August (1889), 'The duration of life' (1881), translated by A. E. Shipley, in *Essays upon heredity and kindred biological problems*, edited by Edward B. Poulton et al., Oxford: Clarendon Press.

Wiggin, M. (1962), Review of *The Offer*, *The Times*, 1 July.

Wilde, Oscar ([1891] 1988), *The picture of Dorian Gray*, edited by Donald L. Lawler, New York and London: W. W. Norton and Company.

Wilder, Rosilyn (1996), *Come, step into my life: Life drama with youth and elders*, Charlottesville, VA: New Plays, Inc.

—— (1997), *The lifestory re-play cycle: A manual of activities and techniques*, State College, PA: Venture Publishing.

Wiles, David (1997), 'Theatre in Roman and Christian Europe', in John Russell Brown (ed.) *The Oxford illustrated history of theatre*, Oxford: Oxford University Press, pp. 49–92.

Williams, Bernard (1973), 'The Makropulos case: Reflections on the tedium of immortality', in *Problems of the self*, Cambridge: Cambridge University Press, pp. 82–100.

Williams, Raymond (1989), *Raymond Williams on television*, London and New York: Routledge.

Wilmoth, Janet M. and Ferraro, Kenneth F. (eds) (2007), *Gerontology: Perspectives and issues*, Third edition, New York: Springer.

Wilson, Brett D. (2011), 'Bevil's eyes: Or, how crying at *The Conscious Lovers* could save Britain', *Eighteenth-Century Studies*, 45:4, pp. 497–518.

Wilson, Melanie (2012a), *Autobiographer*, London: Oberon Books.

—— (2012b), 'Brief encounter with … Melanie Wilson', *What's on stage*, 24 April, http://www.whatsonstage.com/interviews/theatre/off-west+end/E8831335266901/Brief+Encounter+With+…+Melanie+Wilson.html. Accessed 28 July 2012.

Wilson, R. S., and Bennett, D. A. (2003), 'Cognitive activity and risk of Alzheimer's disease', *Current Directions in Psychological Science*, 12:3, pp. 87–91.

Wisenthal, J. L. (1974), *The marriage of contraries: Bernard Shaw's middle plays*, Cambridge, Mass.: Harvard University Press.

Wong, Paul T. P. and Watt, Lisa (1991), 'What types of reminiscence are associated with successful aging?' *Psychology and Aging*, 6:2, pp. 272–79.

Wood, Allen (2010), 'Molière's *Miser*, old age, and potency', in Valerie Barnes Lipscomb and Leni Marshall (eds), *Staging age: The performance of age in theatre, dance and film*, New York: Palgrave Macmillan, pp. 151–61.

Woodward, Kathleen (1991), *Ageing and its discontents: Freud and other fictions*, Bloomington and Indianapolis: Indiana University Press.

Worthen, William B. (1998), 'Drama, performativity and performance', *PMLA*, 113:5, pp. 1093–1117.

Wycherley, William (1996), *Love in a wood; The gentleman dancing-master; The country wife; The plain dealer*, edited by Peter Dixon, Oxford: Oxford University Press.

Index

A

Abendstern, Michele 5
abuse, of the elderly 26, 209, 211, 212
The Act of Being (Marowitz) 143–4
acting 3–5
    benefits 165, 168–70
    and the body 6, 8–9, 41, 110, 143–4
    and consciousness 21, 41
    and gender 44
    and memory 39, 50, 143–4
    Method acting 42, 45
    modern 214
    old age 45–7, 48, 225, 226
    and self-worth 169
    and stereotypes 44, 49, 50, 52
    see also actors; actresses; performance;
        Restoration comedy;
        theatre
acting theory 43–5 *see also* performance
    theory
actors
    Ancient Mysteries 144–5
    definition 35–6, 143–4, 165, 168–70
    and double consciousness 37, 41
    Driving Miss Daisy 130
    Exeter Blitz Project 158–60
    Forever Young 221, 223, 224,
        225, 226
    Gay and Gray 160
    Juliet and her Romeo 213–14, 217
    Krapp's Last Tape 137, 139
    Last of the Summer Wine 113
    Lovesong 139, 141
    Mr Jones Goes Driving 131
    On Ageing 163
    Romeo and Juliet 213

    see also acting; actresses; *commedia
        dell'arte*; performance; stereotypes;
        stock characters; theatre
actresses
    Autobiographer 145–6
    Juliet and her Romeo 214–15
    Restoration comedy 98–104
    see also acting; actors; performance;
        theatre
Adorno, Theodor 66, 67
Aeschylus 62
Afternoon Play (BBC) 128
Agamemnon (Aeschylus) 62
age 3–5, 43–5
    and class 17–18, 25
    and dance 167, 231–2, 233
    and gender 16–19, 28
    and theatrical performance 8–9, 112
    see also age studies; ageing; ageism;
        chronological age; old age;
        social age
Age Concern 167
Age Exchange 155–6
age studies 4, 8, 18–23, 28, 32, 242
    see also age; ageing;
        gerontology
Age UK 167, 209
ageing
    attitudes to 48, 49–50, 205, 237, 241
    and the BBC 8
    biomedical aspects 27–8, 124–5, 170,
        186, 194
    and the body 27–8
    and consciousness 4
    and creativity 66–7
    'crisis' 19–20, 24

Cuffe on 27
cultural aspects 16, 20–1, 25–6, 163
de Beauvoir on 4, 29
fear of 22, 51–2, 205
Forever Young 222, 225, 226
and history 30–1, 241
Kontakthof 231, 233
and liminality 73–4, 75
and literature 31–2
Lovesong 141, 143
The Makropulos Secret 184, 185–6,
    189, 190
and memory 123
Mr Jones Goes Driving 129, 130, 131
Last of the Summer Wine 113
On Ageing 162–4
and performance 6–7, 16, 32
and philosophy 29–30, 57, 58, 190
programmed 182–3
research issues 18
and resistance 8, 9, 73
Restoration comedy 99–100
scientific theories 181, 182–3, 184
Shakespeare on 89–90
as social construct 5, 15, 20–1, 237
and social psychology 5
stereotypes 23, 48, 131, 225–6
and theatre 7, 8–9, 32, 35, 43–5, 79–80,
    149, 225
uniqueness of 17, 18, 37, 43
see also age; age studies; ageism; body;
    decline; gerontology; old age;
    positive ageing
ageing apps 49–51
Ageing Game 47, 51
ageing successfully 21, 125–6, 133, 164–7,
    170, 205, 230, 242
ageism 21, 22–3, 28, 30, 32
    Classical Greece 15, 22
    and dance 231
    modern 46, 47, 48–9
    Restoration comedy 95, 103
    see also age; ageing; old age

ageist suit 52
ages of man (sphinx's riddle) 69
'Ages of Man' (Dutch painting) 90
AIDs 160, 162
Aitkens, Michael 208–9, 222
Aldington, Richard 180
All that Fall (Beckett) 134
American National Institute of Ageing 5
Amoss, Pamela T. 26
Ancient Mysteries (Clegg) 144–5
angry old man 74, 79 *see also senex iratus*
Antigone (Sophocles) 62, 69, 74–5
Applied Drama/Theatre 165–6
Arber, Sarah 23, 24–5
The Archers 144
Arden, John 199–205
Ariosto, Lodovico 84
Aristophanes 80
Aristotle 27, 57, 58
Arts Council England 32, 166
As Far as Thought Can Reach: A.D. 31,920
    (Shaw) 175, 178–9 *see also Back to*
    Methuselah
As You Like It (Shakespeare) 27, 89–90
Asylums (Goffman) 206–7
Auslander, Philip 7
Autobiographer (Wilson) 145–9
Ayckbourn, Alan 140

B
Back to Methuselah (A Metabiological
    Pentateuch) (Shaw) 175–84,
    194, 195
    and *The Makropulos Secret* 186–7
backstage 102–3, 206
The Bad Tempered Man/Dyskolos
    (Menander) 80–1
Badiou, Alain 137
Barnum, P.T. 238–41
Barrett, Andy 222
Barry, Elizabeth 100, 101
Basting, Anne Davis 32
Battye, Marguerite 43–5

Baumgartner, Christiane 222
Bausch, Pina 231–4
BBC 8, 128, 223 *see also The Archers; Forever Young: How Rock 'n' Roll Grew Up; Krapp's Last Tape; Mr Jones Goes Driving; Panorama; Radio 4; Radio Ballads; Steptoe and Son; Waiting for God*
The Beatles 228
Beck, Jessica 158
Beckett, Samuel 134, 205
  Endgame 137
  'Epic' theatre 39, 201
  Krapp's Last Tape 6, 7, 134–9, 142–3, 204
Beethoven, Ludwig van 66
The Beggar's Opera (Gay) 223
Bennett, Alan 38–9, 207
Bennett, D.A. 170
Bennett, Edward 139
Bentham, Jeremy 206, 207–8
The Betrothal of Mary 85–6
Bevan, Aneurin 200
Bible, longevity in 191–2
biblical plays 84–7
Bike Shed Theatre, Exeter 158
The Birth of the Clinic (Foucault) 206
Black, Ian 222
The Blackboard Jungle 228
Blackmore, Susan 135
Blind Boys of Alabama 70
body
  and acting 6, 8–9, 41, 110, 143–4
  and ageing 27–8
  and mind 5, 36, 165, 180–1
  see also ageing
Boston Museum of Science 48, 49–50, 237–8, 241
Botelho, Lynn 30
Bracegirdle, Anne 100, 101
brain 40–1, 170
  and memory 123
  and mind 35, 36, 42
Brambell, Wilfred 107–11

Brecht, Berthold 39, 180, 201
Brechtian style 140, 201, 205
Breuer, Lee 70
Briers, Richard 131, 145
Bristol Old Vic 212
British Medical Association 200
Britishness 7
Brown, Anne Wyatt 31
Brustein, Robert 136, 137
Burke, Kathy 145
Bury-Fair 101
Butler, Robert 22, 28, 123–4, 125
Byrne, Michael 213, 216
Bytheway, Bill 22

C
Čapek, Karel 184–91, 194, 195
care homes 123, 205–12
  and disempowerment 202, 209–12
  as dramatic setting 199
  fear of 202, 205, 206–7, 209, 211
  as metaphor 209
  quality of care 211–12
  and reminiscence theatre 164, 166, 168
  and resistance 155, 209, 221–2, 237
  and workhouses 207–8, 209
  see also Forever Young; The Happy Haven; institutional care; Juliet and her Romeo; Kontakthof; Radio Ballads; Talking Heads; Waiting for God
Care Quality Commission (CQC) 209, 210, 211, 212
Carlson, Marvin 127, 157
Carter, Jimmy 70
The Castle of Perseverence 85
Castlebeck Care Group 211
Centre for Performance Research 227
Cephalus 15–18, 22, 58
Charney, Maurice 31
The Children of Heracles (Euripedes) 62
choreography *see* dance
chronological age 5, 20, 22, 24–5 *see also* age
chronological relativism 23–5

Cibber, Colley 101
Cicero 17
Citizen Kane (Welles) 140
Clapp, Susannah 216
Clarke, Roy 113
class 17–18, 28
  and age 17–18, 25
  Driving Miss Daisy 130
  Juliet and her Romeo 215–16
  Radio Ballads 154
  Randle 114, 117
  Steptoe and Son 109
  Victorian 207
classical drama 57, 59, 80–3
  and love 79–80, 81, 83, 192
  see also Greece, Classical; Greek
    mythology; *Oedipus at Colonus;*
    senex
classical literature 83–4 *see also* literature/
  literary studies
Clegg, David 144–5
The Clod Ensemble 166–7
Cole, Stephanie 208
Cole, Thomas R. 28, 31, 125
Coleman, Peter G. 125
collage technique 213, 223, 225, 226
Collective Encounters 167
comedy
  Classical 80–3
  commedia erudita 84
  Middle Ages 84–5
  The Happy Haven 204–5
  and inappropriate behaviour 80, 83, 112
  Juliet and her Romeo 216
  Mr Jones Goes Driving 133
  The Makropulos Secret 189
  of manners 80, 95, 98, 101,
    103–4, 189
  Randle 114, 116
  Roman 81
  as therapy 107
  and variety shows 113–14
  Waiting for God 208–9

  see also commedia dell'arte; Restoration
    comedy; situation comedy;
    stereotypes
Comedy of Errors (Shakespeare) 81
commedia dell'arte 23, 80, 88–91
  The Happy Haven 201
  Steptoe and Son 110
  stereotypes 88–9, 201
  see also actors; comedy
commedia erudita (learned comedy) 84
conflict, generational 107–8, 111
Congreve, William 95, 96–103
consciousness 35–7, 42, 135, 226
  and acting 21, 41
  and ageing 4
  Back to Methuselah 179–80
  double 37, 41
  and memory 123
  Mr Jones Goes Driving 131, 132
constructive naturalism 36–7 *see also*
  naturalism
Corbett, Harry H. 107–11
Corpus Christi cycle plays 85
Coventry 86, 87
Coventry plays 85–7
Cox, Sam 139, 141
CQC (Care Quality Commission) 209, 210,
  211, 212
Creative Evolution 176, 181, 182
creativity 66–7
crime, fear of 26, 90
Croft, Giles 221, 222, 223, 224, 226
Croo, Robert 87–8
cross-dressing 112, 117
Crowden, Graham 208
Cuffe, John 27–8
culture
  and ageing 16, 20–1, 25–6, 163
  and history 7, 23–5, 80, 183,
    191, 238
  and power 5
  see also society, and ageing
cyber-self 179–80 *see also* self

D

Daltrey, Roger 229–30
dance
    and age 167, 231–2, 232
    ageism 231
    Forever Young 231
    Kontakthof 231–4
    Lovesong 141–2
    Radio Ballads 155
Darwin, Leonard 187–8
Darwinianism 181, 182, 183, 184
Davies, Ann 131
de Beauvoir, Simone 4, 28–9, 30
De Rerum Natura, Book III
        (Lucretius) 190
De Senectute (Cicero) 17
decline, master narrative of 7–9, 21, 23,
        52, 75, 90, 226, 237 *see also* ageing;
        narrative
defensive reminiscence 126, 164 *see also*
        reminiscence
Demastes, William 21
dementia 144, 167–70
    ageing games 47–8
    Ancient Mysteries 144–5
    Autobiographer 145–9
    Sophocles 66
    Timeslips programme 32
    see also memory
Dennett, Daniel 35
dependence 109, 111
The Desperate Doctor 88
Dhuga, Umit 62
Dickens, Charles 207, 208
dirty old men *see Last of the Summer Wine*;
        Randle; *senex*; *Steptoe and Son*
Discipline and Punish (Foucault) 206
'Discover for Life' 167
disempowerment 65–6
    and care homes 202, 209–12
    see also power
disintegration 143–9 *see also*
        integration

dislocation 73, 139–43
double-casting 140, 146
double consciousness 37, 41
Downes, John 103
dramaturgy 52, 102, 140, 205–6
    Back to Methuselah 180
    Exeter Blitz Project 158
    Forever Young 225
    and juxtaposition 225, 226
    Krapp's Last Tape 135
    Mr Jones Goes Driving 127
    The Makropulos Secret 187
    of reminiscence 153–8, 163, 164
    Steptoe and Son 109
Driving Miss Daisy (Uhry) 130
Dunn, Clive 46, 115, 117
Dylan, Bob 225, 230
Dyskolos/The Bad Tempered Man
        (Menander) 80–1

E

Eaton, Mick 107
EHRC (Equality and Human Rights
        Commission) 209, 212
elixir of life 185–6, 187, 188, 203–5
        see also longevity
Ellis, Anthony 31, 89
empathy 40–3, 45, 46, 47, 50–2
Empathy Suit 51–2
Endgame (Beckett) 137
Engaging Audiences (McConachie) 41, 43
Enright, Helena 158
Epic of Gilgamesh 191
'Epic' theatre (Beckett) 39, 201
Equality and Human Rights Commission
        (EHRC) 209, 212
Erikson, Erik 29, 68
escapist reminiscence 126, 127, 164
        see also reminiscence
esse 5
Etherege, George 95, 100–1, 103–4
eugenics 187–8, 202
Euripedes 60, 62

'Every Breath You Take', The Police 227–8
Ewig Jung (Gedeon) 222–3 *see also Forever Young*
The Exeter Blitz Project 158–60
experiments on humans 202–3
'Extravagant Acts for Mature People' 167

F
face-ageing technology 48–51, 237–8
Fair Old Times 154–5, 164
The Fake Magician 88
Falstaff 80, 112–13
Faustus 203
fear
    of ageing 22, 51–2, 205
    of care homes 202, 205, 206–7, 209, 211
    of crime 26, 90
    of the state 199, 202
'Feeling Good Theatre Company' 167
Fevered Sleep 162–4
Fiske, Susan T. 40
fitness 26–7, 167 *see also* well-being
Flanagan, Owen 35, 36–7
flashback 140
Fodor, Jerry 35
Forever Young (Gedeon) 199, 221–6, 231
Forever Young: How Rock 'n' Roll Grew Up 228, 230, 231
Foucault, Michel 206
frailty 26–7, 199 *see also* well-being
Frank, Arthur W. 124
Franklin, Aretha 226
Frantic Assembly 139, 141, 142
Frater, Sarah 233
freakshows 241 *see also* variety shows
Freud, Sigmund 3, 4, 58, 64–5, 68
Fuel Theatre 146

G
Galton, Ray 107–11
Gardner, Lynn 148
Gay and Gray (Pennell) 160–2
Gay, John 223

Gedeon, Erik 199, 221–6, 231
gender
    and acting 44
    and age 16–19, 28
    Classical Greece 80–1
    Restoration comedy 96, 100
    Steptoe and Son 109, 111
    Talking Heads 39
The Gentleman Dancing-Master 101
gerontideology 3–5, 234
gerontology 18, 19–32
    and ageism 22–3
    chronological relativism 23–5
    and 'crisis' 19–20
    cultural ageing 20–1
    and history 30–1, 58–9
    and the humanities 28–9, 42
    inter/multidisciplinarity 28–32
    and literary studies 31
    multidisciplinarity 28–32
    and overcompensation 25–6
    and performace studies 32
    and science 28
    subdivisions of old age 26–8
    see also age studies; ageing; old age; social gerontology
ghosts 127, 157, 206, 216
Ghosts (Ibsen) 127
Gibson, Andrew 137
Ginn, Jay 23, 24–5
'Giving the Elderly a Voice' project 167
Giving Voice Festival 2002: The Voice Politic 227
Glass Shot (Wales) 167
Goffman, Erving 102, 205–7
Gospel at Colonus (Breuer) 70
The Gospel of the Brothers Barnabas: Present Day (Shaw) 175, 176–7 *see also Back to Methuselah*
Gospel music 70 *see also* music
Gostelow, Gordon 202
Gould, Steven Jay 35
Graff, Yvetta Synek 189

Graham, Bruce 144
Graham, Scott 139, 141, 142
Greece, Classical 15, 22, 57–9, 60, 62–4, 66
    see also classical drama; Oedipus at
    Colonus
Greek Chorus 60–3
Greek mythology 57–8 see also classical
    drama
Greig, Noel 156
Griffith, D.W. 140
grumpy old men 131 see also senex iratus
Gullette, Margaret Morganroth 7, 8, 9, 20, 32,
    48, 237–8
Gulliver's Travels (Swift) 178, 192, 193

H
Haley, Bill 228
Hall, Stuart 229
Hamlet (Shakespeare) 3, 4–5, 18, 127
Hancock's Half Hour (Galton and Simpson)
    107–8
The Happy Haven (Arden) 199–205
Haraway, Donna 180
Harrell, Stevan 26
The Haunted Stage (Carlson) 127, 157
Hegel 59
Held, Martin 138
HelpAge 26
Henry IV (Shakespeare) 80, 113
Henry V (Shakespeare) 21
The Heracleidae (Euripedes) 60
Heracles (Euripedes) 62
Heth, Joice 238–41
'Heydays' group 167
HGPS (Hutchinson-Gilford Progeria
    Syndrome) 186
Higson, Charlie 144–5
history
    and ageing 30–1, 241
    and continuity 117
    cultural 7, 23–5, 80, 183, 191, 238
    and gerontology 30–1, 58–9
    life-history 125

of theatre 6, 44, 84, 100, 103, 112
Hoggett, Steven 139, 141, 142
Hougan, Glen 51–2
Human Longevity: Its Facts and Fictions
    (Thoms) 194–5
humanism 83–4
humanities, and gerontology 28–9, 42
Hume, David 42
Hutchinson-Gilford Progeria Syndrome
    (HGPS) 186

I
I Suppositi (Ariosto) 84
Ibsen, Henrik 127, 133
identity
    generational 129, 229, 231
    and narrative 231
    and performance 3–5, 169, 206
    and self 132, 133, 206
    social 5, 235
In the Beginning: B.C. 4004 (In the Garden
    of Eden) (Shaw) 175 see also Back to
    Methuselah
In Full Flow (Greig) 156
inappropriate behaviour, as source of comedy
    80, 83, 112 see also comedy
institutional care 209–12
    Classical Greece 58
    Forever Young 221
    The Happy Haven 200, 202, 204, 205–8
    Juliet and her Romeo 213, 215, 216–17
    and power 202, 206
    and reminiscence theatre 164
    Talking Heads 39
    total institutions 205–7
    see also care homes
instrumental reminiscence 126, 133 see also
    reminiscence
integration 126, 164
    Lovesong 146
    Mr Jones Goes Driving 127–34
    Oedipus at Colonus 67, 71, 73, 75
    see also disintegration

integrative reminiscence 125–6, 127, 133, 164 *see also* reminiscence
interaction 164, 168, 207, 232, 242
Intolerance (Griffith) 140
Itzin, Catherine 5

J
Jagger, Sir Mick 230
Janáček, Leos 184, 189–90
Jardine, Douglas 226
Jarry, Alfred 39
The Jealous Old Man 88
Johnson, Julia 22
Johnson, Paul 30, 37
Jones, James Earl 130
Jones, Robert T. 189
Joseph and Mary plays 85–8
Joseph's Doubt 85, 86
Juliet and her Romeo (O'Connor and Morris) 199, 212–17
Jung, Carl 79, 126
The Just Punishment 88
juxtaposition 216, 225, 226, 228, 231

K
Kazan, Elia 45
Kershaw, Baz 153, 154, 163
Kesey, Ken 222
Kirkwood, Tom 182, 183, 194
Knowlson, James 137, 138
Kontakthof (Bausch) 231–4
Krapp's Last Tape (Beckett) 6, 7, 134–9, 142–3, 204

L
La Cassaria (Ariosto) 84
Lacan, Jacques 3, 4, 65, 67, 74–5
Ladder to the Moon 166
Laetus, Pomponius 83
Lamarckism 181, 182, 194
Langley, Gordon and Dorothy 154
Larkin, Philip 228–9
The Last of the Summer Wine (Clarke) 113

late style, and *Oedipus at Colonus* 64–9
Lavery, Bryony 144
lazzi 88, 91, 102
    The Happy Haven 201
    Songdrama 223
    Steptoe and Son 108
learned comedy (*commedia erudita*) 84
Leigh, Elinor (or Ellen, or Elizabeth) 100–1, 103
The Library Theatre, Manchester 167
Lieberman, Morton A. 125, 126
life review 19, 123–5, 126
    Krapp's Last Tape 134
    Mr Jones Goes Driving 127, 133
lifespan 25, 46–7, 176, 177, 183, 191–2
    see also longevity; old age
lifestyle 20–1, 109, 164–7
liminality 71–5
    Lovesong 142
    Oedipus at Colonus 72, 74–5
    see also marginalisation
Lindsay, R.W. 238
Lipps, Theodor 40
Lipscomb, Valerie Barnes 32
literature/literary studies 19, 28, 31–2, 66
    classical 83–4
longevity 30, 175, 191–2, 241
    Back to Methuselah 176, 177, 181, 183–4, 194–5
    extreme 27, 175, 184, 191–5, 203, 241
    The Happy Haven 203–4
    The Makropulos Secret 184, 185, 188, 194–5
    and politics 183–4
    see also elixir of life; lifespan; old age
love
    classical theatre 79–80, 81, 83, 192
    commedia dell'arte 89
    Juliet and her Romeo 212–17
    Krapp's Last Tape 135
    Lovesong 142
    The Miser 90
    Mr Jones Goes Driving 128, 132–3
    Randle 116

Restoration comedy 96–8
Steptoe and Son 110
Love for Love 101
Love's Labours Lost (Shakespeare) 96
Lovesong (Morgan) 139–43
Lucretius 190
Lukowski, Andrzej 148

M
MacColl, Ewan 153–5
Mackrell, Judith 233–4
Magee, Patrick 6, 137–8
The Makropulos Secret (Čapek) 184–91,
    194, 195
    and *Back to Methuselah* 186–7
Malone Dies (Beckett) 134
The Man of Mode (Etherege) 95, 100–1,
    103–4
Manichaean doctrine 137
marginalization 30, 46, 58, 66, 72, 112, 117
    see also liminality
Marowitz, Charles 143–4
marriage, as financial proposition 79,
    95, 98
Marshall, Leni 32
Marshall, Norman 165
Marx, Stephen 16
masculinity
    Mr Jones Goes Driving 129, 132–4
    Steptoe and Son 110–11
The Master Builder (Ibsen) 127
McCartney, Sir Paul 228, 230 *see also* The
    Beatles
McConachie, Bruce 41, 43
McKenzie, Jon 73
McWhinnie, Donald 137
Medium Fair 154
memory 123, 149
    and acting 39, 50, 143–4
    and ageing 123
    Autobiographer 146, 148
    Krapp's Last Tape 134, 139
    Lovesong 139–40, 142

Mr Jones Goes Driving 127, 132–3, 134
    and narrative 123, 124–5
    and performance 144
    Radio Ballads 153–4
    and theatre 143–4
    see also dementia; reminiscence
Menaechmi (Plautus) 81–2
Menander 80–1
Mercator/The Merchant (Plautus) 83
The Merry Wives of Windsor (Shakespeare)
    80, 113
metamorphosis myths 194
Metchnikov, Elie 184
Method acting 42, 45 *see also* acting
methodology 6–9, 18–19
Middle Ages 84–5
Midsummer Night's Dream (Shakespeare) 79
Mills, Joan 227
mind
    and body 5, 36, 165, 180–1
    and brain 35, 36, 42
Minois, Georges 30–1, 57–9
mirror neurons 40–2
mirrors 3–4
The Miser (Molière) 90–1, 95
Miss Julie (Zola) 36–7
Mitchell, Michelle 209
Molière 80, 90–1, 95
Molloy (Beckett) 134
Monet, Claude 66
Moralia (Plutarch) 66
Morgan, Abi 139–43
Morgan, Gareth 222
Morris, Tom 199, 212–17
Mr Jones Goes Driving (Silas) 127–34
Much Ado About Nothing (Shakespeare) 96
Mulley, Graham 211–12
music 223, 224–5, 234
    The Exeter Blitz Project 158
    Forever Young 221, 223–4, 226, 228
    *Forever Young: How Rock 'n' Roll
        Grew Up* 231
    Gospel 70

The Makropulos Secret 190
music hall 113
music radio 128
and old age 226, 228
pop 226, 228, 229, 231, 234
rock 223–4, 228
rock 'n' roll 224–5, 229
Young@Heart 227, 228, 231
'My Generation', The Who 229–30
Myerhoff, Barbara 3, 73–4, 112, 113, 117, 129

N
Nagel, Thomas 37
narrative 124–7
  The Archers 144
  Back to Methuselah 181–2
  Biblical 85, 87
  commedia dell'arte 88
  Forever Young 224, 226, 230, 231
  Heth 241
  and identity 231
  Juliet and her Romeo 213, 216–17
  Kontakthof 232
  Krapp's Last Tape 135, 139
  Lovesong 142
  and memory 123, 124–5
  Menaechmi 81
  Mr Jones Goes Driving 131, 132, 133–4
  Oedipus at Colonus 64, 69, 74, 75
  Radio Ballads 153
  and reminiscence 126–7, 160
  Restoration comedy 98
  Steptoe and Son 111
  and subjectivity 36–7
  see also decline
National Health Service 199–200, 202
National Theatre 167
naturalism 35–7, 46, 142, 214
Neale, Steve 110
neuroscience 40–3 *see also* science
Noice, Helga and Tony 167–70
Norton, D.L. 29

nostalgia 126, 133, 191, 230
  Last of the Summer Wine 113
  and reminiscence theatre 163–4
  see also sentimentality
nursing homes *see* care homes

O
objectivity 5, 23–4, 37, 39–40, 48–9
  Krapp's Last Tape 134
obsession
  Krapp's Last Tape 134–9
  Mr Jones Goes Driving 129
obsessive reminiscence 123, 126, 127 *see also*
  reminiscence
O'Connor, Sean 199, 212–17
Oedipus at Colonus (Sophocles) 58, 60–75
Oedipus the King (Sophocles) 65, 69, 127
Oedipus myth/narrative 58, 64–5, 69, 74, 75
The Offer 108 *see also Steptoe and Son*
Oglesby, Tamsin 144
old, subdivision of old age 27
old age 23–4, 175, 194, 229
  and acting 45–7, 48, 225, 226
  Classical Greece 57–9, 62
  and music 226, 228
  in Shakespeare 31–2, 133
  subdivisions 26–8
  see also age; ageing; ageism; gerontology;
    lifespan; longevity
Old Age (de Beauvoir) 4, 28–9, 30
*Old Age, Masculinity and Early Modern
  Drama* (Ellis) 31, 89
The Old Bachelor (Congreve) 96–8
The Old Man and the Sea 110
old-old, subdivision of old age 27
Oliver Twist (Dickens) 207
On Ageing 162–4
On the River 156
One Flew Over the Cuckoo's Nest (Kesey) 222
oppression 28, 110, 130
  Forever Young 221–2
  The Happy Haven 208–12, 215

Orr, Jake 148
Other 4, 38, 42
Ottaway, Susannah R. 30
Otway, Thomas 95–6
Our Mutual Friend (Dickens) 207
The Outgoing Tide (Graham) 144
overcompensation, and gerontology 25–6
Ovid 193

P

Pacey, Ben 146
Pageant of the Shearmen and Tailors
    86–8
Panopticon 206, 207
Panorama 211
Pantalone 23, 80, 88–9, 91
pantomime 224
Parker, Charles 153
Parkin, Tim G. 59, 62
Pauper Management Improved (Bentham)
    206, 207–8
Pennell, Steven 160–2
pensions 24, 25, 207–8
percipi 5
performance 6–7, 8–9, 241–2
    and age studies 18–23, 28, 32
    and ageing 6–7, 16, 32
    and ageing apps 49–51
    ethics of 241, 242
    Forever Young 224–5, 226
    front and back 102–3, 206
    and identity 3–5, 169, 206
    Krapp's Last Tape 136, 137–8, 143
    and memory 144
    and radio 8
    Restoration comedy 101–3
    Songdrama 223
    and subjectivity 37–43
    Turner 46–7
    and well-being 165
    Young@Heart 227–8, 231
    see also acting; actors; actresses; theatre;
        theatrical performance

performance studies
    and gerontology 32
    and liminality 72–3
performance theory 32 *see also* acting theory
Persians (Aeschylus) 62
Personal Destinies: A Philosophy of Ethical
    Individualism (Norton) 29
Pherecrates 80
Phillips, Siân
    in *Ancient Mysteries* 145
    in *Juliet and her Romeo* 213, 214, 215–16
    in *Lovesong* 139, 141–2
philosophy
    and ageing 29–30, 57, 58, 190
    Back to Methuselah 175, 176, 182
    and empathy 40–2
    Krapp's Last Tape 204
    The Makropulos Secret 184, 186, 190
    Picture of Dorian Gray (Wilde) 190
Pinker, Steven 35
Plato 15–18, 19, 22, 29, 58
Plautus 81–2, 83, 88
The Play of Jacob and Esau 85
Plutarch 66
The Police 227–8
politics 227, 231
    Back to Methuselah 176–8, 184
    Classical Greece 62, 63
    Forever Young 222, 225
    The Happy Haven 201, 202
    Juliet and her Romeo 215
    and longevity 183–4
    Radio Ballads 153–4
    Restoration 95
    Steptoe and Son 109, 111
    Waiting for God 209
Poor Law Amendment Act 1834 207–8
Pop, Iggy 230
pop music 226, 228, 229, 231, 234
    see also music
positive ageing 21, 68–9, 193–4, 205, 242
    Forever Young 224, 225, 226, 230
    The Happy Haven 205

Juliet and her Romeo 214, 215–16
Last of the Summer Wine 113
Mr Jones Goes Driving 133
Oedipus at Colonus 61, 74
and reminiscence 123–4, 125, 126, 164–5
Republic 16–17, 58
Young@Heart 231
see also ageing; well-being
power
    Ancient Mysteries 144–5
    Back to Methuselah 181
    Classical Greece 60, 62–4, 66
    commedia dell'arte 88
    Coventry elite 87
    and culture 5
    Forever Young 222, 224
    The Happy Haven 205
    and institutions 202, 206
    Krapp's Last Tape 137, 138, 140
    and reminiscence 155, 164
    Restoration comedy 99, 103
    and the *senex* 80, 81–2, 88, 111–12
    Steptoe and Son 111
    see also disempowerment
Power, Ben 213
The Presentation of Self in Everyday Life
    (Goffman) 102
Prinz, Jesse 42

Q
Quetelet, Adolphe 24

R
radio 7, 8, 128, 132, 144 *see also Ancient*
    Mysteries; The Archers; BBC;
    Mr Jones Goes Driving; Radio 4;
    Radio Ballads
Radio 4 8, 128, 145
Radio Ballads 8, 153–5
Randle, Frank 6, 114–17, 225–6
Rapamycin 186
Really Old Like Forty-Five (Oglesby) 144
rebellion 73, 111, 234

Forever Young 221–2, 225–6
The Makropulos Secret 204
Songdrama 223–4
see also resistance
reconciliation 67–8, 69, 125–6, 133, 134, 164
    Krapp's Last Tape 139
Red Megaphones 153
Redgrave, Vanessa 130
Reid, Anne 145
Reinhardt, Karl 74
relationships
    intergenerational 5, 108, 109–10, 111, 233
    with self 124, 135
religion, and *Oedipus at Colonus* 70
Rembrandt 66
Remembered Lives (Myerhoff) 73–4
reminiscence 125
    defensive 126, 164
    discouragement 123
    dramaturgy 153–8, 163, 164
    escapist 126, 127, 164
    instrumental 126, 133
    integrative 125–6, 127, 133, 164
    Krapp's Last Tape 137, 139
    Mr Jones Goes Driving 131, 133
    and narrative 126–7, 160
    obsessive 123, 126, 127
    and positive ageing 123–4, 125, 126, 164–5
    and power 155, 164
    transmissive 126
    typology 125–7, 133
    see also memory
reminiscence theatre 133, 153, 163–7
    aesthetic and ethical issues 156–7
    audience 157–8
    and care homes 164, 166, 168
    and nostalgia 163–4
    see also Exeter Blitz Project; *Gay and Gray*
Report on Elder Abuse and Crime in India
    (HelpAge) 26
Republic (Plato) 15–18, 19, 22, 29, 58
resistance
    to ageing 8, 9, 73

and care homes 155, 209,
    221–2, 237
Forever Young 226
The Happy Haven 221–2
Oedipus at Colonus 75
Steptoe and Son 111
and youth 73
see also rebellion
'Respect', Aretha Franklin 226
Restoration comedy 95–6
    and ageing 99–100
    and ageism 95, 103
    female roles 98–104
    and gender 96, 100
    and love 96–8
    and narrative 98
    and performance 101–3
    and power 99, 103
    senex amans 96–8
    sexuality 95, 98–9, 100
    stereotypes 95–7, 101, 104
    and youth 98
    see also acting; comedy; *The Old Bachelor;*
        Soldiers of Fortune; The Way of the
        World
Rhetoric (Aristotle) 57, 58
Richards, Keith 230
Rifkin, Jeremy 59
rites of passage 72, 73
rituals 129
    Krapp's Last Tape 134
    Mr Jones Goes Driving 129, 130–1,
        132, 133
    Songdrama 223
Rivett, Geoffrey 199
'Rock Around the Clock', Bill Haley 228
rock music 223–4, 228 *see also* music
rock 'n' roll 224–5, 229 *see also* music
Rockaby (Beckett) 134
Rodin, Auguste 66
Rolling Home (Bennett) 207
Roman comedy 81 *see also* classical drama;
    comedy

Romeo and Juliet (Shakespeare) 18 *see also*
    Juliet and her Romeo
Roscius Anglicanus (Downes) 103
The Rover 101
Rowe, Lianne 139
Royal Court Theatre 137, 138, 200,
    202, 204, 213
Royal Hunt of the Sun (Shaffer) 140
Royal Shakespeare Company 213

S
Said, Edward 67, 70
Sales, Nick 155
Scala, Flaminio 88, 89
Schechner, Richard 72–3
Schweitzer, Pam 155–6, 157, 163
science
    and ageing 181, 182–3, 184
    bad science 48, 50, 237
    and empathy 40
    and gerontology 28
    neuroscience 40–3
The Scowrers 101
Segal, Erich 81–2
self 124, 135
    cyber-self 179–80
    and identity 132, 133, 206
    multiplicity of 146
    and subjectivity 36–8, 39, 42–3
    unity of 135
    virtual self 179–80
self-worth
    and acting 169
    Krapp's Last Tape 134, 139
    Mr Jones Goes Driving 133
senex 79–80, 111–12
    commedia dell'arte 88
    female 98–104
    in Greek and Roman comedy 80–4
    Middle Ages 85–6
    and power 80, 81–2, 88, 111–12
    Steptoe and Son 109–10
    and trickster-figures 112–13

senex amans 79, 80
   in Greek and Roman comedy 81, 83
   Middle Ages 86, 87
   in Restoration comedy 96–8
senex iratus 79 *see also* angry old men;
   grumpy old men
senior theatre 32, 160, 166 *see also* theatre
sentimentality 103–4, 132, 133, 148 *see also*
   nostalgia
serenity 67, 69, 124
seven ages of man (Shakespeare) 68, 89–90
sexuality 17, 80, 225
   Gay and Gray 160
   Mr Jones Goes Driving 132–3
   Randle 115–16
   Restoration comedy 95, 98–9, 100
Shadwell, Thomas 95
Shaffer, Peter 140
Shakespeare, William
   on ageing 89–90
   and Elizabeth I 80
   'Golden Lasses…' 228
   influences 84, 88
   Last Plays 67, 133
   and old age 31–2, 133
   seven ages of man 68, 89–90
   and subjectivity 40
   see also As You Like It; Comedy of Errors;
      Hamlet; Henry IV; Henry V; Love's
      Labours Lost; Merry Wives of
      Windsor; Midsummer Night's
      Dream; Much Ado About Nothing;
      Romeo and Juliet; The Tempest;
      Twelfth Night
Shaw, George Bernard 175, 180–2,
   183–4
   and Čapek 184, 186–7, 191, 195
   see also Back to Methuselah
Sierpina, Michelle 28, 31, 125
Silas, Shelley 127–34
Simpson, Alan 107–11
The Simpsons 80
Singing the Fishing 153

situation comedy (sitcom) 107, 110,
   131, 140 *see also* comedy; *Last of the*
   Summer Wine; Steptoe and Son;
   Waiting for God
Small, Helen 16–17
Snow, Charles Percy 20
social age 5, 24–5 *see also* age
social gerontology 5, 15, 22, 23, 26, 28, 125
   see also gerontology
social identity 5, 235 *see also* identity
social psychology of ageing 5
society, and ageing 5, 15, 20–1, 237 *see also*
   culture
Socrates 15–18
Soldiers of Fortune (Otway) 95–6
Songdrama 222–3, 224, 225
Sophocles 65–6
   Antigone 62, 69, 74–5
   Oedipus at Colonus 58, 60–75
   Oedipus the King 65, 69, 127
Southern Cross 210, 211
Spencer, Charles 70
sphinx's riddle 69
Stage Movement (Battye) 43–5
staging/style, *The Happy Haven* 200–1
Stanislavski, Constantin 39–40,
   42, 43, 45
state, fear of 199, 202
Statute of Winchester 24
Steele, Richard 103
Steiner, George 69
Steptoe and Son (Galton and Simpson)
   107–11
stereotypes 22–3, 30, 37, 48, 79–80, 131,
   225–6
   and acting 44, 49, 50, 52
   in *commedia dell'arte* 88–9, 201
   Forever Young 221, 222, 224, 225–6
   Juliet and her Romeo 214
   Molière 90–1
   Mr Jones Goes Driving 128, 131, 133
   Randle 112, 115, 117
   Restoration comedy 95–7, 101, 104

Steptoe and Son 110, 111
    see also actors; comedy; stock characters
stock characters 23, 81, 91 *see also* actors;
        senex; senex amans; senex iratus;
        stereotypes
Strasberg, Lee 43
Strindberg, August 36–7
Stuart-Hamilton, Ian 23–4, 242
subjectivity 3–4, 22, 35–43, 146
suppliant plays 60
The Suppliant Women (Euripedes) 60
Sutton, Dudley 213
Swift, Jonathan 178, 192, 193

T
taboo breaking 115, 117
Talking Heads (Bennett) 38–9
Tanztheater Wuppertal 232
Taylor, Paul 215–16
Taylor, Shelley E. 40
Il Teatro delle Favole Rappresentative 88
technology
    and ageing 48–51, 129, 237–8
    Krapp's Last Tape 134
    Mr Jones Goes Driving 129
teenagers 228–9, 230, 233 *see also* youth
The Tempest (Shakespeare) 18, 67
A Tender Thing (Power) 213
Tennyson, Alfred 193–4
Terence 81, 83, 88
Thane, Pat 30, 90
theatre 7, 8–9, 127, 143
    1950s/1960s 109
    and ageing 7, 8–9, 32, 35, 43–5, 79–80,
        149, 225
    and ageism 23
    benefits 165–6
    and empathy 41, 50
    'Epic' 39, 201
    history of 6, 44, 84, 100, 103, 112
    of ideas 175
    intergenerational 155, 156, 158, 160, 163,
        166, 167

and memory 143–4
Middle Ages 84–5
and naturalism 36–7
and objectivity/subjectivity 39–40
Restoration comedy 100, 103
senior 32, 160, 166
see also acting; actors; actresses;
        performance; reminiscence
        theatre; theatrical
        performance
Theatre of Action 153
Theatre Workshop 153
theatrical performance 5–6
    and age 8–9, 112
    and empathy 42–3, 50
    as social construction 21–2
    see also performance; theatre
The Thing Happens: A.D. 2170 (Shaw) 175,
        177 *see also Back to Methuselah*
Third Age Acting Company 167
Thompson, Evan 42
Thompson, Paul 5, 30
Thoms, William 194–5
Timeslips programme 32
Tithonus 192–4
Titian 66
Tobin, Sheldon S. 125, 126
total institutions 205–7
        see also institutional care
Townshend, Pete 229–30, 231
tragedy 59 *see also Juliet and her Romeo;*
        Oedipus at Colonus
Tragedy of an Elderly Gentleman: A.D. 3000
        (Shaw) 175, 177–8 *see also Back to*
        Methuselah
transmissive reminiscence 126
        see also reminiscence
The Travelling People 153
Treatise on Man (Quetelet) 24
The Trial of Mary and Joseph 85, 86
trickster-figures 112–13, 117
    Forever Young 225–6
    The Last of the Summer Wine 113

Randle 114–15, 225–6
Steptoe and Son 111
Trueman, Matt 148
Turner, Janice 46–7
Turner, Victor 72, 73, 74
Twelfth Night (Shakespeare) 81

U
Ubu Roi (Jarry) 39
Uhry, Alfred 130

V
van Gennep, Arnold 72, 73
variety shows 113–14 *see also* freakshows
Violet (in *Talking Heads*) 38–9
virtual-self 179–80 *see also* self
Viva Voce 158–60
Voluntary Longevity 176, 177, 181

W
Waiting for God (Aitkens) 208–9, 222
Walker, Stephen 227
Washington, George 238–9
Watt, Lisa 125–7, 133, 134, 137, 153, 164
The Way of the World (Congreve) 95, 98–103
Webb, Eugene 136, 137
A Wedding Story (Lavery) 144
Weismann, August 181, 182, 183
well-being 51, 125, 126, 153, 165, 169 *see also*
    fitness; frailty; positive ageing
Welles, Orson 140
West Yorkshire Playhouse 167
Whannel, Paddy 229
'When I'm Sixty-Four', The Beatles 228
Whitehouse, Paul 145
The Who 229–30
Wilde, Oscar 190

Wiles, David 84
Williams, Bernard 184–5, 190–1
Wilson, Melanie 145–9
Wilson, R.S. 170
Winterbourne View, Bristol 211
Woman from Samos (Menander) 80–1
Wong, Paul 125–7, 133, 134, 137, 153, 164
Woodward, Kathleen 4, 20, 31
workhouses, and care homes 207–8, 209
Wrinkled Deep in Time (Charney) 31
Wycherley, William 96, 100–1

Y
Young Vic Theatre, London 162–4
young-old, subdivision of old age 27
Young@Heart 227–31
Young@Heart (Walker) 227
youth 32, 234
    Classical Greece 57–8, 69, 192–3
    The Happy Haven 204
    Juliet and her Romeo 213, 214, 215,
        216, 217
    Kontakthof 231–2, 233
    Krapp's Last Tape 136, 143, 204
    and liminality 73–4
    The Makropulos Secret 185
    meanings 229
    Medieval comedy 84–5
    Mr Jones Goes Driving 133
    and resistance 73
    Restoration comedy 98
    Songdrama 224–5, 226, 228, 229–31
    Steptoe and Son 108, 109, 111
    teenagers 228–9, 230, 233

Z
Zola, Émile 36–7